genesis

genesis
chapter & verse

TONY BANKS   PHIL COLLINS   PETER GABRIEL

STEVE HACKETT   MIKE RUTHERFORD

EDITED BY PHILIP DODD

WEIDENFELD & NICOLSON

CONTENTS

INTRODUCTION

In the beginning, there were five schoolboys from Charterhouse who formed a band called Genesis. There is nothing unusual in that *per se*. There have been many groups who grew up together in the same city, the same neighbourhood, the same classroom.

But let's take another look. At the time, in the mid-1960s when this tale begins, Charterhouse was, then as now, one of the premier public schools in Britain, a bastion of the English – and I choose that word deliberately – establishment. The school was part of the very fabric of the nation. The staff and the parents of the boys who played cricket and rugby on its playing fields had survived a World War, had sworn never to let it happen again, and having emerged triumphant were determined not to see the traditions they had saved be further threatened.

In other words, this was almost precisely the kind of environment that would have, that should have, stifled Genesis at its inception, have sucked the very musical marrow out of the group, and spat its husk out as far away as possible. In short, Charterhouse was the unlikeliest spawning ground for a rock band ever.

Yet Genesis – where so many other school bands foundered – survived, and survived again, and went on from strength to strength. Maybe something of the spirit of Charterhouse persisted, some jot of 'up and at 'em', Charge of the Light Brigade pig-headed valour had stuck.

And then, when the Charterhouse lads who remained – Tony Banks, Mike Rutherford and Peter Gabriel (drummer Chris Stewart had been an early casualty, Ant Phillips a victim of his

own insecurities) – had gone as far as they could, they wisely brought in new and different blood. It was very different, a chirpy, cheeky, self-confident drummer who came from a theatrical, stage school background, a serious-minded guitarist from the backstreets of London's Victoria. Again, after Peter jumped ship, the survivors called on the cream of British and American jazz-flavoured session musicians, or much later on, for *Calling All Stations*, brought in a Scottish singer who arrived with a bagful of attitude.

Each infusion coursing through the band's veins provided additional longevity and durability, so that the band survived the high-profile departure of not one vocalist, but two (Peter and Phil), their most influential guitarist (Steve) and their best-known drummer (Phil).

It was like the Stones losing Mick Jagger, Keith Richards and Charlie Watts. Genesis, however, simply got stronger and bigger – matching the huge solo success of Peter Gabriel, Phil Collins and Mike Rutherford's Mike + the Mechanics. Genesis had the adventurousness and awareness to continue evolving. The band moved on from their position as pioneers of progressive rock (even though they might dispute that term), at a time when other prog rock bands like ELP and Yes were being hamstrung by the 'dinosaur' tag, to emerge triumphant as global hitmakers.

Against the odds – OK, against all odds – Genesis always did it their own way. There is an Englishness about this story, about the reticence and pride, or sheer stubbornness as Mike

Rutherford calls it, that permeates their reminiscences. It might seem a surprising description, for those who think of them as mild-mannered gents, but Genesis is one tough band.

Genesis: Chapter & Verse is as authentic a history of this group as we could possibly make. That is why the voice of each member is relayed direct and uncensored. This is a story patchworked together from their memories, their stories, their personal take on what they have achieved. History of any kind is a fickle business, but by combining all their stories, here is the closest we can get. We don't claim it is definitive, but it is real.

Perhaps what is most remarkable in this book is that, unlike almost every major band of forty years' existence, not only have all the musicians who have been part of Genesis contributed, but they are still alive. Amongst their contemporaries, excess, self-abuse, suicide or murder have reaped a toll of casualties, or filthy lucre, mutual distrust and legal constraints have distorted the re-telling of a band's history.

Only Tony Stratton-Smith, the charismatic Charisma boss, could not add his voice to proceedings – he died in 1987 – but his presence is here within the memories of those who knew him. The photos of Strat convey a glimpse of the man whose enthusiasm and support picked up Genesis at a critical moment, when they were seeking a new outlet for the music they believed in, and became a guide and mentor who believed in the music just as much as they did, and segued them towards a long and healthy life.

Was this also down to the diet provided by their schoolfriend, road manager, cheerleader and chef Richard Macphail: cauliflower cheese, yoghurt and home-made bread? John Mayhew, who drummed with the band for the year they recorded *Trespass*, said he didn't drink at the time, and anyone seeking the revelations of excess and drugs and rock'n'roll would be better advised to buy Mötley Crüe's autobiography. That was and is not Genesis's style. But if you want to understand who these musicians are, what made them gel and occasionally fall apart, and how their music developed its individuality, then read on.

Throughout the course of the book the voices of each of them mesh together, like a radio play, giving us their take on the development and history of the band. They are drawn from interviews conducted with Mike reclining on the sofa at the Farm studios, Phil in a hotel suite high above Broadway, Tony during rehearsals in Brussels, Peter at his Wiltshire base (a rich vegetable soup-cum-stew providing sustenance for both of us). Ant Phillips was at home in Clapham, Steve Hackett at a café near his Twickenham studio, Ray Wilson up in Leith on a blustery St Andrew's day, the band's very first drummer Chris Stewart on a sunlit February morning on the ledge of his farm in southern Spain. Separate places, but a shared story.

And around them there is a play of sidelighting from a diverse group of colleagues, observers, helpmeets and fellow musicians, each adding a separate shade, a different hue to the central story, bringing their friends into relief.

The final knockings and finishing tweaks of this book were undertaken in the Hall 5 of the Brussels Expo Centre, a vast 1930s ziggurat-shaped extravaganza that Mussolini would have been proud of – the only building the band's production team could find that was big enough to house the stage set for the *Turn It On Again* tour. Under the gaze of nine shining steel spheres of the futuristic Atomium, one of Brussels' iconic sites. Here, amidst a hectic schedule of run-throughs, technical rehearsals and press interviews, the band found time to apply care, insight and thought to improving and coalescing this book, with a constructive attention to detail that is the mark of the craftsman and the professional.

Phil has said, 'People think of us as "Genesis", this sacred cow, which mustn't do anything else, like a brand name. We think of ourselves as songwriters, who can do a bit of this, a bit of that…'

Genesis: Chapter & Verse is, we hope, a book that will surprise some readers, undermine a few pre- and mis-conceptions – and allow the band to dispatch more than a few sacred cows… Amen to that.

PHILIP DODD

CHAPTER ONE
PROLOGUE

TONY BANKS: There was always a piano in my house. It was a boudoir grand, which had a distinctive sound that I came to love. My mother loved music and was a pianist with a wide repertoire, though she never performed professionally, and I grew up listening to her playing Chopin on that piano. But she could only play if the music was in front of her. If you took the music away, she couldn't play, because although she had a good technique she simply wasn't able to play by ear. Which is extraordinary, because I'm exactly the opposite. My father, on the other hand, was completely tone deaf, but he would play along, in the sense that he would let her enjoy her music, although he didn't really understand music at all. He was a teacher who used to cram boys to make sure they got into the public schools of their choice.

We lived in the same house in East Hoathly in Sussex for eleven years. I went back to see the house recently and found it had been turned into a nursing home, sprawling all over the place, a complete nightmare. But in my memory it is still a beautiful home, a lovely house to have been born in, and where music was a large part of our family life, whether we were listening to 78s or later LPs, or hearing choral music in church.

I have one brother and three sisters, all older than me. I probably had the closest relationship with my brother, who was ten years older, but when I was about eleven or twelve he went to Jamaica for three years. So there were never that many people around. I was a very shy child – I still am, actually – but I was really quite self-sufficient. I loved being on my own at home and doing things alone, reading or just walking around. I was very self-conscious, pretty irascible and used to have a lot of tantrums. Looking back I don't think I would have particularly wanted to be friends with me at the time, so I'm surprised that I did have some friends. But I hated parties or any social events. I still don't like crowds of people, which is not so good if you're playing in a rock group. I much prefer a smaller party.

After going to a local kindergarten school, I went to board at prep school when I was seven. I never liked boarding; I hate the way you're restricted. So I was not happy. I had been taken away from home and suddenly left there, a little boy of seven years old, with all these people around me, and with compulsory food, which I hated too. And then there were the beatings. It was not a great period for me. But you do form incredibly strong friendships with other pupils by virtue of being thrust together. That's the one thing I'd say in favour of those boarding schools. I remember, when I left the place, waking up in the middle of one night and thinking, 'I'm never going to see these people again', and feeling really sad.

From prep school I went to Charterhouse. My brother had gone there; I don't know why. He didn't like the place and although he is quite a bright guy, I remember seeing old school lists where it looked like he was bottom of the bottom class. As far as I was concerned, I didn't have any strong feelings about going there. When you attended prep school and you turned thirteen you were going to go to public school; that was what happened. Again, Charterhouse was a boarding school, so I didn't like that aspect of it. I had won a scholarship, but after two years at the school I really wasn't achieving what I should have been. In the end it was a relief to be able to drop some of the subjects that I didn't enjoy: I concentrated on science for my last two years there and found that much easier. The subjects I had done least well with were English and history, which is strange, because since leaving school those are the things that interest me far more than anything else. I think I'm OK with words. I read a lot, and obviously I've written hundreds of lyrics, although that doesn't come as easily to me as writing music. Perhaps it was the way those subjects were tested at school that meant they didn't really appeal to me at the time. I liked science and maths because there was usually a definite answer; you knew if you'd got it right. Whereas in English, for example, you'd sometimes write what you thought was a really good essay but get marked down, and you'd think, 'I don't understand why'.

I was never very good at team sports. I used to like playing tennis, squash or fives, which I played with Peter quite a lot. We were great friends and also great rivals, and although neither of us was particularly talented at any of these sports we used to have good competitive moments. I suppose there were about sixty or seventy boys in my house – I was in the one known as

Opposite: Snaps from the family albums. Clockwise from top left: Peter aged eight with a canine friend; Mike in his prep school sports sweater with his Hofner jazz guitar and his friend and fellow musician in the Chesters, Dimitri Griliopoulos; Tony, learning how to check out backstage catering, at home aged four or five; and Ant fresh from the pampas in 1957.

Duckites. The house itself was all right, but when I went there no one was allowed to have a radio or a record player. We used to go to the local record store so we could listen to music. I remember going with a friend, Paul Grumbar, into a listening booth in Record Corner in Godalming, a shop which still exists, and listening to *Rubber Soul* for the first time: it was so exciting.

I loved music, it was really the main thing for me. There was a piano in the house which anybody could play. A few of us would go in there and I'd either play along to sheet music, to pieces I didn't know, plonking out the chords, or I'd play by ear. The first piano teacher I had at Charterhouse, who was a good musician, unfortunately had no time for me. While I was studying with him I almost gave up playing piano completely, but then at his suggestion I went to one of the other teachers there, a guy called Leonard Halcrow, who was much more sympathetic to the way I wanted to do things. We got on very well and he helped me develop as a player. I was never going to be a great classical player – I made too many mistakes – but I've always played with a bit of fire. At the same time I was playing by ear, which was more interesting to me, and I was able to combine the two ways of playing in the early days of Genesis.

MIKE RUTHERFORD: My father was in the Royal Navy and was away much of the time when I was young. In fact, I didn't see him until I was two, I believe. He was actually off ships by the time I was around, but he had seen active service during the war. I never knew much about that until I read a book he had written about his experiences. He came from a services background: my grandfather was an Army doctor, who also wrote a couple of books, one of which had the wonderful title *Soliloquy With A Stethoscope*.

Like any services family we moved around a lot, so we never had much of a fixed base, although both sets of grandparents lived in Surrey, in Farnham, so I got to know that area of the country. But my first memories are of Portsmouth, where my father was serving as Gunnery Officer at a naval training establishment called Whale Island for three or four years. My mother came from a large Scottish family and had been brought up in Liverpool before her mother remarried and moved the family to South Africa; my father met her when he was out there on leave. They married and then decided to come back to England after the war because they could see the troubles in South Africa were on the horizon, and thought it was not going to be a good place to live, as much as they loved it there.

So they brought me back for a fine English education. At seven and a half I was sent to boarding school at the Leas Hoylake up in Cheshire on the Wirral. Bit of a mind-blowing moment. Suddenly after a very happy childhood you're boarding. I remember my father saying to me, 'You've got to be strong, Michael, don't cry or anything'. It was probably a week before it dawned on me that I'd been dumped and I promptly burst into tears. My father had also promised me he wouldn't make me have dancing lessons and of course in week two the list for dancing lessons was read out and there was M. Rutherford. Dancing with your peers, with some thug your age with a snotty nose, was not my idea of fun.

At prep school, I was never very sporty. I like sport but I prefer golf and tennis, not so much team games. I was never a great mixer, quite a shy boy, and I didn't have many friends because of the constant moving around, but it was what it was. You didn't get out much at school: maybe twice a term and at half-term. So the whole experience was quite a wrench. Boarding school wasn't much fun in those days. There were outside lavatories, for example: the loo was covered but the passageway wasn't, so you'd be trudging out in the snow in your slippers. And I suppose that's partly why, when I was aged about ten, myself and a friend there, Dimitri Griliopoulos, started making music together. It was something to do. If you weren't sporty it was important to find something else to inspire you, to help get you through it, a form of escapism.

At home there hadn't been much music at all. My mother loved music but didn't play any instrument, and we didn't have a record player – so there were no sounds in the house – until my older sister acquired one and started playing Elvis records, but the record player was in her bedroom and I wasn't allowed in there, which probably made it seem more attractive. My first musical recollection is of performing in an end-of-term concert. I think I was singing either 'Michael Row The Boat Ashore' or a Cliff Richard number. Funnily enough I remember having no nerves; it's weird. When you're young you're often fearless. I couldn't sing at all, but it didn't really matter.

I started learning guitar at eight. It was a very slow start. I had no training and it never really crossed my mind to have any kind of lessons. From then on I mastered about three chords a year. And until I met Ant Phillips when I was about fourteen it was still three chords a year. So after six years that would have been about eighteen chords. No, actually, that's way too many.

I liked the shape of the guitar. It felt good and although this was prior to the Beatles, had I started when the Beatles were around I definitely would have chosen the guitar because they made it cool. Even an old-fashioned acoustic guitar seemed cooler to me than a piano. And around the time the Beatles did arrive my week had a high point on Sunday afternoons. My parents would come and take me out for Sunday lunch at a hotel and in the afternoon between two and four I'd sit and listen to a music show on the radio. You can't explain to kids today what it was like, the concept that pop music was only on radio once a week for two hours. It's inconceivable. But that's what made it such a special thing at the time.

Luckily, my parents were supportive of my music-making. When I was about twelve my mother took me to buy an electric guitar in Manchester. I'd seen all the cartoons in the papers, where you had a picture of a kid playing his guitar and the father holding his hands over his ears, and it always showed the guitar plugged straight into the mains socket on the wall. So when we went in to buy an electric guitar and the sales guy asked me, 'Do you want an amp?', I said, 'A what?' – I didn't know what an amp was – 'No, no, I don't want an amplifier, I just want an electric guitar', because I thought the noise came straight out of the guitar. My mother bought me a Hofner guitar with an action designed for a jazz player where the strings were about an inch away from the fretboard and a Little Giant or a Fender amp. My father used to walk around the house inspecting the foundations, convinced that I was going to knock the house down. Quite seriously. He wasn't complaining, because he was a very, very understanding man, but it was more that this was a new phenomenon: loud music which could shake the floorboards. In those days, no one quite knew what might happen. Maybe he was right: I could have been shaking the cement out of the joints.

At first, with Dimitri, who played drums, we covered some Shadows songs, the hits, whoever was in the charts that week. It felt a very insular activity, just me and Dimitri, and perhaps one other guy, although I can't remember what he played, and I think there was another drummer at one point. As usual, there's always two of what you don't need two of.

And then it was Charterhouse. Big school was a bit scary at first: 800 boys. At the time my parents had moved to Cheshire and Charterhouse was down in Godalming, so they got it all back to front: when I'd been at prep school in Cheshire they'd been living in Farnham. So they couldn't come down very much because it was too far away. I found Charterhouse a less friendly place. The Leas had been quite a small, warm school, with a good atmosphere. Which meant you went from being a big fish in a small pond to the opposite. It was a shock, and I didn't really enjoy the first year at all. I was always in trouble at Charterhouse, whereas I never had been at prep school. My housemaster had a massive downer on me. He was convinced during my entire time there that there would be a huge revolution in his house caused by me, and that he'd be ruined, so he was very repressive. When *Sergeant Pepper* came out, much later on, there was a kind of common room where you could play music, but by eight at night you had to be back upstairs. I thought, 'Fuck that', and was playing the album downstairs in the common room because there were some good speakers there and this housemaster stormed down, dragged me out by the scruff of my neck and beat me...

Ant was the first person I connected with at Charterhouse. Here you were in an environment you didn't really like, under quite a severe, unnatural regime, and there wasn't much contact with home. So once again music became something you clung on to, a little chink of light in what was a difficult time.

ANTHONY PHILLIPS: I was brought up in south-west London, in Putney and Roehampton, and sent away to prep school – like the others – at the age of eight. It was a very Draconian time when it was thought that going to boarding school made a man out of you, which was all very well-intentioned. My father always came out with the line that in his experience the people who had kept their heads in the war were the public school boys – and he was a grammar school boy, so he had no reason to be biased.

My initial experience was most bizarre. It seemed pretty much like being in a prisoner of war camp. In the 1950s meals at school still consisted of food like powered egg, and you had to sit there until you ate it: one night I threw up all over my teddy bear and destroyed him. I used to dread fish pie day, because this wasn't some delicious melt-in-the-mouth fish pie with buttered beans. We are talking stuff that needed oxyacetylene gear to cut through it, just disgusting.

My parents hadn't known how to break it to me that I was being sent away to the school, which was St Edmund's in Hindhead, but they were convinced it was going to be good for me. I had no idea what it would be like. I had nobody to compare notes with. I arrived at the school, went up to the headmaster and asked him, 'When am I seeing my mummy and daddy again?', and he said, 'Not for four weeks, boy'. He had been badly injured in the war, shot down in the Battle of Britain, and for an eight year old to be thrust into this place and find a headmaster who had bits of fingers missing and whose face had been burned to shreds was like walking into a horror film. He was a kindly man, but he looked like an ogre. However, there were other masters who were actually quite sadistic. There was very little scrutiny of the prep schools, and there were some pretty rum cookies there, I can tell you. And of course you didn't sneak, you didn't tell your parents, you just got on with it.

Music didn't really crop up until I was eleven. There hadn't been any significant musical heritage in my family. I think my father had scraped his way through a bit of coarse violin playing, and he and my mother both liked music: I can remember hearing the famous musicals of the era, although they didn't mean much to me at the time: *West Side Story*, *High Society*, *My Fair Lady*. And I wasn't a natural musical talent at all; I certainly wasn't Mozart creeping downstairs at four in the morning to pen my next concerto. When I did start getting involved in music it was singing Lonnie Donegan's 'My Old Man's A Dustman'. There was an impromptu concert where I was the singer for some reason. But I forgot the words and remember thinking, 'Maybe I should take up guitar instead'. There was only one other guy in the school who was any good at the guitar and I thought, 'Well, I'll see if I can be better than him', but it wasn't really a consuming interest until the Beatles came along – and I'm dating myself now – in 1963, when everything suddenly changed. Immediately music became a real passion. I got the bug big time and from then on that's what I did all the time.

We had a school group at St Edmund's. The only other musician there who was really competent was Rivers Job, who was later in one of our Charterhouse groups, dear old Rivers. The others were hopeless, absolutely hopeless. We called ourselves the Spiders, which was obviously our version of the Beatles. We had a drummer who was so free form that he would just stop playing for about thirty seconds and then throw himself at the drums. In a way he was ahead of his time, but as far as staying on a beat was concerned it made things difficult for the rest of us. We also had a guitarist who used to play a D7 chord the whole way through every song.

When I went to Charterhouse, Rivers had already been there for a year, which made going to the school relatively easy for me. Because going to public school is pretty terrifying. At prep school the masters had been frightening, but at Charterhouse it was less the masters who worried me than the boys. For some reason my parents made me join the school in the summer term and I was the only one starting that term. New boys were called 'New Hops' and all the other boys paraded past jeering and laughing, which made for quite a tense introduction. However, I quickly made friends with the other musicians. That was the great thing about Charterhouse for me: when I turned up people almost immediately came looking for me because they knew I was a guitarist. At St Edmund's I had just been a complete squit like everybody else.

PETER GABRIEL: My mum's father was a carpenter, and my dad came from a family of timber merchants. On his side they'd made some money, which is where the funds for a private education had come from, but it wasn't a traditional, conservative, public school family. My father was a quiet, thoughtful inventor and electrical engineer. My mother was the one who was interested in music and performing, running on adrenalin. My dad was more meditative. He would come back from a day working in London and stand on his head in the garden doing yoga.

I always loved music and the thing that excited me most as a kid was the drums. I acquired a bass tom-tom from a friend's brother and that was my first instrument: just the one drum. But it was a start and that one drum gradually evolved into a kit: I think I'd got roughly eight drums by the time I went to school.

I wasn't really thinking about writing songs at the beginning. I had been advised by an older cousin not to join the school choir because it was too much work. I wanted to learn oboe but I didn't feel good enough or qualified enough. Nowadays in my book the only qualification required for any art should be the desire to do it. I think 'talent' is a really overblown concept. There is a wonderful computer pioneer called Alan Kaye who is very interested in education and talked about visiting a school where there were just enough pupils for all the instruments of the orchestra, so there was no question about only the musicians being allowed to play in the orchestra. Everyone had to play. And it wasn't a problem. It was like learning a language. Clearly some people will excel and are able to pick a language up much more quickly but every one can find their level. In brain research they've learnt that the brain is actually a much more plastic environment than was previously thought, and that it rewires itself based on environmental experience and can, even into very late years, continue to do that.

A wonderful educationalist called Ken Robinson tells a story about a girl who was having severe problems at school, very much a problem child. Nowadays she would be given Ritalin or some other drug for attention deficit disorder. After a long interview with her and her mother the educationalist took the mother out and left the girl in the room with the radio on. The girl started dancing. There was a little window into the room and he said to the mother, 'Look through there. Your child isn't sick. She's a dancer, her skill is movement'. The girl went on to become a very successful principal dancer in the Royal Ballet and a choreographer for Andrew Lloyd Webber. It's simply a question of recognizing what everyone's talent is.

At school I started playing drums in a kind of trad jazz band called Milords, pretty badly. I was a very enthusiastic drummer but really not very good, although I have always loved rhythm and that led me down a particular path. In fact, in the old days, with the earlier drummers in Genesis, there was room for Ant and me, who were both particularly into drums, to spend time with the drummers trying to evolve rhythmic arrangements. Then of course as soon as Phil came along, he was so much better at it than we were that all that came to a halt.

Going to Charterhouse was a family tradition. But I hated it. I had started boarding at a prep school to get a year's preparation for the big board exam and I had actually enjoyed that quite a lot because I could cycle home at the weekends. And then at Charterhouse, suddenly I was stuck there, trapped in this dormitory. I remember my first night at the school very well. There were no curtains and it was near a road, whereas I'd grown up on a farm. So I could hear the noise of cars going past and see their headlights moving across the ceiling like anti-aircraft lights, and the air was full of the sounds of boys either crying or masturbating, or both. It was 'Welcome to grown-up school'.

TONY: The first time I met Peter was on our first day at Charterhouse at the beginning of the autumn term of 1963. We turned up in the same house on the same day because the new boys arrived slightly earlier than everybody else so that they could have a chance to meet each other and get acclimatized. I remember Peter very clearly. He was a slightly tubby, friendly guy. We became friends from the beginning, always got on well and started playing music together. I would play piano and Peter would sing along, unless Pete got to the piano first in which case he'd play and I would do my best to nudge him aside. I was quite happy to sing in terms of demonstrating a melody. I had been in my prep school choir and used to have a good treble voice. When it broke I could still sing in tune but it wasn't something I really wanted to do. I always thought Peter had a great voice. It had a lot of character even when he was quite young.

PETER: What drew me to Tony? It could only have been desperation! We were both struggling away at the piano, trying to write songs, he with his more classical chops and me playing with one finger, which later developed into two fingers... I think Tony figured out that he didn't have a particularly strong voice and thought I had a better voice, so I suspect that was his main motivation for trying to work with me. And I certainly knew he had skills on the piano that I definitely didn't have. Initially we had no real intention of getting a band together. Ant and Mike, on the other hand, were band players and out there doing it. Tony and I were more shy and although I do have an exhibitionist side I am also not very comfortable just getting up and performing. So it was this kind of backroom songwriting that fired me up originally, with Tony and me trying to find interesting chord sequences and melodies that other people weren't using, and looking at lyrical approaches that might avoid the usual romantic clichés.

TONY: Anthony Phillips was in the same house as Peter and me but in a different year to us, which meant that our paths didn't cross much. But we always got on well with Ant, and music was probably what brought us together. We were also friendly with Chris Stewart, who became the original drummer in Genesis. However Mike I hardly knew at school. It's strange, because we've ended up spending over half our life together. But he was in a different house and not someone I particularly came across. He was notorious as a bad boy, a bit of a lad.

MIKE: Because my housemaster had such a downer on me, there was a time when I wasn't allowed to play the guitar in my house, because it was 'a symbol of the revolution' as he called it – his words! So I was banned from playing the guitar, which of course was just going to guarantee I would play it. He made my life pretty horrible, actually. So I ended up sneaking off. Later on I had a motorbike which I kept in a garage around the corner and I'd head off to London in the evening to go and see bands. But I never got caught.

As at prep school, music was what got me through Charterhouse. I think it would have been hard otherwise. Thursday afternoons was when we used to get together: no games, so we'd pick up the gear after lunch, lug it over to a classroom – that took up most of the afternoon, actually – set it up, make it work, write for a couple of hours and then go back again. That was the high point of the week, regardless of the quality of the session. I started playing with Ant: in those days if you were in a school and someone else played guitar you knew about them, there weren't that many.

> **ANT, IT SEEMED, WAS THE ONLY GUY IN THE SCHOOL WHO OWNED A GUITAR AND AN AMP, SO HE WAS IN EVERY GROUP. FORTUNATELY HE WAS A PRETTY GOOD GUITARIST TOO.**
>
> **TONY BANKS**

Opposite: Charterhouse School. Founded in 1611 with money bequeathed by Thomas Sutton, a wealthy Jacobean merchant, the school was originally based in London, in a former Carthusian monastery at Charterhouse Square near Smithfield – hence the terms 'Carthusian' for a current pupil and 'old Carthusian' for a former pupil. In 1872, the school moved to its present site, a few miles southwest of Guildford and just outside Godalming, in Surrey. The school's illustrious list of old Carthusians includes John Wesley, the founder of Methodism, Robert Baden-Powell, founder of the scouting movement, the composer Ralph Vaughan Williams, the writers Max Beerbohm and Ralph Graves, and the Dimbleby brothers – along with Messrs Banks, Gabriel, Phillips, Rutherford, Stewart, Macphail and King.

ANT: I was in Duckites with Peter and Tony, but to start with I didn't know them because they were older and I had my friends out of house. It was all very antediluvian, and there was a lot of inter-house rivalry, especially in the housemaster's mind, so when I started fraternizing with people outside the house I got a lot of questions as if I was being disloyal. I was quite good at sport, though ironically not cricket which is the one I've carried on playing or trying to play, but once I realized that it clashed with guitar practice I skipped the sports. Quite quickly I had a school group going called Anon, which included my old prep school friend Rivers Job, a friend of Rivers' called Richard Macphail on vocals, and Mike Rutherford.

MIKE: Ant had an outgoing personality and was an impressive musician. He knew all the songs I didn't know and he had the right amplifier, so in my mind he was way ahead of me as a musician. He was also the most developed in trying to think about learning chords, learning to play lead, writing songs. All of which made me want to catch up.

The first thing Ant and I really did together was Anon. Ant was the dynamic, driving force, Richard Macphail was a good front man, and we had Rob Tyrell on drums and Rivers Job on bass. Rivers was equally impressive, and the first of any of us to turn pro: when he left school he joined the Savoy Brown Blues Band. We learned Beatles and Stones songs and would rehearse probably all term and half the holidays to do one party at somebody's house. But playing covers was quite a good thing: by learning other songs you could get your guitar playing up to speed a little bit.

This page: Peter (left) and Tony (right). Despite the trophies in front of them, they were not huge fans of the organized sports at Charterhouse. Tony recalls, 'I was never interested in team sports, but I did like games like tennis, squash and fives, all of which I played with Peter. We were great friends and great rivals. Neither of us was very good at any of these sports, but we were able to be very competitive against each other.' Tony says he feels sorry for their schoolmate sitting in the middle who has had to see himself immortalized between Tony and Peter.

ANT: The first show that we ever did was just before Christmas 1965, during 'School Entertainment', a multi-arts event with a mix of film, theatre and music. So the curtain is about to go up. And Mike Rutherford has got no lead. We just couldn't believe it. We managed to race round and get him one in time. And when the curtain did go up, there was the headmaster sitting right at the front with his hands clamped over his ears, which was not encouraging.

Anon were pretty rough and when the Beatles' songwriting got too complicated we piled out of trying to cover their songs. Even so, at one point Mike decided all this practising was far too serious, so he left and formed a group called Climax with another bunch of guys who were a little more *laissez-faire*. We brought in Mick Colman, who was a brilliant piano and violin scholar, terribly, terribly gifted, but he didn't quite fit in with the rest of the band. Climax was Mike's journeyman band, but we were convinced we had the best musicians, so we would sit there and say, 'They're never going to make it.' And sure enough, Mike came back pretty quickly.

By this time the blues era had started and I was trying to copy Eric Clapton, not that well to be honest. We were given permission to give an impromptu concert by the music master, Geoffrey Horder, 'but,' he said, 'no announcements'. We had a huge equipment breakdown during the set, with leads not working and the audience growing very restless so Richard had to say something. 'Sorry, folks', he said. 'This is all part of the act. And now the next number is one of our own'. Luckily we did have one of our own, but suddenly I saw this Vesuvian master looming up on my left shouting, 'Last number, off, off,' and he stopped it with two numbers to go. In fact, he didn't know what a service he'd done us because we hadn't rehearsed what was going to be our final number and had only listened to it in a record shop, so the gods were moving in mysterious ways. But there was almost a riot, boys rocking the school clock and Rivers Job was heard to say 'Where's that bugger Geoffrey?' and threw a lead at him, which must have contributed to Rivers getting thrown out of Charterhouse.

MIKE: After Rivers left, I played bass, because although Ant and I both played guitar he was a much better guitarist. Funnily enough in those days, it wasn't like a demotion. It was simply, 'Oh, you're better than me, I'll play the bass', very matter of fact.

TONY: Anon were actually pretty good. The singer, Richard Macphail, ended up working for us much later on after we became Genesis, which is bizarre. Richard would have liked to have been a Mick Jagger type of vocalist; he probably ended up being a bit more like Dennis Waterman, but he was still an effective singer. And he was happy being up on stage and the centre of attention, which is something I think Pete initially found quite difficult.

PETER: I am pretty shy, and usually in two minds about performing, but once, and if, I can break through that, I quite enjoy it...I think I was an awkward teenager, which is still how I feel today sometimes! But I did have another kind of adrenalin fix. When I was fourteen or so, I had come across these hats that looked slightly Cromwellian, with a nice brim and a high central crown. I started schlepping them round the trendy places in Carnaby Street and the Kings Road but no one was interested until I got to a place called Emmerton & Lambert in the Chelsea Antiques Market, this very cool place in the King's Road where the Stones used to hang out, with a café up on the second floor, Moroccan, a bit smoky, very avant-garde for the time. The guy there said, 'Yeah, I like these, bring me some in pink and lime green', and I persuaded Dunne & Company, who had a shop in Piccadilly, to manufacture the hats for me. I heard that Keith Richards had bought one and when I went home one Saturday from school and switched on *Juke Box Jury*, which was a regular music fix, there was Marianne Faithfull sitting on *Juke Box Jury* wearing my hat: she'd stuck a feather in it but I was very happy that my name was embossed on the leather strip around the inside. I never did continue my career as a milliner, although I have had a few silly things on my head since then. But I did possess an entrepreneurial streak, a determination, which I think really helped Genesis at times.

TONY: Pete and I eventually became part of this group called the Garden Wall, which had originally been put together by a guy called Johnny Trapman who was a trumpeter. It was supposed to be a jazzy, bluesy outfit and I was roped in on piano – and organ when we could find one to steal or borrow. Pete would sing, Chris Stewart ended up on drums and Ant was the guitarist. I can't remember who the bass player was. Perhaps we didn't have one. We did one stage show which wasn't very brilliant: since the piano was too heavy to lift onto the stage I was sitting out in front of the stage so no one even knew I was there until I played the introduction to 'When A Man Loves A Woman' and everybody went, 'Christ, there's a guy down there'. And of course you couldn't really hear anything. God knows what it sounded like.

Overleaf: A Duckites house photograph. Tony and Peter are top left, back row. Ant is fourth from the right in the second row from the back, with Chris Stewart to his right. The house was in fact called Girdlestonites, but had gained the nickname Duckites supposedly from the duck-like walk, not of Chuck Berry, but of its founding housemaster Mr Girdlestone. To a certain extent the houses were self-contained communities. Mike Rutherford was in a different house, Lockites, and as a result Tony, for example, didn't know him so well: 'I'd met Mike once or twice but he wasn't someone I came across. He was notorious as a bad boy, a bit of a lad.'

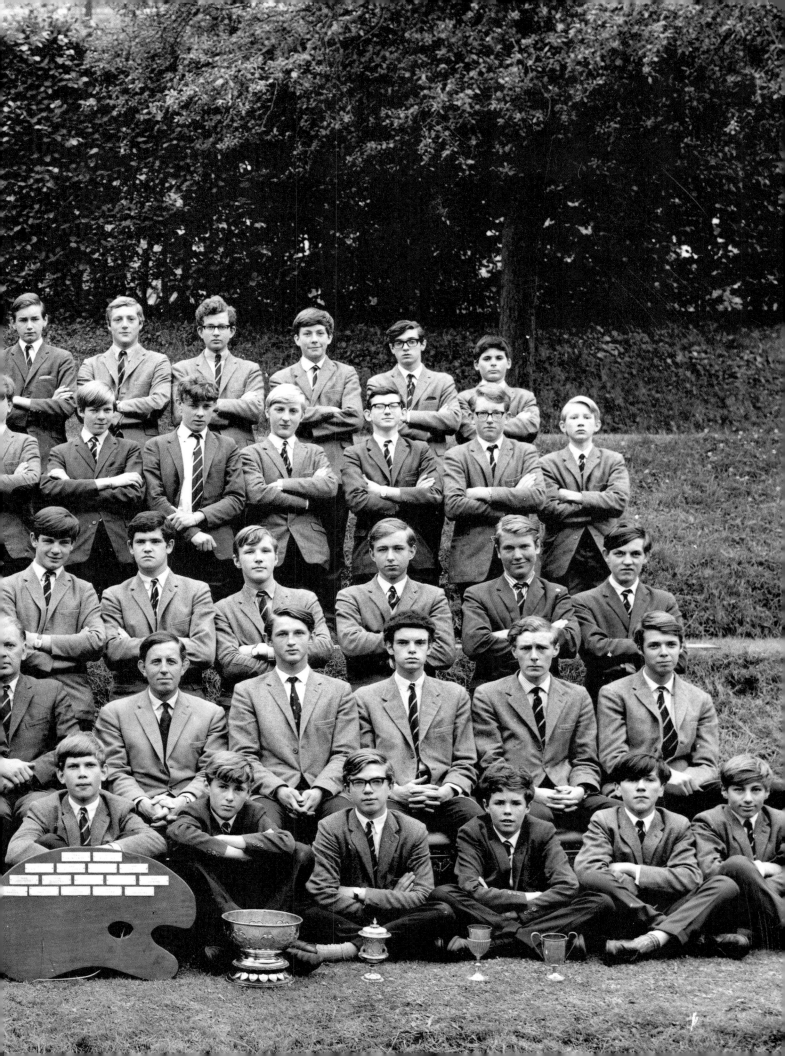

MIKE: One of Anon's main shows at Charterhouse was on the same bill as Tony and Peter, who had another band called the Garden Wall, who were not at all as good as us, whatever they may tell you. They had trumpets and pianos and we had rock and noise and racket, which was what I liked.

ANT: It's a complete misconception to think that Genesis existed as a group at Charterhouse. It didn't. It existed only as four songwriters. Richard Macphail left to go to Millfield School, Mike and I had become very close friends again and were writing together, and then we joined forces with the other two. Mike and I were caught in a strange time warp between doing bad blues numbers and trying to create something new with twelve-string guitars, and I think at that stage we were still a bit backward. So when we wanted to make some demos towards the end of 1966 we asked Tony to come and add keyboards and he said, 'Well, can I bring Pete and do one of our own numbers?'

TONY: Ant was the one who instigated doing some recordings. We had a friend at school called Brian Roberts, who had a makeshift studio at his home, egg boxes on the walls. Ant was doing some recording at Brian's with Mike and he asked me if wanted to come along and play organ on it. I said, 'Yeah, and why don't I get Peter along as well', because we'd written a song together and Pete and I thought, 'Well, we can record that at the same time'. We turned up, and because Pete couldn't come straight away we started off with Ant singing the vocals on the first song. I stopped them and said, 'Look, we should really wait for Peter because he's got an awful lot better voice than you and it would just sound so much better if Pete was to sing'. When Pete turned up he ended up singing on all the songs, not just the one song he and I had written, which was called 'She Is Beautiful'. Ant had a voice a bit like mine: he could sing in tune, and in the right situation he'd have been fine, but he just didn't have the character of Pete's voice. Pete could get across depth and excitement at once. Even on that early tape you can hear it.

PETER SANG ALL EVENING. HE SOUNDED GREAT AND THAT MADE ANT REALIZE THAT HE WASN'T REALLY A SINGER AND PETE WAS. IF ANT HADN'T REALIZED THAT WE MIGHT HAVE MISSED THE MOMENT. Mike Rutherford

PETER: Richard Macphail had been the main singer, but eventually, as things were juggled around and re-assembled, I was effectively asked to move in as the main singing entity. Tony and I inched our way in there, because we had a few other songs and I think Ant felt my voice might be a useful tool for his material. And that was the start of our recording.

ANT: Both Peter and Tony were incredibly friendly, I have to say. Tony was great fun. I'd grown close enough to him to feel completely at ease about asking him to come along and play the organ for us. He wasn't pushy at all. And Peter was actually very different to how he became. He was very much part of what I call 'the safe crowd', not particularly charismatic, very nice but really quite a conventional guy. He used to lend us his drums but he was very old-womanly about it, very nervous, coming along to check everything was all right. On the other hand he would also jump up on the dining room table and do this Motown turn. In a way Mike and I had the R&B, the raw side, Tony had the classical influence and the thing that Peter brought in, which the rest of us didn't have naturally, was the soul, that slightly soulful voice.

PETER: As well as interesting and creative bands like the Who, the Beatles, the Yardbirds and John Mayall – I know Ant and Mike were very much into John Mayall – Tony and I were also listening to Otis Redding, the Stax/Atlantic artists, Tamla numbers like 'Reach Out (I'll Be There)', as well as the Beach Boys, who were important, particularly for Tony, because these records were where some of the real innovation was happening. Whereas at that time Ant and Mike were more in a blues band mode.

ANT: Brian Roberts had one of the early tape machines and he loved recording: groups, choirs, anything. Bit of a classic boffin in a way, but very generous. His father was a doctor and they had two houses opposite each other in Chiswick. As Anon we had recorded some sessions over in the main house, pretty much just with a tape recorder in a domestic room, but later on Brian used an upstairs room over the garage of the house opposite, which he had converted into a studio, with room for drums and a couple more mikes.

MIKE: Anon had also done one recording at a studio called Tony Pike Sound in Putney, a song called 'Pennsylvania Flickhouse', which Richard Macphail sang. In those days there were no young, hip engineers, only old-school technicians who weren't used to recording loud amplifiers, so we had a real old-fashioned BBC-type engineer. I didn't realize that if we were in the studio he could hear what we were saying. He kept telling us, 'Don't play so loudly, mind my compressors', and I muttered, 'Stupid old git'. He said, 'I heard that'.

ANT: One of the most awful things is that when Brian left his house, he suddenly remembered the tapes in the attic. He went back and they'd been chucked out. A lot of early stuff disappeared. I always maintain that the original 'Pennsylvania Flickhouse' demo that Anon recorded with Brian was much, much better than the one we did later in the studio, which was dreadful.

PETER: Having made a demo, our original intention – at least as far as Tony and I were concerned – was to sell our songs to other people. So when we heard that Jonathan King was coming down to visit the school on Old Carthusians Day we got our friend John Alexander to go up and give him a copy of our tape.

Above: Mike (right) in 1965, with his friend Dimitri Griliopoulos using Mike's Little Giant amp, and Mike's sister Nicky posing as the singer. Mike and Dimitri had met at prep school and started playing music together – Mike's first foray into a group format.

This page: The programme for Anon's first gig, in which Richard Macphail's name was left out because his parents didn't want him to take part.
Opposite: An early performance by the Charterhouse band.

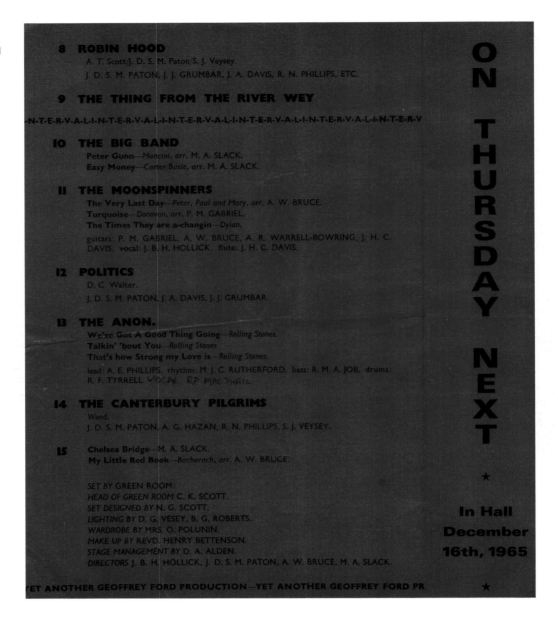

8 ROBIN HOOD
A. T. Scott/J. D. S. M. Paton/S. J. Veysey.
J. D. S. M. PATON, J. J. GRUMBAR, J. A. DAVIS, R. N. PHILLIPS, ETC.

9 THE THING FROM THE RIVER WEY

-N-T-E-R-V-A-L-I-N-T-E-R-V-A-L-I-N-T-E-R-V-A-L-I-N-T-E-R-V-A-L-I-N-T-E-R-V-A-L-I-N-T-E-R-V

10 THE BIG BAND
Peter Gunn—*Mancini*, arr. M. A. SLACK.
Easy Money—*Carter/Basie*, arr. M. A. SLACK.

11 THE MOONSPINNERS
The Very Last Day—*Peter, Paul and Mary*, arr. A. W. BRUCE.
Turquoise—*Donovan*, arr. P. M. GABRIEL.
The Times They are a-changin—*Dylan*.
guitars: P. M. GABRIEL, A. W. BRUCE, A. R. WARRELL-BOWRING, J. H. C. DAVIS. vocal: J. B. H. HOLLICK. flute: J. H. C. DAVIS.

12 POLITICS
D. C. Walter.
J. D. S. M. PATON, J. A. DAVIS, J. J. GRUMBAR.

13 THE ANON.
We've Got A Good Thing Going—*Rolling Stones*.
Talkin' 'bout You—*Rolling Stones*.
That's how Strong my Love is—*Rolling Stones*.
lead: A. E. PHILLIPS. rhythm: M. J. C. RUTHERFORD. bass: R. M. A. JOB. drums: R. F. TYRRELL. *vocal: RP MacPhail*

14 THE CANTERBURY PILGRIMS
Wood.
J. D. S. M. PATON, A. G. HAZAN, R. N. PHILLIPS, S. J. VEYSEY.

15 Chelsea Bridge—M. A. SLACK.
My Little Red Book—*Bacharach*, arr. A. W. BRUCE.

SET BY GREEN ROOM.
HEAD OF GREEN ROOM C. K. SCOTT.
SET DESIGNED BY N. G. SCOTT.
LIGHTING BY D. G. VESEY, B. G. ROBERTS.
WARDROBE BY MRS. O. POLUNIN.
MAKE UP BY REVD. HENRY BETTENSON.
STAGE MANAGEMENT BY D. A. ALDEN.
DIRECTORS J. B. H. HOLLICK, J. D. S. M. PATON, A. W. BRUCE, M. A. SLACK.

YET ANOTHER GEOFFREY FORD PRODUCTION—YET ANOTHER GEOFFREY FORD PR

ON THURSDAY NEXT

★

In Hall
December
16th, 1965

★

ANT: I think we were actually ambitious. It seems a ridiculous word to use because we were a group of people who had got together for one demo tape, hardly played together, just thought it was all great fun. Why not give somebody our tape, and who better to give it to? Jonathan King was the only accessible famous person we knew: he'd had a big hit with 'Everyone's Gone To The Moon' a year or so before, and he'd been a pupil at Charterhouse.

TONY: We were looking for any contact we could find in the music business. There were two possibilities. One was David Jacobs, who hosted *Juke Box Jury*, because his son was at the school, and the other was Jonathan King. Of course, we didn't have the guts to give him the tape ourselves.

MIKE: Someone said, 'Go on shove it in his car' or something, and John Alexander was the only one with enough nerve to go and put the tape in Jonathan King's car. Which was odd, because, to be honest, Pete's never afraid of doing things. We're all fairly fearless really, Pete especially, so I don't know why John Al ended up having to do it.

PETER: Eventually we heard back from Jonathan King, after what seemed quite a long time. He phoned up and invited us up to London. We were very excited at this prospect of bright lights, big city.

TONY: I think what Jonathan King liked was Peter's voice, and on that basis he thought it was worth going on. The song 'She Is Beautiful' was the one which seemed to be attracting the most attention at the time, so Peter and I were a bit smug about that since that song had been our contribution to the tape.

MIKE: Jonathan King played a really important part in the history of Genesis. Because we ended up making an album, these four or five guys who couldn't really play their instruments. In those days being given a chance to make an album was pretty unusual. It didn't happen very often to people of our calibre, and the experience really whetted our appetites.

ANT: Many years later when Jonathan King presented an award to Peter either he said, or the impression was given, that he was the man who had managed Genesis to success, which is just not true. I'm as damning of that claim as I am overflowing with gratitude for what happened at the start. Without him we would probably have never got going. He was hugely patient and indulgent with us. We were all pretty shy and retiring and despite Peter being very practical and very good when it came to getting gigs, I'm not sure the rest of us would ever have done anything. He gave us a lot of confidence: we liked what we were doing but we really didn't think anybody else was necessarily going to like it.

PETER: Jonathan gave us our first break without any question. And he was really smart at hearing songwriting. I've talked about this sometimes with the 10cc guys, who he also launched. Genesis has done extraordinarily well over the years because, I think, it's a group of songwriters as opposed to a group of musicians, which has given it longevity, with Mike and Tony and myself all doing our own things, as have Ant and Steve, and Phil, the most successful of all. And that you rarely see in any other band, although 10cc was an example of a similar group of people who were there for the songs more than for the playing.

Right and opposite: Jonathan King was a pop star while at Cambridge, when he wrote and released 'Everyone's Gone To The Moon' and quickly made a name for himself as a producer and A&R man at Decca Records. Ant remembers, 'Jonathan King was famous; he'd had that big hit. But he was hugely patient with what we wanted to do. I think he saw a talent, and let us do the singles and the first album without interfering too much. He gave us a lot of confidence.'

'SHE IS BEAUTIFUL' IS THE NUMBER JONATHAN KING LIKED AND WE GOT THE DEAL ON THE BASIS OF IT, WHICH MIKE AND I WERE ALWAYS MORE THAN HAPPY TO ADMIT.

ANTHONY PHILLIPS

TONY: We went up to London to Jonathan King's flat and found ourselves at least on the fringes of the music business. We originally only wanted to be writers, we didn't really want to be performers, so we agreed a publishing deal, a pretty stupid contract initially which fortunately, because we were minors, we managed to get out of.

PETER: Of course Jonathan had waved these pieces of paper at us, and told us, 'Oh, these are deals I signed' and then he showed us one with his signature on which looked similar, and we all went, 'Sure.' Our parents were quite worried that we'd signed these contracts and got hold of Goodman, Derek & Co., who were actually pretty hopeless but represented the Beatles at the time and they did then manage to improve the terms a little, but I think at that point we got to two and a half per cent royalty, UK only, one and three quarters for the rest of the world. So it wasn't the most generous of terms. But it was fairly standard for the time.

TONY: We used to see Jonathan King quite a bit. He was always very friendly. He used to play up on the conceit thing which has always been part of his personality. I think it's a sort of front he puts on. He was always very enthusiastic and he was kind to us and I think he liked the fact that he was the star working with these impressionable young guys.

PETER: Jonathan King was pretty much exactly the same as he is now. Very enthusiastic and with ideas of controlling everything. He gave us the name Genesis. Actually, his first choice was Gabriel's Angels, which I thought was pretty good. But for some reason I still can't fathom the others in the band didn't like it as much. When Genesis was suggested I think we thought, 'Well, if this guy's going to pay for us to go into a studio, we'd just better go along with it'.

MIKE: We didn't have a name when Jonathan King came up with Genesis. We couldn't agree on anything, and we didn't have any great alternative to offer him, so that became the name. Genesis was never a name that I thought was very good, but after a while it is what it is and you get used to it. I mean, the Beatles is a crap name really, if you think about it.

TONY: We'd spent an awful lot of time thinking up names and they were all crap! And we knew they were too. Ant came up with Champagne Meadow, which gives some idea of the kind of brick wall we were hitting. So the name Genesis was something of a relief as far as I was concerned.

ANT: Jonathan King got us working on more demos. It's ironic that the group later ended up recording all these long pieces because that's what we kicked off with: five-minute epics with lots of elements, more 'A Day In The Life' than 'Get Back'. But Jonathan King was hugely patient with that. I think he saw a talent and he let us do this first album and two singles that missed, without interfering too much with the material.

PETER: I think Jonathan was of the opinion that if he'd got the vocal performance he could fix the rest. And the drumming wasn't that locked in: Chris Stewart is a lovely man, but was not a wonderful timekeeper. We somehow got through the first set of demos and that led us into a second phase. Jonathan was very excited about getting these new songs from us, and then we heard nothing; he seemed to have lost interest at that point because we were getting too experimental. Pop music is his forte and always has been, and the songs we were giving him weren't poppy enough, so I think he was a bit disappointed.

TONY: Because King couldn't find anyone to perform the songs, he suggested, 'Why don't you do them yourselves?' So we thought, 'OK, we'll try doing that'. He was getting less and less interested because we were trying to get more and more ambitious, with these slightly longer pieces. We felt we were losing him, so Pete and I actually sat down and said, 'Let's write a song which he *is* going to like'. We did a pastiche of a Bee Gees song – the Bee Gees of the late '60s – which turned out quite well, called 'The Silent Sun'. King said, 'Yeah, I love this, it's fantastic'. We went in the studio and made a proper recording of the song, which was released as our first single in the beginning of 1968.

Overleaf: A shot by Brian Roberts – who was a keen photographer as well as a recording buff – on his father's Leica. The band are in woodlands near Ant's house in Send. From left: Tony, Mike, Peter, Chris Stewart and Ant.

PETER: It was as a reaction to Jonathan's disappointment in the second bout of demos – which we thought were wonderful and very exciting – that we then deliberately tried to write a more poppy song with this 'Gibbish' vocal. On 'Silent Sun' I was trying to imitate Robin Gibb, who had the more emotional soulful voice, which was Jonathan's favourite voice at the time. We'd figured that if I could steer things a little bit in that direction we might have a chance of getting back in the studio. So that's what got us back I think in recording. I've told the Bee Gees this story since, which amused them…

Above: The first version of Genesis, kitted out in black and white by Jonathan King, and shot for publicity purposes.

ANT: I was very headstrong and not very realistic, so when Jonathan King tried to get us to start writing these very simple things, I wasn't too keen. I didn't really like 'Silent Sun' very much, but Mike and Tony were much more sensible and they realized that this was the way to go. I think what I didn't like was the idea that King was trying to turn us into a sort of facsimile of his own material. The best thing that ever happened to Genesis was that it wasn't successful with the first singles, because if they had been successful the band would never have developed and gone down the line it eventually followed.

TONY: I think 'Silent Sun' could have been quite a big hit if other factors had been right, but it didn't work out that way. And probably from our point of view it was a great thing the single wasn't a hit because if it had been we would have been very much stuck in a rut as a Bee Gees copy band.

MIKE: When 'Silent Sun' was released we all rushed out to buy our outfits for *Top Of The Pops*. It's a lovely concept, isn't it? We thought we should be prepared just in case we had to appear, so we all bought black and white outfits, black trousers and white tops or the other way round.

FAME AND FORTUNE…JONATHAN KING TOOK US ALL TO CARNABY STREET TO GET DRESSED UP FOR TOP OF THE POPS. AND, OF COURSE, WE NEVER GOT ANYWHERE CLOSE TO BEING ON THE SHOW. PETER GABRIEL

TONY: We recorded a second single, 'A Winter's Tale', which was released in May of that year, 1968, and we started discussing an album. King said that he had talked to some other people and that he, and they, felt we really had to get ourselves a better rhythm section. We said, 'We're not sure about a new bassist', because Mike was very much a part of what we were doing, so we had to have a change of drummer. Chris Stewart was a lovely guy, but he was not a great drummer. He is now, of course, a world-famous author, so he's done all right in the end. I remember talking to him about the decision and he sort of nodded and said, 'Right,' but God knows what was going through his brain. In any business you have to be ruthless, but at that stage we were nothing, and the chances were that we would continue to be nothing so perhaps he didn't think it was so bad.

MIKE: I had to fire Chris. They picked on me and said, 'You go and tell him'. They all chickened out. I think Chris would agree he wasn't a great drummer. Although having said that, were we that good to be able to say he wasn't that good? I might have been chosen to fire him because he was in the same house as Peter and Tony, and if you're in the same house you're very close so maybe they got me in so he wouldn't like me rather than them. I walked down to the house, with John Alexander, who'd given the tape to Jonathan King. John came to support me morally. We walked down this long corridor to tell Chris the bad news, got to his study, I knocked on the door, went in and said, 'Oh Chris, hi, John Al and I want a word'. I looked round, Al had pissed off! He'd chickened out too! I was on my own. But Chris was always a happy guy; I'm not sure he really worried about it too much.

PETER: It was very hard with Chris because we'd grown up together, but I think we did feel that our chances were being diminished a little. He was very sad but I think he sensed that it wasn't taking off.

We found a replacement in John Silver, who was studying at the same crammer in London as me. John was a jazz fan: Stan Kenton in particular was his hero. But he was also the person who introduced us to Randy Newman, who I've been enjoying ever since, and was a big Beach Boys fan along with Tony. He was a real enthusiast and a great source of energy.

TONY: We now had a collection of songs and then had this great idea to write an album based on the story of the Bible, absolutely pathetic. But it did give us something to hang everything around and we re-wrote some of the lyrics to fit the concept. Since we were English public schoolboys towards the introverted end of the scale it was difficult for us to write about reality. It felt easier for us to hide behind a big story. In the early days of Genesis we tended to use myths and legends as a way of writing to avoid having to say anything real, and for the time that was quite original.

PETER: Jonathan may have edited or picked the songs, but we'd pretty much finished the songs prior to his input. So he might have steered them a bit in the studio – though he may have a different take on that – and the concept of the album was broad enough to allow us to include all kinds of songs. Actually a lot of artists still work like that, as have we. You have your grand dream and that actually allows you to peg in lots of old shit.

TONY: *From Genesis To Revelation* was really a composite of all the best tracks we had up to that point including songs from the early tapes we'd done for Jonathan King which had sounded quite good. It included 'The Serpent', which had originally been 'She Is Beautiful' on the very first demo. I think we always felt this was a song which had an excitement about it we liked – and it still sounds pretty good as a song, I think.

There was also one quite ambitious long piece called 'A Place To Call My Own', mainly written by Ant, which was originally about three times as long as the version that ended up on the album, a first example of us heading towards a longer format. But at that time we decided in the end to use only the final section on the album, and get rid of the other sections, which were probably not as consistent all the way through.

Above: Jonathan Silver during recording sessions for *From Genesis To Revelation*. 'I can remember during one of the recordings, on 'The Conqueror', Jonathan King told me, "Play like Charlie Watts". He wanted it to sound like 'Get Off My Cloud', so I duly did, because if Jonathan said jump or stand backwards or stand on your head, you did it. This was the nature of the relationship: he was completely omniscient in a truly decent way.' Overleaf: Another stop on the exhausting tour of fine English country houses that the band undertook in the summer of 1968: here in the grounds of John Silver's home: Tony, Ant (with that pith helmet again), John Silver on bongos, Mike, and Pete on flute.

JONJO MUSIC CO. LTD.

DIRECTORS:
J.D.A. RONCORONI
K.E. JONES
KENNETH G. KING

37, SOHO SQUARE
LONDON W1
01-437 9405
CABLES—MARQUIMUS, LONDON

29th November, 1967.

JR:CB

Mr. Peter Gabriel,
CHARTERHOUSE COLLEGE,
Godalming,
Surrey.

Dear Peter,

I must apologise for not writing to you before about the tape you left with me of your songs. The reason I have not written is that it has only been possible for Jonathan to hear these this week and I am sorry to tell you that we were not very impressed - the previous batch you did are, in our opinion, much better.

If you are coming to town this side of Christmas perhaps you would give me a ring or come in and see me and we can have a chat.

All the best to you all.

Yours sincerely,

Joe Roncoroni.

One of the other tracks which was significant for me was 'Fireside Song'. The verse was something I had originally written using really quite complicated chords and one day I sat down and thought that the melody line itself was nice, but why didn't I just use the most bog standard chords I could underneath to see how it sounded. And I thought, 'That sounds actually a lot better'. Being a keyboard player you are always a little prone to using lots of funny chords, and over the years I've obviously done a lot of that, but I have also always liked things where everything has been kept really simple, and I think working on that song in particular taught me that.

PETER: The recording of *From Genesis To Revelation* was done very quickly, as all recording was in those days. We had no real control over the way things sounded, although you can hear where we were starting to explore things melodically, especially on some of Tony's pieces.

MIKE: The album only took three days. There must have been a bit of overdubbing, but it was only on a four-track machine so there wasn't the scope to do much. We would do a few different takes and get a version we liked.

We were hardly a band and we couldn't play our instruments that well. I was probably the least proficient technically. I was definitely the slowest developer, and I played bass pretty averagely on that first album, though I'm not sure it was that obvious to the outside world.

Also recording techniques were not yet that advanced. For many years I felt that the sound we made in the room was a lot better than what we managed to capture on tape. We used to get a severely dodgy sound. It makes you realize what an incredible job George Martin did with the Beatles. Obviously they were a great band, but the records sounded fantastic and the guys at the Regent B studios or wherever were getting the most horrible sound. Actually, it was us probably.

PETER: We were definitely conscientious about doing the recording. We were determined that we should make the best of the chance we had. But I was struggling because I didn't realize that singers often take longer to get to a performance – not every singer does, but I certainly do – and I don't think we could do much patching in then, so as the singer you'd have to do take after take until you got the whole thing right, which was tiring. Each time the previous attempt would be erased, so you just had to wait for a good take. I don't think I had any techniques for looking after my voice in those days. I guess it just used to hurt the next day.

ANT: Peter and Tony were way out front on the first album, no doubt about it. Mike and I were playing catch up. I had started to write on piano, independently of Mike, and so I had my own thing going with a couple of tracks. In fact we did a version of 'Visions Of Angels' for that album which didn't get on, it just didn't work out – a much better version ended up on *Trespass*. So I did have a couple of my own things, although everything was a group composition. There was no competition at all, and I can hardly remember a single argument in fact. This was partly because it was a part-time activity, we were recording it during a school holiday. Mike was the only one who didn't really have a forum as a writer on that album. But it didn't matter: Mike was a bit like the guy who turns up with the jokes and the cravat and makes everybody feel good; he'll admit that himself... And even when Mike started writing a hell of a lot more and playing a far more prominent part in the group, that side of his character was vital to us, as a source of lightness and as a peace maker and provider of good vibes.

MIKE: We were quite industrious. We wouldn't go there and get pissed all day. We worked quite hard. And the other thing is there was very little drugs around. Peter and Tony didn't really partake and I was smoking a bit of dope, but nothing very much. I'd survived my first acid trip,

Opposite: The less than encouraging letter Peter received from Jonjo Music – the publishing company set up by Jonathan King and his business partner Joe Roncoroni – in response to a second set of demos the band had recorded in autumn 1967.

when I went to see the Cream at the Marquee Club with Richard Macphail, aged sixteen or seventeen, and someone had spiked my Coca Cola with acid. I had the most horrendous bad trip in Richard's house in Holborn that night. The next day I was going to join my parents to travel to France for a family weekend and I arrived at the Victoria Station Hotel, just coming down from the trip, wearing a big Afghan coat, with sweat pouring off me, my T-shirt wringing wet. My mother, bless her, said, 'Oh, poor boy, he's got a cold. Put him to bed and we'll go a day later'. I just lay in bed and tossed and turned and threw up. It never occurred to her that I had anything more than a bad dose of flu.

PETER: Jonathan King would be there at the studio, although he may have gone off early because he was living the high life a little bit and driving around in his E-type Jag. And he had a lot of male friends that didn't all add up at that point, but like John Silver, he was a real enthusiast, and when he's hot and getting into something, it suddenly seems everything's possible. When, however, he gets interested in the next thing, he hops away and you're forgotten about, so it was sunshine or nothing.

The recording was finished in the summer of 1968, but the album wasn't released until the following spring. When we did hear the final version, I don't think we were completely happy with all the performances and certainly we didn't like the sound of the record.

MIKE: Jonathan King had gone away to put some strings on our first album. We were thinking it would be like the Moody Blues, we're going to sound great – and when we heard it, it was like, 'Oh gawd'.

TONY: I thought the strings were good on some of the songs. I don't think they were that bad. They were just pop arrangements. I think a song like 'In The Wilderness' sounded better without the strings, but it wasn't a big thing for me. However, I know Ant in particular always found it annoying.

ANT: Ah, the strings on *From Genesis To Revelation*. I was the one who really blew my top about it. To this day I still don't understand how the others could be so much more mature and sensible about it. I remember I had to live for about a year afterwards with all my friends saying, 'How could you have let Jonathan King do that?', because they'd heard the original four-track versions before the arrangements were added – the originals were rough but at least they had some power. And I was saying, 'But we didn't know, we didn't know.' I felt really angry because it was a complete *fait accompli* and of course in those days you couldn't get back to a previous version, it was too late, good night, erase, there was no 'undo' button. And I completely freaked out.

I know Jonathan King was looking for something, and to be fair to the man, he thought it needed a more commercial edge. With modern technology it would be just fine, but at that time, once you had reduced that backing track to mono it was gone forever. And I can only quote all my other friends saying, 'He's butchered it'. So that I can't really forgive him for, partly because of all the grief I got from other people, although I can understand why he did it. And I remember the others just stood there and I thought, 'How can you just stand there?' I tore out of the room and I went and lay down for about two hours wondering, 'What else is going to go wrong in my life?' – I'd just been going through a very emotional break-up. It was an indescribably awful feeling. I felt as if my whole world was caving in.

I HAVE QUITE A LOT OF AFFECTION FOR FROM GENESIS TO REVELATION. I DON'T LOVE IT OR ANYTHING, BUT IT WAS A PART OF MY CHILDHOOD.
TONY BANKS

Opposite: Peter in the studio and, inset, a tape box from one of the Central Sound sessions in March 1968.
Overleaf: Outtakes and memories of the sessions for the band's debut release, *From Genesis To Revelation*.
Following pages: Alfresco rehearsal in the summer of 1968, Tony on acoustic far left, Ant still in his pith helmet on a twelve-string, Mike on bass, on the roof of their friend David Thomas's family house at South Warnborough in Hampshire. David, who is just visible beyond Tony, was and still is one of Tony's closest friends: he sings the lower harmony on the chorus of 'In The Wilderness' on *From Genesis To Revelation*, and his flat in Earls Court was Tony's base in London in his early days there.

CENTRAL SOUND STUDIO
9, DENMARK STREET, LONDON, W.C.2.
TEMple Bar 6061/2

CLIENT GENESIS

SUBJECT 1) *Keyl*
2) 1m *Here*
3) 2·30 *Pink Line [am.p.m]*
4) *This was a movement*

DATE 13/3/68

TAPE SPEED 7½

RECORDING ENGINEER

EDITING/DUBBING ENGINEER
FRED

COPYRIGHT 1968

JONJO MUSIC

GER 9405 37 SOHO SQ.

THE IMPRESARIO'S TALE: JONATHAN KING

Although I hadn't been much involved in music at school I was, from an early age, very keen on pop music. That started in my prep school days when I picked up on a song called 'Singing The Blues' and, typical, I adored the original American version by Guy Mitchell. My mother took me round all the shops to try and buy it. Everywhere we went they had the Tommy Steele cover and I kept saying, 'No, that's no good, I must have the original.'

After Charterhouse I got a place at Trinity College, Cambridge, to read English literature, but before I went up I travelled, and met Brian Epstein and Derek Taylor, the Beatles press officer, amongst others, who gave me lots of very helpful advice. I had also started to perform as the lead singer with a group called the Bumblies, writing songs – not very good ones, I have to say – and trying to record, including a couple of songs with the great, late Joe Meek, who to me was almost like Phil Spector was in America.

At Cambridge I was enjoying myself, but frustrated to hell that I couldn't become a pop star. Then I fell ill with a Meckel's diverticulum, and was put into the college sanatorium; I did all my course work for the whole year within about two weeks, and wrote letters to people in the music industry. Tony Hall at Decca wrote back encouragingly, so as soon as I was better I went down to see him and he put me together with Joe Roncoroni and Ken Jones who managed the Zombies, and who later became my partners in Jonjo Music. And as a result I had my first hit singing 'Everyone's Gone To The Moon', enjoying all the fame and all the glory.

So of course I wanted to go back to Charterhouse when I had the opportunity, to flaunt myself around. The school couldn't quite make up their minds whether I should go on the old boys list as the most famous old boy, which by then I far and away was, but on a list which contained people like Baden Powell, it was deemed not really appropriate. If I remember rightly, I'd also been accepted back as an old boy because I'd gotten into Cambridge. That was what really counted. Then I became a pop star and they thought, 'Oh god, maybe we should throw him off again'.

I was down for an old boys' day, and a young lad came up to me as I was getting out of my car – an MGB GT or an Austin Healey Sprite, I had both at the time – and handed me a tape. I asked him if he was in the group, and he said, 'No, but they're friends of mine and we think they're really good.' I asked, 'What's the name of the group?' and he said, 'Well, they don't have a name', which I thought was ridiculous, but I told him, 'OK, I'll listen to it'.

I had already become a producer at this point, because a year or so earlier I'd written a song called 'It's Good News Week' that I'd wanted to make into a hit. I had found a band of RAF guys up in Lincolnshire to front the record, and this Hedgehoppers Anonymous single had been another hit for me. So I was receiving a flood of tapes and demos, and 99.9 per cent of them were awful.

I carried on poncing about at the old boys' day, seeing my old friends and some of the staff. Then I drove back to London, put the tape on and that was when I immediately went, 'Fucking hell, this boy has got a lovely voice'. I was absolutely staggered by the quality of Peter's voice. It had a smokiness to it, which is something I've always gone for. All the people I've really liked as singers, like Peter Frampton, for example, as well as Peter Gabriel, have got that slightly smoky sound to their voice which is a bit soulful, and Peter's voice was even better in 1967 because it was full of youth and enthusiasm.

There was a phone number on the cassette, I think, which was for the telephone in the Duckites house, and I called them up. My first contacts with the group were with Peter, who was a very good spokesman for them. He wasn't a stunning-looking boy, and I didn't think he was going to be a heart-throb, but he did have a really sweet, angelic look about him. He was a very quiet, innocent, very decent person – and I don't think my opinion of Peter has changed at all since.

Although he was terribly, terribly shy, very polite and soft-spoken, he knew what he wanted to do and where he wanted to go. He was the perfect go-between, because I used to have quite a few problems with Tony Banks and Anthony Phillips in that they both wanted to feature quite strongly. They were very young kids at the time, playing music they weren't really quite good enough to play, and very self-indulgent so that their pieces would go on for hours. Of course, after we parted company, Genesis became typically progressive rock and their tracks did get longer and longer, which in many ways was part of their mass popularity, but it was not my thing at all. And even to this day the Genesis tracks I like are the ones that are really nice, pretty pop songs.

At that stage, they were probably destined not to go anywhere, because although they had little bits of talent, they were just fitting this in between their school lessons. I made them into something that actually had the potential to be a proper group. I encouraged them by getting them to make demos, then singles, then an album – and by giving them a name. I wanted to call them Genesis because I felt this was going to be a genesis, the start of my serious production career.

Whenever I read their stories of trying to sound like the Bee Gees because they knew that was the music I liked, I don't remember it as such at all. I remember very clearly that they had electric instruments which were very cheap and rather noisy, and would go out of tune because they liked to play it all terribly loud, and they couldn't actually hear their own mistakes. I made them go acoustic for that reason, because they were still learning and I knew if they were playing acoustically they would actually hear their mistakes and correct them. And by that time I'd come across Crosby, Stills and Nash, who I thought were going in a really interesting direction; and of course I also loved the Bee Gees, that acoustic folk-style pop.

Peter's voice was always much more suited to a slightly more soulful approach, so that's why I very deliberately pointed them down that slightly more acoustic route which they have since always followed. They never went down the road of loud music and raucous rock. Although they were a rock band to a degree, they were very much an acoustic rock band.

There was a moment when I was summoned to a meeting with all the boys and their parents, who said to me, 'Look, you've been in the business a couple of years now, would you really advocate that these sons of ours, who have been to a very expensive public school and who are destined for very good careers as accountants, lawyers, bankers and so on, should actually concentrate on having a pop career, because it's pretty grubby.' I could see that the only thing that was influencing them to listen to me was that I myself was a Charterhouse boy, and I had been to Trinity College, Cambridge, which was quite impressive to these parents; they were thinking, 'Hang on, maybe this guy isn't so flaky'. I told them, 'I would say, "No, don't go into music," to 99 out of 100 people. I don't think it's a world for most people. But I truly think these guys have got talent'.

And I really did. Peter deserved to be a huge star, and I loved his attitude, because he was very down to earth and honourable. Mike was just what you wanted in a bass player, a very solid, reliable, decent guy. Tony on keyboards was very sensible and creative, even though I felt far too self-indulgent, Anthony the same, although sadly he didn't last very long. And all of them were contributing to the songwriting. We just didn't have a drummer. Neither Chris Stewart or John Silver were very good drummers and they knew it; the result was that the drums are very low in the mix on the album. It's the only thing that makes it sound quite old-fashioned. But I thought little Chris was a sweetheart – and I'm delighted he's gone on to success with his books – and John Silver also seemed like a nice kid.

We recorded the album at Regent Sound's second studio on Charing Cross Road. I was very hands-on in the studio. I can't be anything else. We had arguments over the length of solos and other bits and pieces. What I liked about them is that even though I was two or three years older than them, and a great success, they had the balls to fight their corner. I was likewise quite prepared to let them try things; whilst I was as dominant as I always am when I'm producing, it wasn't my project and they weren't my songs, so I was trying very hard to bring the best out of them rather than make a Jonathan King record. A prime example is that Peter had learnt the flute very, very badly and wanted to put in a few flute passages. I thought I could bring a session musician in to do this, but he wanted to do it and he did it, and it sounded really nice, because he wasn't trying complicated things, he was working within his limitations.

The part that the band really didn't like was that I added the strings. I wanted to give them a slightly more progressive, but also more professional, feel with a string section adding little bridges between the numbers, but sometimes playing on top of the numbers as well. I think they work terribly well, actually. It gives the songs a sweetness that wasn't there in the original thing and covers up some of the slight amateurishness of the basic tracks. The album came out and got slagged off, especially by Chris Welch on Melody Maker, who was extremely lethal about it, not flattering at all. But it was the beginning of what I'm glad to say went on to be a really great career.

Jonathan King's first hit, 'Everyone's Gone To the Moon', launched an entertainment career of many facets. He was a record exec with Decca and set up his own label, UK Records, aged twenty-five. As a producer, as well as launching Genesis, he discovered the Bay City Rollers and 10cc, and released many singles of his own under various pseudonyms. He was a TV presenter – with his own show *Good Evening: I'm Jonathan King* in the 1960s and *Entertainment USA* and *No Limits* in the 1980s – became a radio presenter and newspaper columnist, and ran the *Brits* and *Song For Europe*. He is currently fighting to overturn the conviction for sexual abuse he received in 2001.

THE DRUMMERS' TALE, PART I: CHRIS STEWART

For a thirteen-year-old, Charterhouse was big and frightening. There were people there of extremely advanced years with blue stubble on their chin and Clearasil on their acne. There was a smell of burgeoning manhood about the place which was really quite unpleasant. I went back there many years later on an open day where you could tuck into strawberries and cream in a tent and watch the cricket. I was struck by the extraordinary beauty of the architecture, the lawns and the gardens. I thought, 'Jesus, did I really get educated in a place like this?' I had been too much of a nihilistic yobbo ever to appreciate it at the time. But although the surroundings were stunning, school life was pretty Spartan – there was no hot water to wash in, for example. This was to make a man of you. The public schools were set up to teach our young to run the British Empire. But of course the Empire had long gone by the time I got to Charterhouse, so this was simply gratuitous and anachronistic unpleasantness.

On arrival you had to master a whole new set of ropes, and the ropes were very, very complicated. You could only walk round the tables in the common room in an anti-clockwise direction until you'd reached a certain stage of seniority. In your first year you were not allowed to have any of the buttons of your jacket undone, even in high summer, and you had to be right at the top of school before you could take your jacket off at any time. There was a completely different language to learn: your bicycle was a 'grid', work was a 'hash', prep was 'banco'.

And there was cruelty. When I first arrived there was a system called 'fathering': a boy in the year above was your 'father' and it was his responsibility to teach you all these rules and regulations. The fathers treated us appallingly. They made our lives a misery. I remember turning on them one day and saying, 'Why are you so unnecessarily and mindlessly vicious in all your dealings with us?' It was quite an outrageous thing to

say, and they were a bit stumped by this, but after a while they said, 'For a perfectly simple reason – because it was done to us.' But we didn't do it when it was our turn. There had been a generational shift, a change in philosophy. We were not cruel to our charges when we were fathers; we treated them normally. I felt this really was quite an important thing.

One of the most disagreeable aspects of Charterhouse was its Cadet Force. You had to dress up as soldiers one day a week and march around like a ponce on a parade ground, the most mind-numbingly stupid waste of time that anybody could ever have devised. There was only one get-out, to join what was known as the 'Band and Drums', which meant that instead of square-bashing, you got to sit in the drum room and learn how to do paradiddles and flam paradiddles and ratamacues. It was the rhythms and the way the sticks worked that got to me. We would all practise at lunch by drumming our knives and forks on the table, to the fury of whichever master or mistress was supposedly supervising us.

I then became aware of the fact that deep in a cellar, in a hideous old room at the bottom of Duckites, there was a drum kit, a dark red Pearl drum kit. It belonged to Peter Gabriel, who was playing jazzy stuff with a band called the League of Gentlemen. Peter was a year above me, and normally you would never get to know somebody who was older. One looked upon them as slightly different beings. But for some reason I knew him well enough that he let me fool around with his drum kit.

It was Peter who taught me how to play. He needed somebody to take over the drums in his band so he was free to play flute and sing. I was a young oik around the place who seemed able to use a pair of drum sticks. He was a wonderful teacher. My strongest memory of Peter is his gentle buffoonery. In his quiet way he would play the fool, taking the piss out of the ludicrous situations in which we constantly found ourselves. He was, like me, not very academic. He did not come across as confident – he was a rather nervous person – and he wasn't light and zappy, more sombre, but in the most enchanting way. He had a big aura. I guess he was born a rather extraordinary man and he remains an extraordinary man. At the time I saw him as a bastion of good sense, somebody to admire. I would often think to myself, 'Now what would Peter do in a situation like this? That's the way I should comport myself.'

All of a sudden, under Peter's tutelage, I became absolutely passionate about playing drums, to the extent that I would feel sick with longing at the very sight of a drum kit. It was an adolescent crush: I would come over all funny. This was the time of the Stones and the Beatles. You could see this was the hub of a universe that was just being born, and to be sitting behind a drum kit just did it for me. Previously I had fooled around with a guitar, having realized that it was a powerful tool of seduction, but I had no talent for it. Not only could I not tune the thing, but I could never tell when it had gone out of tune. I would practise 'The House Of The Rising Sun' and people would walk past my cube in the dormitory with expressions of appalled pain on their faces.

So there I was in Peter's band, which was going to perform at House Entertainments. I can still conjure up the shuddering of excitement I felt at the prospect. We played 'When A Man Loves a Woman' – Otis Redding was Peter's big thing – with 'Sitting On The Dock Of The Bay', 'Green Onions' and maybe Lee Dorsey's 'Get Out Of My Life, Woman'. I wanted to do 'Anyway, Anyhow, Anywhere' by the Who but the others told me, 'Don't be ridiculous'. I said, 'I know I've only just started playing drums, but maybe we could use a tape recorder so it sounds like I'm playing when in fact I'm not'. It was dismissed out of hand.

The show was well received. Everybody was conscious of these great musical movements going on in the outside world, and they felt here was something of their own, a band in their house. Later on we started to play our own stuff. I can't really say 'our own stuff', because I didn't have much of a hand in writing it. That was down to the others.

Tony was a contemporary of Peter's, but somehow less approachable, and Mike I never really knew. Ant, though, was a good friend of mine. He was younger than me, so he had somehow managed to approach me from beneath, so to speak. I had dinner with Ant a few years ago and he was just the same as he was when he was at school, a constant clown. He is one of these people about whom it is said, with some exasperation, that they never take anything seriously at all. If he hadn't been in early Genesis he would have been a part of Monty Python or something like that.

I was not a natural drummer. I was an appallingly crap drummer. There was a guy called Rob Tyrell at school who was a fabulous drummer. Aaah, the crispness, the smoothness of his rolls, the lightness of his stick work. I would plod away and my rolls were crap and scruffy. They always were and they still are. Rob probably should have been the drummer in the band because he was brilliant, but he might have been a more difficult character than I was. In general musicians are difficult folks, egotistical and self-absorbed and generally a pretty bad lot, so I imagine that when the others found somebody who was easy to get on with and who tended to help everybody else get on with each other, they thought, 'OK, he's a crap drummer, but he's quite a nice guy to have around'. I was a steadying influence, and I was not a writer, so I did not represent another dissenting voice. What paltry success I ever had was due to that.

The only recording I can remember doing was 'The Silent Sun' and 'That's Me'. My involvement in both was pretty minimal. The recording took place in a studio in Denmark Street and was, in reality, unspeakably boring because we had to do the thing over and over and over and over again. But it didn't matter, because I felt, 'This is it, I'm here, I'm where it's at', which in contrast was mind-bogglingly exciting. We also had some publicity photographs taken in a studio in Kensington Church Street, in the black and white clothes we'd been sent off to buy in Carnaby Street. It was not a very glamorous place or occasion. I adopted what I imagined was a look of teenage angst. I wasn't actually suffering from any teenage angst, and my natural demeanour was that of a cheerful buffoon, but I guess we'd all been reading Melody Maker and NME and seen photos of bands all looking angst-ridden, so I did my best.

Shortly after the second single had been recorded, I learnt that I was no longer in the band. The moment when I was told is a blank. It's absolutely vanished. I know that while I was in the band I was thinking, 'Music is it. This is going to be the future for me', so I must have been absolutely heart-broken when they said I was out, but I have no memory of that, which is odd, because I have always been quite an emotional sort of person. The others were right to fire me. They had the potential to get somewhere bigger and better and with me banging away badly in the background they probably wouldn't have got where they are today.

Peter turned up at my house one day after I'd left school and announced cheerfully, 'I've got a cheque here for you, Chris, £300'. I went, 'Three hundred quid, Jesus!' He said, 'Yeah, but first, you have to sign this piece of paper which signs away all your future rights'. 'For £300, I'll do anything.' So I signed. I was really happy with the £300. I thought it was more than I deserved. I forgot all about it until 2006 when a letter reached me with a cheque for 'part of your earnings from 'The Silent Sun''. I couldn't believe it. I sent it back, saying, 'I've actually signed all my rights away…'

I hardly listened to Genesis's music after I left the band. I did listen to some of Peter's music, which I liked very much, and I kept up with Ant for quite a while. I thought Trespass was really great, but that was the last album I listened to. I have never been to a concert of theirs. I've always said blithely that Genesis just didn't do it for me, but on reflection it might have been because I had suffered a great hurt. 'Schoolboy drummer leaves band' is hardly earth-shaking stuff, but for the schoolboy drummer in question it would have been pretty earthshaking. Now I feel I really ought to see what all the fuss is about. Maybe I'll get the box set.

After Chris Stewart's untimely departure from Genesis, he spent time variously working in farming, playing drums in the two-man band of Sir Robert Fossett's Circus, shearing sheep in Sweden and writing travel guides to China and Andalucia. In the 1980s he moved to Spain with his wife Ana and bought El Valero, a remote farm in the Alpujarras Mountains of Southern Spain, an experience he described in his 1999 book, *Driving Over Lemons*. It became an international bestseller, which he followed with the sequels *A Parrot In The Pepper Tree* and *The Almond Blossom Society*.

CHAPTER THREE
CHRISTMAS COTTAGE

ANT: After we'd finished the recording for *From Genesis To Revelation* over that summer of 1968, three of us – Mike, Peter and I – suddenly found ourselves confronted in September with the prospect of studying for A Levels for the following year, and Tony was going off to university. Although we did get together during the Christmas holidays at the end of that Autumn, it was a period of hiatus. We were waiting for the album to come out, and we didn't know what was going to happen with it.

TONY: I went to Sussex University, originally to study chemistry, but then changed to logic with physics. I wasn't really enjoying the chemistry very much and wanted something that offered me a little bit more, and the new course had a hint of philosophy, which interested me.

I was really too shy to make the most of university. The campus at Sussex had not yet been finished, so I was in a kind of bed and breakfast place, run by a woman who ruled about twenty of us. I had one or two friends, and it was fine, but I don't think I had a fantastic time. I did like the fact that I was free and unrestricted. And I used to love going walking round the area, driving off into the downs behind Brighton and then down to the sea, to little places along the coast like Rottingdean, where I could wander for hours.

The one thing I didn't get to do at Sussex, which I would have liked to have done, was meet girls. There were plenty of them there, but having come out of Charterhouse, and not really knowing what a woman looked like, apart from my sisters, I didn't adjust very well and I certainly didn't make the most of my time. The trouble with science was there were only three girls doing science – one of whom was very pretty actually – but if you could imagine one pretty girl amongst 500 young gentlemen, it certainly wasn't going to be me who was going to win... Every weekend I used to go to Peter's place or his parents' house. They were very tolerant of me, and kind to me.

PETER: My parents still have the guest book, and Tony was clearly a long-term resident: there are countless entries for A.G. Banks.

TONY: I had also bought an organ, a Hammond L122, this huge thing which we lugged up to my room in these digs. I plugged some headphones into the organ instead of using the speaker, kind of hardwired them in. And I wrote a few things there, including bits and pieces that we later used in 'Supper's Ready'. And I also used to play guitar, which I enjoyed because it allowed me to experiment. I knew the keyboard so well I had to try and fool myself on it, whereas with the guitar half the time I didn't know what I was playing.

ANT: By that Christmastime I hadn't yet heard the album and didn't know what had happened with all the string arrangements, so we were feeling OK, except that I had just been given the elbow by this girl Lucy Burge, a dancer who later became a principal for Ballet Rambert, so I was in no frame of mind at all. The big irony is that Lucy had been very much into Peter and I think had taken me on as a sort of second-best.

Peter had been transformed from this slightly old-womanly, not a curmudgeon, but a bit reserved, old bloke. Suddenly, this chrysalis had burst open and here was this extraordinary, colourful, good-looking, dynamic, eccentric guy, dyeing our shirts for us, writing all these strange lyrics and driving a London taxi – he was one the first people to get a decommissioned cab. He had become hugely charismatic, so all the women were suddenly flocking to him. But Peter was very loyal to his girlfriend Jill, and the rest of us were left as a less good option. Anyway, I got dumped by Lucy, which was great for my songwriting...

There didn't seem much point in making any great plans while we were waiting for our album success. And then it came out in the spring and nothing really happened, apart from one nice review in *International Times*.

PETER: The *IT* review was by Mark Williams, who was quite a hip reviewer, so for us that was a big excitement. But apart from that the ripples were few and far between.

Opposite: Christmas Cottage in the snow. The cottage, at Wotton, between Dorking and Abinger Hammer in Surrey, was owned by Richard Macphail's parents. This was where the band lived, rehearsed and wrote throughout the autumn and winter of 1969-70, 'the first time', in Mike's words, 'we worked like a real band'. Having the space and time to innovate also appealed to Peter, who says, 'Throughout my musical life, one of the things that turns me on is the sense that you're on virgin snow...' Overleaf: Loading equipment into a horse box outside Anthony Phillips' home. Ant's father, the pipesmoker, watches proceedings.

THE ALBUM, AFTER A YEAR OR SO, HAD SOLD 649 COPIES, AND WE KNEW ALL OF THOSE PEOPLE PERSONALLY. IT WASN'T A VERY AUSPICIOUS START. TONY BANKS

Opposite: The *East Grinstead Courier* gets a scoop. On the far right, holding a guitar, is Tony Hill-Smith, one of the band's ever-positive supporters, who stepped in to make up the numbers. Brian Roberts, the Charterhouse boy whose recording expertise gave the band vital support on their early demos, is sitting at the back, next to Tony. Brian played a significant role in the transition of Genesis from school band to recording artists. He says he is indebted to Charterhouse, where he was head of the choir, because the school allowed him to pursue his interest in recording techniques, from recording a full orchestra in concert to demos by a band of schoolmates. He built up a collection of equipment – a microphone here, a few cables there, and brought them down to the Radio Society room, in the basement of the science block, which gradually filled up with kit. Brian's audio and technical interests were fostered in particular by the head of music, William Llewellyn – so much so that after Brian left school the two of them set up a company called Roblyn Recordings. Brian went on to start at the BBC as a cameraman, and he still works in the business, running a television facilities company. Brian wanted to record Anon because they posed a different set of problems to an orchestra – trying to capture and separate the sound of the individual instruments – and invited them to his family's house in Chiswick, where, above a couple of stables, using 'a valve mixer from the school, with huge black knobs like a BBC outside broadcast unit's' and a Ferrograph tape recorder, he recorded their first demos. The 'studio' was not very sound-proof, and Brian remembers 'loud music blasting out across Chiswick'. He later mixed some of the earliest Genesis demos, which the band were preparing for Jonathan King.

MIKE: I guess we were the first of our bunch of mates to actually make a record. Just doing that was an achievement, even if it didn't sell. We were still amateurs really. We weren't drawing comparisons with other bands. There were no criteria to judge it by because we hadn't really joined the music world. We were still doing our education, still studying. This was like having a fun part-time hobby. So it was hard to be disappointed.

PETER: The first time you get a physical product in your hand is genuinely exciting. You want to show it off to all your friends. I think Jonathan's idea had been that the black cover for the album was a response to the Beatles' *White Album*, which wasn't a bad idea, but I didn't want to have any text on the front. Even now I still fight the battle of trying to keep text away from the images, but at least in that case I could console myself with the fact that the cover was a fairly simple image.

ANT: We took our A Levels, and the question was, 'What next?' The summer of 1969 was a really moochy one. We hung around in the corridors of the BBC thrusting this album on disinterested people. It was a very confusing time because suddenly there was no more school, no cocoon any more, and we had to make a decision about whether we were going to go to university, get a job or actually try to do something with this music. And what basis was there to think that this fledgling group of songwriters could turn itself into an active live unit? There was no reason to think that, because Tony Banks, who was so much the fulcrum of the group, didn't like the idea of playing an organ and you couldn't mike up a piano in those days – terribly impractical live. The odds were probably that a couple of us might have said, 'Well, actually, I don't think this is really possible.'

Jonathan King tactfully gave us a bit of breathing space. He'd given us a lot of opportunities and nothing ever really happened. We'd had a fair crack of the whip. He needed us to come up with some more dynamic, more commercial material, and we couldn't. We were going through a metamorphosis and producing what for him was a very ugly style, and he very much lost interest in us.

MIKE: We did have some more songs but Jonathan King didn't like any of them and we thought we'd try and get out of the contract. I can't remember now if we offered him some dodgy songs. It just drifted off naturally.

TONY: We realized that King would never want to follow the direction we did. The more complicated we wanted to make the music, the less he liked it. We were writing pieces that went on for ten, fifteen minutes. And we felt that he would be holding us back. So we actually started rehearsing without telling him and finally we told him that we weren't going to go with him any more and started looking around for other possible management situations. It wasn't acrimonious, and although we weren't totally honest with him, I don't think he was really too upset about the fact we parted company.

ANT: Our album hadn't made it and finally we'd had our dose of bad vibes. We'd led a fantastic, charmed life for a couple of years when everybody was getting on fantastically well and now there had to be some tension. Again, it's a time for gratitude because there was a guy called Tony Hill-Smith who knew Peter. He was a bit of a bounder, always going round in a cravat like David Niven, but a great chap, hugely positive. We'd be thinking, 'Are we going to go on, are we going to stop?', hoping a miracle would happen and this chap Hillie was always really encouraging to us and along with one or two other people helped keep us going whenever we were thinking there was no point in carrying on. He'd always keep dropping by while we were rehearsing, in a rather aimless way, in these lovely country houses.

FOLK-BLUES-MYSTICAL group Genesis with the man who has managed all their recordings to date, Brian Roberts, of Maher Lodge, Dormans Park (centre back), at a practice session in the house

GENESIS—A NEW CREATION IN SOUND

A LYRICAL and delicate alchemy of sound drifted across Dormans Park last week when Genesis came to stay.

On holiday, rehearsing, writing new material and trying to decide the pattern of their future, this unusual recording group were staying at Maher Lodge, Dormans Park, home of 19-year-old Brian Roberts who has recorded all the group's work to date.

With a curious combination of all-acoustic sounds and vocal harmonies they have so far had three singles released on Decca and one album "From Genesis to Revelation" all produced by singer and controversial "pop" columnist Johnathan King.

Brian Roberts, now an assistant cameraman, said: "We all met at school at Charterhouse and began writing together. A group was formed from this. I began to record work and have continued to do so.

"So far all their work has been done from the recording studios. But thinking very seriously of becoming professional, they are looking for the type of work where audiences are prepared to sit down and listen — as on the present college circuits. Their music is essentially for the listener, not the raver."

"Progressive is a violently-abused term at present but although they all admit admiration for certain other artists, their material is all original and written by themselves," said Brian.

The line-up is Peter Gabriel lead vocal and flute, Ant Phillipps lead 12-string and acoustic guitars, Michael Rutherford six-string and bass guitars, Tony Banks organ piano and six-string guitar, and John Silver percussion (not simply drums).

R.A.

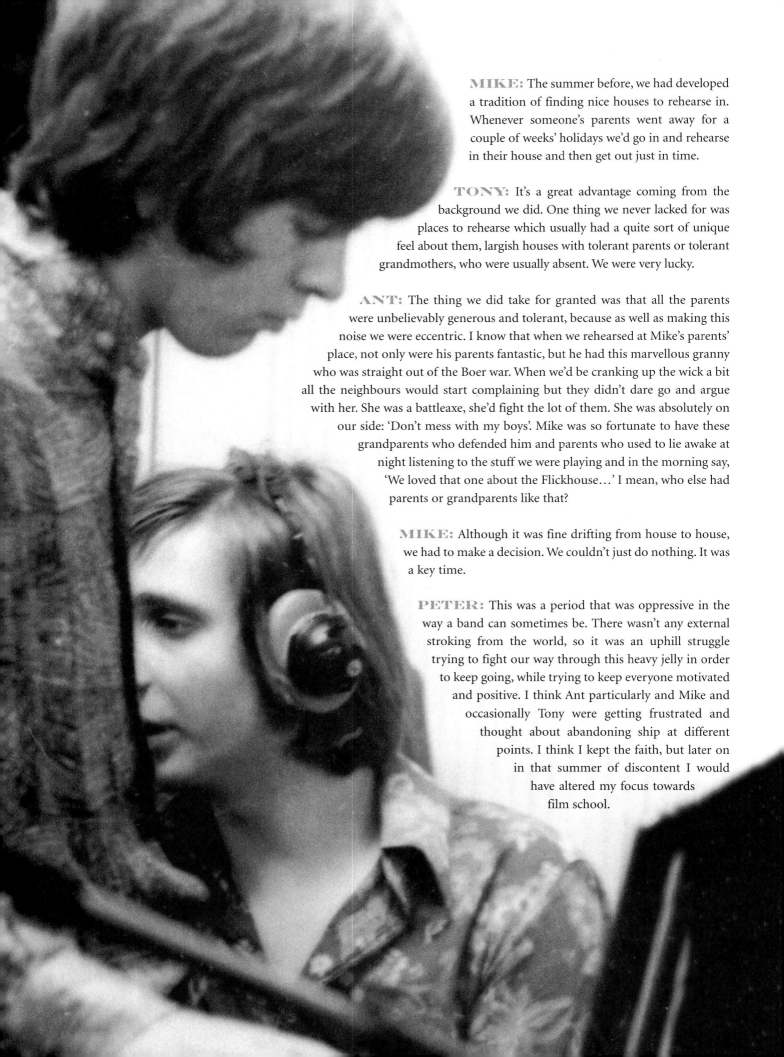

MIKE: The summer before, we had developed a tradition of finding nice houses to rehearse in. Whenever someone's parents went away for a couple of weeks' holidays we'd go in and rehearse in their house and then get out just in time.

TONY: It's a great advantage coming from the background we did. One thing we never lacked for was places to rehearse which usually had a quite sort of unique feel about them, largish houses with tolerant parents or tolerant grandmothers, who were usually absent. We were very lucky.

ANT: The thing we did take for granted was that all the parents were unbelievably generous and tolerant, because as well as making this noise we were eccentric. I know that when we rehearsed at Mike's parents' place, not only were his parents fantastic, but he had this marvellous granny who was straight out of the Boer war. When we'd be cranking up the wick a bit all the neighbours would start complaining but they didn't dare go and argue with her. She was a battleaxe, she'd fight the lot of them. She was absolutely on our side: 'Don't mess with my boys'. Mike was so fortunate to have these grandparents who defended him and parents who used to lie awake at night listening to the stuff we were playing and in the morning say, 'We loved that one about the Flickhouse…' I mean, who else had parents or grandparents like that?

MIKE: Although it was fine drifting from house to house, we had to make a decision. We couldn't just do nothing. It was a key time.

PETER: This was a period that was oppressive in the way a band can sometimes be. There wasn't any external stroking from the world, so it was an uphill struggle trying to fight our way through this heavy jelly in order to keep going, while trying to keep everyone motivated and positive. I think Ant particularly and Mike and occasionally Tony were getting frustrated and thought about abandoning ship at different points. I think I kept the faith, but later on in that summer of discontent I would have altered my focus towards film school.

TONY: We never originally intended to make a career out of music. It didn't seem appropriate. Back in 1969, it was still a pretty unusual career choice. Somewhere like Charterhouse was designed to prepare people to go into the law, the army or the priesthood, not into the rock business, so it was very much against the grain.

Peter and I had conversations about this deep into the night. One of us would be leaving and the other one wouldn't and then – from my memory of it, anyhow – we ended up sort of persuading each other to give it a go. I certainly couldn't bear the idea of thinking what might have happened. And there was another keyboard player around, a friend of Ant's called Harry Williamson – the son of Henry Williamson, the author of *Tarka The Otter* – who was a good player and certainly would have fitted in fine. So perhaps knowing that there was a potential substitute available made me think twice as well. I felt there was something special going on, and in life you only get given one chance, so you've got to give it a go, haven't you?

MIKE: I remember Tony was very torn over what to do. I think he only came because he felt what if he'd missed out? I never thought about giving up music. If it hadn't worked out I quite fancied going into journalism, and my father fancied the Foreign Office for me. Look at what we ended up with.

ANT: I'd had glandular fever in the March and April just before my A Levels and I was feeling rough. But just before I got the glandular fever and just after the end of the affair with Lucy, Mike and I had started writing on two twelve-string guitars. We hadn't done that on *From Genesis To Revelation*; although the album did have some acoustic guitar playing, it wasn't Mike and me in tandem. So when we tried that, in February and March of '69, by complete accident we found that for the first time in our lives we weren't really copying anybody. We used to love it. One of us would play a chord and the other would play a different inversion and we'd marvel at this dual sound. It was like we were entering a magical new world.

Some of the stuff that ended up on *Trespass* was written during that period in the kitchen at my parents' place: 'Dusk', 'White Mountain' and early bits of 'Stagnation'. It was really, really exciting. In fact, I've got a tape somewhere of us playing the first part of 'White Mountain' and you can hear Mike's girlfriend saying, 'Ooh, that's nice'. So although as a group we were having a depressing time, Mike and I were having some great sessions as a duo. We'd finish rehearsals with the others and then stay up late to do some more together and the others used to get a bit angry. This is where we had some tension starting, because I would be shattered in the morning. Nobody had told me that with glandular fever you've got to be careful and on top of the stress of a failed album, and not being sure whether to keep going, of course that wasn't good at all. I was pushing myself with the excitement of the music with Mike but then feeling shattered as well and not knowing why.

It reached crunch time at the end of the summer when Mike and I were so simpatico and my relationship with the others was OK but not so close. There was a crucial moment in the kitchen. Tony asked Mike, 'Are we going to go on?' and Mike said, 'Yeah', so I said, 'Yes' too. If Mike had said, 'No', I would have said, 'No'. I don't think I've ever told anybody that. Mike's response was crucial because he was a bit of a father figure to me. I was much more bothered about my relationship with Mike because that was the music I really loved... And so the decision was made.

MIKE: The summer was drawing to a close, and we were still enlisting drummers, as you do. Jonathan Silver had left. He had decided to go to Cornell University to study Leisure Management. He wasn't in pain about the decision, it was his own decision.

TONY: We would never have kicked John out. He just felt this wasn't a career for him, and he probably had the greatest family pressure on him not to do it. Because he'd joined later on it didn't seem to be such a crucial decision. We felt that we could replace him. But we were sad to lose him, he was a nice chap. We're still friends.

> **THERE WASN'T A DEFINITE PLAN TO CARRY ON. I THINK WE WERE SIMPLY ALL RELUCTANT TO SAY, 'THAT'S IT, WE'VE FAILED'.**
> ANTHONY PHILLIPS

Opposite: Peter and Mike
in the studio.

In the auditions to replace him, we were most impressed by this guy called John Mayhew, because not only did he bring his own kit which not all of them did, but he sat down and played a riff all around the kit ending with a crash on the cymbals, and we thought, 'Hey, we've been looking for that for years', because that was what Rob Townsend of Family did. John was a professional and was good for us playing live because he had the experience of how to behave on stage. He wouldn't get flustered, could keep us going and would rescue us from all kinds of shaky moments. He helped us learn our trade.

ANT: John was quiet, but seemed very nice and he was certainly the best drummer we had had. He was three or four years older than us, and I think didn't know quite what to make of us to be honest. I quizzed him about this recently. I asked him, 'John, were we dreadful to you? Who was the worst, was I the worst?' and he said, 'No, you were all fine', but I always imagine we must have seemed insufferably squitty and toffee-nosed to him.

PETER: John Mayhew was a pretty good drummer, but I think it was quite difficult because the rest of us had really grown up together, and had our own shorthand way of talking to each other. From his side, there was probably a bit of a class barrier in some ways, and when we couldn't fulfil what we were dreaming of in our heads he got frustrated and we got frustrated. But he definitely helped us move forwards. He was more like a professional musician than anyone we'd met before. We happened to be amateur enthusiasts, whereas John had been a gigging musician on the road with other bands. He knew the life and he had the hair…

ANT: We spent some time at my parents' place, where we knocked into shape the basic parts of two or three of the main numbers that we would do on the road, including 'The Knife' and 'Looking For Someone', which were the two long, long tracks with lots of sections – what became characterized as 'prog rock'. What we were really doing was like sellotaping one section onto another. There's not necessarily anything wrong with that and certainly it was acceptable once the Beatles had produced tracks like 'A Day In The Life'.

So even at this stage we had a lot of the main material that turned up later on the *Trespass* album, because as well as 'Looking For Someone' and 'The Knife', Mike and I had already written the basic parts of 'Dusk' and 'White Mountain' and as a group we had worked on this piece called 'Movement' that became 'Stagnation', an experimental piece with twelve-string and organ and Peter's wonderful lyrics. And 'Visions Of Angels' had been kicked out of the previous album, which was a godsend. These half-dozen pieces formed the entire material for what became the next album.

This period at my parents' place was really good. We sat and played in a circle and people would come and sit and listen in the middle which is a great way to listen to a band because you have a completely equal sound. After the summer of doubts, we were in a very positive frame of mind.

TONY: I always think of this as the time when we decided we were moving on to the next stage, writing songs like 'Pacidy' as well as 'The Knife' and 'Going Out To Get You', both of which became the main strengths of our live show, the two heavy long numbers. 'Going Out To Get You' went through hundreds of changes and never made it to an album, which was strange because it was such a key song for us. I think it might have made it onto the album after *Trespass*, but by that time Ant had left the band and the song part of it was his bit, so it kind of went with him. All of these songs started emerging around this sort of time, as we began rehearsing to try and play as a group, which we'd never done before. When we had recorded *From Genesis To Revelation*, we'd just gone into the studio and played.

ANT: Once we had decided to go for it things went incredibly well. It all seemed to slot into place. We had been back in contact with Richard Macphail, who had been the singer in Anon, and Richard persuaded his parents to, incredibly generously, let us use their cottage near

Opposite: Peter during recording. He says, 'You had to do take after take until you got tired. Each time everything would be erased and you just had to wait and carry on until you captured a good performance. It was pretty hard on the vocal chords. Now I'd take a lot of hot water or honey. In those days it just used to hurt the next day.'

Dorking over the autumn and winter of 1969. They didn't like to go down there because in the winters – 'it were in them days when we had proper winters, lad!' – it was very cold and in the middle of nowhere. So we were ready to move in there, Richard was going to be our housekeeper, roadie, wet nurse, the whole lot, and one of my friends, called Dave Rootes, also came on board to help.

RICHARD WAS A GOOD SINGER. IF HIS BEST FRIENDS HADN'T HAPPENED TO BE GENESIS, HE MIGHT HAVE HAD A CHANCE TO MAKE IT IN HIS OWN RIGHT. Mike Rutherford

TONY: There had been some break-in at the house, and I think that Richard's mother had got a bit spooked by the place and didn't want to stay there. And Richard's father had got hold of this old bread van from his work at Rank Hovis McDougall, which we were welcome to use as our group van. It did forty-five miles an hour top speed. Forty-eight if you pushed the accelerator to the right. It was bloody slow.

PETER: In stupid fashion, I had bought a London taxi thinking that it was a wonderful thing because I could get my drums in there and carry the band's gear around, but what I hadn't realized was that it meant I had to drop everyone else off first and then help with humping the organ. So this next phase, when we were in the country cottage and Richard persuaded his dad to sell us the old bread van, was a vast improvement.

ANT: I knew Richard's parents well. They were great, a slightly more grandparenty age, or so it felt. When I was at school I used to tell my parents I was coming up to London to stay at Richard's parents' flat, which I was. What I didn't tell them was that his parents went down to the Dorking cottage at the weekend so we were up there by ourselves and there was a whole crew of us going off to the Ram Jam Club in Brixton at the age of thirteen or fourteen. Rich was a year and a half older than me, nearly fifteen and very responsible. If our parents had really known. And we thought Richard's parents were stuffy! Which is amazing, looking back on it.

MIKE: Richard was very funny, very outgoing, very enthusiastic. At Charterhouse, in what was quite a dark school environment, he had always been a ray of sunshine. He was always 'up' and when we turned pro he was not only our road manager but also general cheerleader. He cooked all the meals, and was a driving, enthusiastic force. I think every band needs one of those guys in the early part of their career.

PETER: Christmas Cottage was a beautiful place and it was cold, too, I remember. There was snow around sometimes. Nowhere to escape to. Dark and steamy and not very healthy, but at least the music was getting written.

MIKE: Christmas Cottage was small but beautifully picturesque. It was a little cramped, and we argued like fuck, actually. But it was the start of us being a real band, the formation of what we became, rather than just two sets of songwriters who wrote a bit. It was a formative time, quite a playful time in this very close environment, a collection of quite volatile people, who were strong-willed musically. There was a lot of arguing and you had to stand your ground if you wanted to win your argument. But it was also a very creative time, and we came out of that period, some six months later, having established a mood and located where we were going to plant our musical flag in the ground.

And interestingly what we had done was to go outside the music business – not that we were ever in it. But we didn't go up to London to watch other bands and hang out. Otherwise we might have been constantly thinking, 'Oh, we should do it this way'. Instead we headed off for six

Opposite: Mike describes his own bass playing on the first album as 'pretty average, I was the slowest developer,' but nevertheless he brought to the studio, according to Ant, an all-important feel-good factor.

months down to our cottage. It was a time many bands were doing that: 'Get it together, man, in a country cottage'. And we just wrote and wrote and wrote. There was no real pressure. And we had no reference points. The canvas was so blank we could do what we wanted.

TONY: Endless writing! Organizing bits and pieces and improvising and learning how to play, for me, because I'd never really played an organ very much. I had started by trying to play an organ like a piano, which is quite difficult to do although some things transferred very well like 'The Knife', which was originally written on the piano, but also sounded very good on an organ.

FOR MANY MUSICIANS IT IS ALL ABOUT PLAYING RATHER THAN WRITING, AND WRITING IS SOMETHING THEY HAVE TO DO TO GET TO THE NEXT SOLO. WHEREAS FOR US, WRITING WAS THE CENTRE OF IT ALL. Peter Gabriel

ANT: It was great to move away from writing verse chorus, verse chorus, which has its virtue but can be pretty restricting, certainly in instrumental music. I think everyone got a spring in their step then, we felt very excited.

We didn't really work in the evenings. We would knock off at maybe six o'clock and start again in the morning, not fantastically early with somebody banging the gong, but it also wasn't guys pitching up at one in the afternoon and rolling a joint. It was fairly disciplined. Our relaxation time was probably the last couple of hours of the day, and Rich would prepare the food for the evening.

PETER: We spent time making yogurt and bread, because our budget was very limited. Richard was the principal breadmaker. Yogurt was I think generally my thing – a big bowl put in the airing cupboard overnight with a bit of the culture – and we were probably making our own muesli. It was a cheap way of eating.

TONY: Every time *Monty Python* was on, we'd stop for that. And we also listened to the first King Crimson album, *In The Court Of The Crimson King*, which came out that autumn. I felt this was the way forward, that you could have expansive pieces of material and really excite people. We loved the sound of the Mellotron, the whole grandeur of the music, which was something we'd been trying to do, taking the early Moody Blues and developing it one stage further.

PETER: We talked. I don't think there was much else to do really. There was a certain amount of discussion about what was going on in the world but the main focus was the obsession with music. There were all the dramas of relationships, working and struggling going on in the background, but the music was good, definitely, and there was a feeling that we were entering new territory. And throughout my musical life, one of the things that turns me on is the sense that you're on virgin snow.

Opposite: Tony had gone to Sussex University to read chemistry, then changed to logic with physics, but took a sabbatical at the end of his first year. 'I wanted to take a year out to try and make the group go. My parents weren't very happy about that but in the end they thought, "That's fine, it's only a year off." At the end of that time, I said I wanted another year off, even though we weren't really getting anywhere. There was nothing much to pin my hopes on.' So far, Tony hasn't gone back.

ANT: The thing about the cottage was that you had five musicians and two roadies living in a small cottage for six months and we virtually never went anywhere apart from going out in the van to gigs and coming back.

We had made an unspoken commitment to each other. We didn't fraternize outside, we didn't go to the pub, we didn't go back and see our parents other than at Christmas. It was almost like a monastic vow and we would go out and minister together and then come back in again. So no steam was ever let off. No walking in what was the most beautiful countryside, deer everywhere. Football, anything, would have been good, so physically we were probably very unhealthy as well. There were no weekends off. I didn't have a girlfriend at the time, but it was even worse for the other guys because they hardly ever saw their girlfriends. And of course the girlfriends got very uptight and there was quite a lot of 'It's me or the group'.

PETER: Ant had broken up with his big love at that point so he was totally work-obsessed. I think I was with Jill, who became my wife, and Mike had a girlfriend called Josie, so those of us who had relationships were expected to pretty much abandon them. It was like signing up for the army, and Ant in particular expected rehearsals to run seven days a week. It was a slightly obsessive thing, not very healthy at all. It was a little bit like *Big Brother*, this very enclosed world, and if I saw anyone else doing that now, I would suggest that they get a life.

ANT: Peter used to get picked on quite a lot, partly because he didn't have a power base. I could thwack out a chord and say, 'It goes like this'. Peter didn't have an instrument which he could explain his ideas on, and he was quite slow at explaining his ideas. And the thing is that Tony Banks and myself are, I have to say, impatient. Peter and Tony in particular started to go at each other hammer and tongs and towards the end even my relationship with Mike was a little frayed – or it just got distant. I think Peter was ahead of us in some of his ideas about arrangements because we were all big block chord men and the sound was very thick at times. Peter could see that some songs could be more powerful with fewer notes, but that would have meant denuding us of our power base and it was like, 'Well, who are you to tell us this, show me,' and of course he couldn't.

TONY: Money was always a bit of a factor. We didn't really earn enough. In order to finance buying instruments we had borrowed money from our parents, £150 from each parent. After that we probably lived off savings. We had free rental at the cottage, which obviously made a lot of difference, and occasionally food parcels would arrive from Ant's parents. And then when we got a few shows there was enough to keep the whole thing going, just about enough.

ANT: Peter would spend a lot of the time on the phone trying to find us gigs, because the paradox with Peter was that he was, at one and the same time, the most mystical of us but also the most practical. He was the one who knew that if you didn't get on the phone and find an agent no one was going to ever hear this supposedly wonderful music. And he really did put the time in on that so we would lose him for chunks of the afternoon.

MIKE: Peter was very proactive. I remember his little notepad by the phone with lists of people to call. Peter was very good at ringing up guys who advertised in the back of *Melody Maker* and saying 'Here we are, what are we going to do?'

PETER: I wouldn't give up, and Richard helped hustle too. But it was extraordinary because agent after agent would ring up and say their car had broken down on the way over. It was only out to Abinger Hammer, which is twenty-five miles out of London. I think there were about three weeks when we were given this same excuse as the reason why these Londoners couldn't make it down our way. And then we had one classic moment where we were excitedly offered an interview with, I think, John Martin of the Marquee Martin agency. He listened to the tape, smiled and said, 'Listen boys, whatever you're doing now, carry on doing it. Don't do music, you're never going to make it'. And I think we owe a lot to him because, perverse buggers that we are, we were going to prove him wrong.

TONY: We did eventually manage to tempt an agent or two down, which led to some work: we played at a students' union in London where there were some promoters and that led to us getting a few more performances, which was really useful. We were able to develop as players and artists in that way. Because we really didn't have any experience and we needed time to try and work out how to do it.

Above: Supporting Jackson Heights, the band formed by the ex-Nice bassist Lee Jackson, at the Marquee. It was through their gigs at the Marquee that Charisma Records were alerted to the existence of Genesis.

I'd hardly even seen anybody play live at that point. Peter and I had been to see the Nice play at the Marquee. It was the first concert I'd ever seen. I found it staggering, incredible, the most exciting moment in my life up till then. The sound was wonderful: they had the guitarist Davy O'List with them at the time and I think the combination of all of them was really good. And Keith Emerson, keyboard player extraordinaire, was very impressive. I'd never really considered playing live before that.

PETER: Our first public performance had been a school dance at the end of the lane by my parents' house, at the home of some family friends called the Balmes. We thought we were fabulous but the small audience wanted to hear what was in the charts. That was a lesson it took us a long while to learn, but that's part of the education of being a performing musician: learning how to choose what out of the material you play is going to work with a particular audience on a particular night. And it was something some of the band learned better than others.

MIKE: When we first started playing at places like Brunel University it was a steep learning curve. We'd been playing in the living room of Christmas Cottage sitting in a circle. So we got to Brunel and no one had a clue how to set up, who was going to go where. We were completely lost. There was no plan. That was quite scary, the first gig. But again we started to learn to play as a band. Apart from the writing stuff we learned how to perform and play as a unit.

ANT: That first proper professional gig at Brunel University was lovely because we were so naïve. Peter kept moving the PA forward and somebody else kept moving it back and there was this stand-off between Peter and whoever it was. We'd been working in a small little living room and suddenly we were in a big hall and we didn't know how to make the transition. The acoustic guitars had pick-ups which would feed back because the pick-ups were ancient and too close to the amps. The stage area was usually very small and then Mike wouldn't know which one of us was feeding back, so we'd both turn ourselves down, and there would be silence, with Peter left singing on his own.

We were still doing a song off *From Genesis To Revelation*, the kick-off track called 'In The Beginning'. It bit the dust pretty badly that night because I'd restrung my guitar too soon before the gig and I hadn't stretched the strings. The guitar had a dodgy machine head and when we reached the instrumental riff about forty-five seconds in, a string had slipped and so there was a miasma of sound, nobody could tell where we were, who was doing what. I was looking at my guitar, thinking 'Which string is it?' and turning the machine heads willy-nilly. Oh, it was a bad moment.

MIKE: One weekend we headed off to do two gigs. We had all the gear packed up in the back of the bread van, which had the front part of the rear space converted into a bench seat, with no windows, probably all highly illegal. We were about to leave and I suddenly saw Peter coming down the hill carrying his double mattress, trying to push it into the back of the van, just in case he wanted a good night's sleep. There was no room, but he was always stubborn and he managed to get the bloody thing in.

TONY: Richard was our roadie. But he couldn't actually drive, so Mike and I had to do all the driving. And to be honest Mike and I were also much better with soldering irons at that stage than Richard. But Richard was vital because he was a huge support at a critical time.

MIKE: That weekend we did a show in Wolverhampton for Guest, Keen & Nettlefold, a company who made nuts and bolts. It was their Christmas bash. They probably stood there thinking 'What is this?', because the trouble is we weren't a covers band, we did our own stuff. And we often started softly, acoustically, and there were no drums until the third or fourth song, so when we were playing in places with noisy bars half the audience wouldn't know we were on stage until the drums came in.

THERE WAS DEFINITELY ONE GIG UP NORTH WHEN THERE WERE MORE PEOPLE ON THE STAGE THEN THERE WERE IN THE AUDIENCE. IT WAS SUGGESTED THAT WE SHOULD STOP AND BUY THEM A DRINK. IT SEEMED A BETTER WAY TO ENTERTAIN THEM.

PETER GABRIEL

We also played a gig in Bramhall, at some youth club near where I used to live up in Cheshire. We hadn't arranged anywhere to stay, we couldn't afford hotels, and then someone at the gig said, 'I've got a house in Buxton', Buxton which is in Derbyshire. 'You can come and stay there'. I told the guys and they said, 'OK, it's not far away,' and I said, 'It's bloody miles away, it's in the Derbyshire Hills'. Nevertheless off we went, it took two and a half hours, and then it started to snow, so eventually this little old bread van crawled up to this house that was just full of hippies. It was freezing cold, and the guy was chopping up furniture to heat the fire. It was the most horrible night.

PETER: This guy had told us he had a 'bloody big house in Buxton', but it was a squat. We didn't know what a squat really meant and of course the windows were all smashed. When we got up in the morning he said, 'Oh, don't worry, I'll get breakfast', and we discovered what that meant, following the milk van around and nicking bread and butter, eggs and milk from people's doorsteps. It was an educational experience.

ANT: I had to take to my bed every six weeks or so. I think the others just thought, 'Oh god, he's got another cold'. But given that I had had glandular fever only six months or so before I was contravening nearly all the basic things that I should have been doing. You were supposed to sleep well. Rich did his best with the food, but when we went out we didn't have a lot of money so we wouldn't eat very well. The van was terrible for travelling in, it was cold, there was no exercise, but a lot of stress. If you present that to any medical guy he will tell you that's probably going to lead to some problems. It's not rocket science. But none of us knew much about the after-effects of glandular fever at the time, so I must have seemed like a sickly weed.

MIKE: We often made life more complicated for ourselves. Somebody's aunt or grandmother had given us a cello, and I started trying to play it on the song called 'Pacidy'. I couldn't play the cello at all, so I had to put white tape on the fretboard so I could work out where to put my fingers. Hopefully it was miked up but I'm not sure if it ever was.

ANT: I would be doing this twiddly bit on the twelve-string to give Mike enough time to put his bass down and get set up with the cello, but there were two important elements. One was that the roadie's torch had to be working because if the roadie's torch wasn't shining on the cello Mike had no idea where it was. And the other thing was the fret markers had to be there, but the trouble with the cello was that the splicing tape would often work loose. And many were the nights they'd have to pull him out of the PA. Oh dear, Mike did make me laugh a lot. And the other famous time was when were playing Blazes nightclub, and all the audience wanted was a bit of dancing, some smoochy stuff, and here was this weird band with their prissy English music who kept changing instruments and fiddling with leads and stuff, and in the middle of all this Mike accidentally stuck the bow of the cello up some girl's skirt.

Peter also had a marvellous thing. He felt too exposed because there was nothing in front of him, just a mike stand. So he used to play his own bass drum. Of course John Mayhew wasn't too keen on this, and Pete's drum often wasn't nailed down and would just start advancing towards the audience...

Pete was also quite a good, intuitive flute player, although he wasn't that versatile. 'The Knife' was in A Flat Minor and Pete couldn't really play in A Flat Minor, a tough key on a flute, but he had a solo part. So what he used to do was pull the flute out a bit so he could use the keys in A Minor, which was easier for him to play. Tony Banks would always remember, just before the start of the song, to tell him, 'Pete, flute!' and Pete would go 'Oh, yeah' and adjust his flute. But very occasionally this was omitted and so you'd hit this point where the song would go quiet for this lovely solo, and suddenly Pete's flute would come in a semitone out of tune. Fantastic.

WHEN PEOPLE USED TO ASK ME WHAT OUR INITIAL GOAL WAS, IT WAS TO PLAY THE MARQUEE CLUB. OF COURSE WHEN YOU GOT THERE, YOUR GOALS HAD ALREADY GONE MUCH HIGHER, BUT I ALWAYS THOUGHT, 'GREAT GIG!' Mike Rutherford

TONY: Pete started to develop a stage personality because he found it very difficult up on stage. He was a self-conscious guy, quite shy, and he suddenly found this way of talking drivel between songs, a way of communicating with an audience that seemed to go down quite well.

ANT: We played at the Kingston Hotel with Mott The Hoople, who were really nice people: very generous, very gracious. They were proper Shropshire lads, really damn genuine, and extremely encouraging to us at a point when we were pretty rough. Pete used to forget all the words and at that stage was a sort of slow bumbler. And we'd hear him floundering with the lyrics virtually every night. Funny, nobody knew the songs so it didn't matter. It was probably the tuning of the twelve-string guitars that saved him because the tuning would take forever and that forced him to have to do something, so he assumed this kind of slightly mad demonic personality telling these weird stories which we never listened to because we were worrying too much about the twelve-strings. After a couple of months we thought, 'Whatever Pete's doing, he seems to be making a good fist of this'.

TONY: A significant step up was playing at the Marquee Club in February 1970. We thought we'd made it, even though we were the support act, obviously. Supporting Rare Bird was really the only time I'd ever felt, 'This group is much better than us. God it's not worth it, they're too good'. I'd never thought that about anybody else, not out of conceit; I'd simply never had that feeling before. They were very impressive and had a line-up with two keyboard players, including the guy Dave Kaffinetti who ended up appearing in *Spinal Tap*. He played the electric piano through some kind of fuzz box, which is something I did later when Ant left the group and I had to reproduce all the guitar parts on the keyboard. The other guy, Graham Field, played the organ and Steve Gould, the singer, had a lovely voice. It also showed me that it was possible to learn from other groups; they could give you ideas that you could apply to what you were doing.

MIKE: Like Tony, Rare Bird is the only band I've ever seen on stage and been depressed by them because they were so good. That gig was significant in another way. John Anthony, who was Rare Bird's producer, saw us and talked us up to their label, Charisma Records. And so it was that Tony Stratton Smith entered our lives.

Below: Peter and Ant recording at Regent Sound. Former drummer John Silver says, 'There was one hell of a lot of tambourine playing in Genesis. Tambourine playing was "perfectly valid, man". Everybody liked to get in there and play the tambourine, up against the microphone.' Overleaf: The Genesis line-up that recorded *From Genesis To Revelation*, complete with John Silver (far right), a preponderance of pith helmets and Peter's decommissioned black cab.

THE DRUMMERS' TALE, PART II: JOHN SILVER

Let's get this thing in context. Whilst it would give me immense pleasure to be remembered as Jonathan Silver and his band Genesis, the fact of the matter remains that I'm a very minor cog in this whole exercise. The serious success of Genesis all happened after I left, so I have merely coat-tailed behind their success over the years. And because my time with Genesis was before I went off to university, not only am I a very small cog, I was a very short-lived cog. Although bits of the drum kit I played on From Genesis To Revelation *are somewhere in my house, it's not a working drum kit any more. I never really progressed a great deal, and wasn't, as a drummer, much cop even then.*

I was at school in Oxford, at St Edward's. I was the founder member of the first pop group in the school, which was probably the best gig I ever played in my life. I was scheduled to go to Oxford or Cambridge, but I didn't get the grades I needed, so my parents sent me up to Davis Laing & Dick, a crammer in London where Peter was also studying. We hit it off and I must have mentioned that I was a drummer, because Peter said, 'Well, come and meet these people and see whether you like them'. So we had a few sessions together and we got along well. Peter explained that through Jonathan King they had the opportunity to go into a studio and record some demos. Exactly why Chris Stewart was not asked, I honestly don't know. I was there, hustling myself in one way or another, and I didn't ask, 'Hey, where's the other guy?' That's not the sort of question sensible people ask. In these days of completely unlimited access to recording equipment and music it's difficult to explain to people just what a rare opportunity it was to get into the Regent Sound Studios in Denmark Street for three or four days. It would never have occurred to me to turn it down.

As we started preparing for the album, we traipsed around the south of England and the Midlands, mostly in Peter Gabriel's taxi with all the gear in the back, driving from place to place. This rehearsal period was the most wonderfully 'English' experience in the main. It involved going to bed at all hours and getting up late, surrounded by a long-suffering retinue of domestic staff, parents and others who treated us with a most amazing leniency. As a parent I would now be going through the roof. But at the time, we were completely oblivious to this indulgence.

At one stage we were at my parents', a large house in north Oxford. There was half of an old garage downstairs which we used as the recording space; my dad owned an old Ferrograph reel-to-reel recording machine which was on all the time as we rehearsed, and we played for hours and hours and hours. Because the acoustics in the place were good enough neither the neighbours nor my parents ever complained as we worked through the night. My brother and my younger sister were also

there and of course for Caroline and her school friends this was wonderful fun: her older brother in a group who were meant to be making a record. I think she was allowed to bring the tea in. Tea figured strongly in the early days of Genesis for some reason.

I can remember at some stage getting up, jumping into a Morris Austin or one of those cars, with no shoes on, just in my underpants with a blanket around me, and driving with the rest of the band, similarly attired, to the local shops in Summertown, roaming around in the middle of the day and buying a roll or two or a bottle of Coca Cola before swinging on back.

And there was a chap, David Thomas, whose parents had what in hindsight must have been a lot of property, including a kind of country mansion with a swimming pool, where we stayed in that summer of 1968: sleeping in beautiful old-fashioned beds with eiderdowns, waking up with the sun streaming in through true Brideshead-type rooms, wonderful breakfasts being brought to us, and our job that day was to go by the pool and write another piece for this magnum opus which was on the way.

I remember it as this truly golden snapshot of time when we had no responsibilities other than to make music all day, all the time. And there were girls. Remember we were all from public schools. I'd just come in to this crammer where there were all these wonderful London society girls. It was a time of amazing fun and indulgence, so young love was very important throughout all this.

But what today seems quite incredibly indulgent was nevertheless the way it was in those days, because we had the potential for a recording contract and so were treated slightly differently from other waifs and strays who had no opportunity of a recording contract. My parents' view, and the others' too, I'm sure, was, 'You've all had a good education, you're destined to go to university and you can be indulged in this whim for a period of time but at some point: 'Enough is enough, Sheldon!''

Because we had a recording contract we'd already got 'success'. It was socially acceptable, certainly amongst our peer group, to be in a pop group. We hadn't achieved any commercial success, but there was some evidence to support the fact that this was not complete indulgence. And there was a real innocence about this whole thing. It was not tainted by any real world experience at all. What the record company liked about us was that our innocence made us so incredibly malleable. We had no streetwiseness at all and that must have been rather endearing.

On the first demos I had managed, like all drummers, to include some flash drumming. That's what the object of playing drums was in those days. Most of the tracks featured me playing a biscuit tin. For some reason I couldn't get a drum kit into the studio, so I was playing brushes on, and I can still see it now, a square Huntley & Palmers blue and gold biscuit tin. After the demos we had to wait around to see whether they were going to

allow us to make the album. We were all hanging around at a flat in Bramham Gardens in Earls Court.

We would be pretending to rehearse or simply waiting around and somehow somebody would bring a message to the flat, 'Quick, get over to Jonathan King's flat, because Paul McCartney's turning up'. We would scurry over as quickly as possible because the art was to be there, looking casual, before the next famous person arrived, so that Jonathan King could say, 'Hey, these are my new protégés'. I treated him as a god, because he knew these people. It wasn't celebrity like it is now. There were only a few famous people and he knew them. If Jonathan said jump or stand backwards or stand on your head, basically you did it. This was the nature of the relationship: he was completely omnipotent, in a decent way.

When we did start recording the album, there were no real fallings out other than the usual, because we had to work so bloody fast. We had a list of songs to do which we had rehearsed so you got on and banged through them in the hope that you didn't screw up the execution. And even if you did screw up in the execution it would probably be OK anyway.

Everybody had serious input into what was going on. Ant Phillips was a very important voice in the style and manner of what we were doing, and I recall he was always walking around wearing a pith helmet, and stabbing at his guitar chords: the track called 'Image Blown Out' was quintessentially what Ant was all about. He and Mike I think of as a unit coming up with ideas, ways of doing things. I am truly in awe of what's happened with Mike Rutherford. It is so brilliant. But at the time he was a bass player. He wasn't the most demonstrative person, and because the technology of the electric bass was so poor, you couldn't hear much of him any time.

Tony was the guy who would be forming the whole structure because he was the pianist and he had the Farfisa organ; we managed to stick drawing pins in the hammers of the piano, which is why there are these fiddly bits that sound a little honky

tonk, a wonderful sound. Tony always was the musical heavyweight of the band, no question about it, and the most musically proficient. Peter was the singer and the voice. Singing was much harder for him than anything we were doing and so worrying about Peter's voice – and he was a worrier – was incredibly important, because his voice was constantly being stretched.

A constant theme was equipment. We had to borrow kit all the time and at the end of the studio sessions in the night, I would go with one of the others, carrying a guitar or guitars, to a room somewhere in Soho above a Greek restaurant where we had to give the guitars back to Cat Stevens – he was signed to Decca too, probably Jonathan King had set it up – and we'd pick them up the next day for another session.

I don't think anybody in their right mind listens to From Genesis To Revelation much. It's completely swamped by the wretched strings, which is a shame. When the single came out there was a moment of true nirvana and eternal happiness when we got a message to say that somebody like Brian Matthew was going to play it on the radio, and I had the chance to phone my mum who in turn had some of her friends there. At the time I thought we should do whatever it took to get publicity: I would have been perfectly ready to dress up like any other pop group at the time and run round Trafalgar Square with a publicity photographer if that was necessary to get some success in the age of pirate radio, before the tabloids. But I knew that amongst the misery guts of the rest of the band this was never going to be part of the deal, and I kept my counsel.

Before the album came out, I started feeling family pressure coming back on me. My father in particular said, 'Look, you don't want to do the regular thing. What about going to university in the States?' I got accepted at Cornell University. I had no real interest in studying management but I did fancy the idea of going to university in the States. I went there absolutely sure that Peter would phone me at any moment to say we'd been offered a slot on The Old Grey Whistle Test, 'Get back over here now'. That is what I really wanted to happen, no doubt about it. I played in various bands at Cornell, I would go and do regular interviews on the college radio station there, telling them about how it was in swinging London, and I began to enjoy that vicarious existence. Meanwhile I waited to get the call. But it never came.

Jonathan Silver was Chris Stewart's successor on the drum stool. He left the band in August 1969 after the recording of their debut album *From Genesis To Revelation*, and went to study at the School of Hotel Administration of Cornell University. He subsequently changed direction to work in TV production, specializing in news and current affairs for Granada, Reuters and Thames Television, and later moved into IT and computing applications, most recently working on the Lightworks high-quality video editing system.

CHAPTER FOUR

AT THE SIGN OF THE MAD HATTER

PETER: I had been trying hard to find us a record deal. I was particularly keen on Island because I was a big fan of Chris Blackwell and at the time Island had Fairport Convention and Free on the label; they also had a visual style which really appealed to us, whereas most of the other labels seemed to have no sense of the visual world. We had supported Mott The Hoople on one date and they went back and enthused to a guy at Island called Guy Stevens, who had been working with them. He met us, big fuzzy hair, and took us into his office in the Island building; there was nothing in the room, just one telephone. He was, I think, in an alternative universe most of the time. And consequently, although he was initially very interested, we weren't really pursued by Island.

TONY: We also saw Chris Wright at Chrysalis, and I'm sure it was him who told us there was no question of any women coming out on the road, which was quite a big thing for us because we're family kind of people, and we didn't want someone telling us what to do. The Moody Blues were launching their Threshold label – Mike Pinder was quite keen on us and we actually recorded a version of 'Looking For Someone' for him. What put me off was that we finished the recording and I had made a mistake towards the end, just a fluff, a brown note; nobody noticed except me of course. I said we'd have to redo it and Mike said 'No, no, we'll live with that'. Now, I can't put out something that has a brown note on it and that's one of the reasons we didn't go with Threshold in the end.

ANT: There was pressure to get a deal. We needed a proper record company to back us because we had no money. We were surviving, just, on what we made from the gigs, which was quite piecemeal. And of course we wanted to record. But by that stage we were beginning to have some confidence, clearly, because we didn't rush at the first person who expressed interest. Peter in particular was very shrewd, very watchful. I think otherwise we might have been prepared to go with Threshold, because the Moody Blues was a big name. Eventually, it seemed that Tony Stratton Smith's Charisma label was going to be the best fit for us.

PETER: I think I'd read about Tony Stratton Smith in *Rolling Stone* when he was managing the Nice, who were an incredibly exciting, hard, pioneering band at the time. So much so that Hendrix asked to join, not a commonly remembered fact. Strat's connection with the Nice was certainly one of the things that excited us about him.

I might have sent a tape to him off the back of that article, but then Rare Bird's producer, John Anthony, started lobbying on our behalf and encouraging Tony Stratton Smith to come and see us, trying to lure Strat away from Le Chasse, the drinking hole on Wardour Street where he could be found with Francis Bacon and a few other, I was going to say stars of Soho, but they were probably more like black holes.

MIKE: We had this residency upstairs at Ronnie Scott's club. It looked good on the schedule, although most nights there were only seven people in the audience. But Strat came, liked us and saw something.

ANT: The showcase gigs at Ronnie Scott's didn't have a great atmosphere because there weren't that many people there, but you knew damn well that virtually everybody there was very serious: Strat came in for us on the basis of seeing us there.

MIKE: Charisma was an independent label which had a quite classy feeling to it. And Strat was a larger-than-life-character. He had this wonderful ability to convince you that you were great. That was the key thing for us because our career went very slowly on record after we signed to him, and without someone as fully behind us as he was we would have floundered a bit.

Opposite: The *Trespass* line-up, in which Ant, Peter, Mike and Tony are joined by drummer John Mayhew, far right.

ANT: In a way, Strat seemed quite upper-middle class and old school, a guy who liked to go racing, a bit like my father in a way: very dignified, intelligent, cultured, well-dressed. And he really believed in us. I am convinced that if Genesis came along now, the group would not be successful, because nobody would have the patience and the time to allow them to mature into a money-making machine. It took a long time. Maybe I'm getting old but it seems to me that decisions are now made by record companies on the basis of numbers and profit within a year or two. These old-style patrician record label bosses – I don't think they really exist any more – were prepared to take a loss on certain things. For example, Strat funded an album of modern hymns which Mike and I contributed to and which was never going to be a big money-spinner. He had a lot of idealism, which was delightful.

TONY: He was very enthusiastic. He loved the music and he grew to like it even more. That kind of belief was vital. It was very important to have someone who believed in us when things really weren't happening. And Charisma really stuck with us; we didn't make money for years.

PETER: I think Strat had come from very humble origins and yet he had a lot of gentlemanly ways about him. He had a lot of heart. He was a gambler: before he settled any royalty statements or any money owing in one quarter he'd spent it all on the next exciting thing. He'd been a sports journalist originally, and often wore a sort of dishevelled suit. You could imagine him emerging from a pub in Fleet Street with his shirt undone... There were rumours that he'd been a spy in Brazil, always a sense of mystery about him, and because he was uncomfortable about being gay, he also moved in a world which was still ninety per cent hidden. Strat could blow hot and cold, but he was a wonderful man to have working behind us, really driven and with a great soul. He worked exceptionally hard for all his artists whether that was Vivian Stanshall, John Betjeman, or Monty Python... His tastes were remarkably catholic.

YOU'D GO INTO A MEETING WITH STRAT DEPRESSED ABOUT HOW YOUR CAREER WAS GOING AND COME AWAY ELATED, THINKING YOU WERE THE GREATEST. HE HAD AN ABILITY TO MAKE IT ALL SEEM WONDERFUL: 'IT'S GOING TO BE OK, BOYS.' MIKE RUTHERFORD

PETER: I had been slightly holding off signing to Charisma, just in case Chris Blackwell came though, because Island were still my number one choice. But we couldn't resurrect any response from them, and Strat seemed to be really passionate. What we were worried about was that his main project at the time was the Nice; our concern was that we might only be a little fringe project while he got on with managing the Nice.

MIKE: I remember going for a meeting when he agreed to sign us and put us on a wage, £10 a week. In fact, he offered £15 and it was John Mayhew who said 'No, £10's enough' and John was the working-class boy; I don't know where that came from. We all rounded on him afterwards and virtually did him over! But what Strat did do was to make available to us funds to buy better equipment, so that we could become a proper on-the-road band. He was an inspirational person but also very proactive. Bands like Rare Bird and Lindisfarne would be playing all the time and had brand-new PAs and gear, so he was the real thing.

Opposite: Photo session at Newark Priory near the village of Ripley in Surrey, September 1969 – shortly after John Mayhew had joined Genesis. These photos were taken by Bob Rootes, brother of Dave Rootes, another friend who handled roadie duties along with Richard Macphail.

PETER: I see it from the other end now because here I am at Real World trying to help musicians from all around the world get started. They expect you to sort out their lives and pay their rent. From Charisma we were getting ten quid a week, which eventually went to fifteen. It wasn't really enough to pay our bills, but it was some money, and it was regular – although occasionally there would be weeks when the horses hadn't done very well and the support fell through...

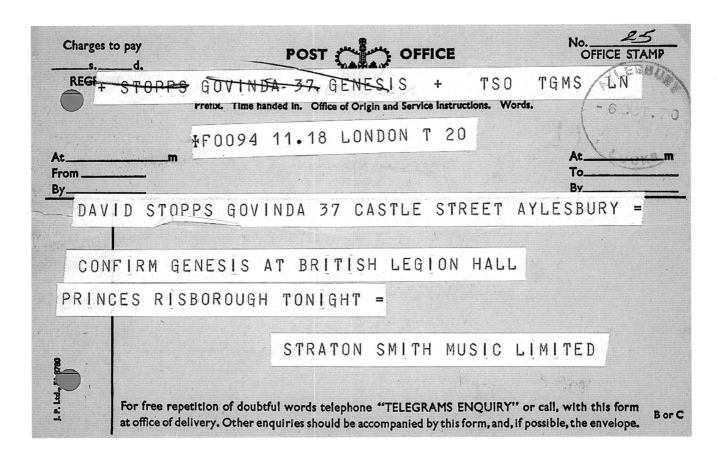

Charges to pay	POST ⚙ OFFICE	No. **25**
s. d.		OFFICE STAMP

REG: + STOPPS GOVINDA 37, GENESIS + TSO TGMS LN

Prefix. Time handed in. Office of Origin and Service Instructions. Words.

+F0094 11.18 LONDON T 20

At_____m At_____m
From_____ To_____
By_____ By_____

DAVID STOPPS GOVINDA 37 CASTLE STREET AYLESBURY =

CONFIRM GENESIS AT BRITISH LEGION HALL
PRINCES RISBOROUGH TONIGHT =

STRATON SMITH MUSIC LIMITED

For free repetition of doubtful words telephone "TELEGRAMS ENQUIRY" or call, with this form
at office of delivery. Other enquiries should be accompanied by this form, and, if possible, the envelope. B or C

Above: The recipient of this telegram from Tony Stratton Smith's office was Dave Stopps, founder of Friars in Aylesbury, one of Genesis's favourite regular venues in the early 1970s.

TONY: The Charisma office in Soho consisted of Strat, his assistant Gail Colson, Fred Munt, who later became Gail's husband, Gail's brother Glen who handled press, and Eve Slater. That was the entire personnel. So the whole operation depended very much on Strat's enthusiasm. God knows where the money came from.

PETER: Chris Briggs, who worked with Charisma, who now works with Robbie Williams and who I've always got on well with, once called us 'a bunch of snotty-nosed bastards'. I think most of the people in the rock world who had come from middle-class homes had pretty successfully covered it up. But it had never occurred to us, or we weren't smart enough, to do that and so we picked up quite a lot of flak – occasionally deserved, but mainly not – for being public school boys who had been silver-spoon fed. There was always a degree of that natural resentment and in particular Glen Colson, whose humour and cynicism I've always enjoyed, would be very happy to put us in our place at any opportunity.

ANT: We were continuing to build our range of live venues. We did a gig at the Roundhouse in Camden, which is the only visual proof I've got that I was with Genesis because a film of the event exists somewhere. I remember the cameras on stage and David Bowie and Tony Visconti dressed in spaceman suits and capes. Kind of weird, really.

PETER: We were Bowie fans. In fact I think it was Tony who first picked up on David Bowie with one of his very early singles, 'Can't Help Thinking About Me', which Tony used to play regularly downstairs in the billiards room.

And then we ended up performing at this thing called the 'Atomic Sunrise Festival' in the Roundhouse, with – yet again – more people on the stage than there were in the audience, pretty extraordinary. Somewhere someone has the film of that show. I'd love to see it; it's probably really bad, but definitely of the time.

MIKE: We were still travelling to gigs in the van. At one point some journalist got hold of the fact that backstage we used to have a kind of picnic hamper and one of the papers made it sound like we had servants and fine silver. It was actually economics: we couldn't afford to go and eat out in restaurants or cafes. It was cheaper to cater for ourselves. We'd started preparing our own food during the Christmas Cottage days. Richard would have prepared baked potatoes, sausages and boiled eggs and always, when we were setting out from London, by the time we got to Hendon we had finished the whole lot off! Twenty minutes into the journey, and a seven-hour drive stretching ahead of us.

ANT: Around the beginning of that year, 1970, I had suddenly started getting chronic stage fright. I remember we were playing at Watford Tech supporting Atomic Rooster, Vincent Crane and Carl Palmer's band. We were starting the song called 'Let Us Now Make Love', just twelve-string and voice. And I remember looking down at my guitar and thinking, 'What comes next?' It was an awful moment. I was frozen in time. I really didn't know what had happened. I later heard Derek Jacobi talk about exactly the same thing, how he was about to do Hamlet, the speech, and suddenly thought, 'How does it go?' I tried to dismiss it, but the next night it started coming on and on and on, and I began anticipating its onset.

I'll never know to this day whether I would have been able to come clean about it if I'd been living a more sensible life. All I can say is that it was sufficiently frightening to feel that I *couldn't* talk about it, at the very time when I should have been. I remember thinking the others would think I was cracked and also that I ought to be able to deal with it and make it go away, because that's the way I'd been brought up at school: you don't squeal.

The trouble was that I had my good days where it wouldn't happen. What was great for me was when things went wrong on stage. I know that sounds awful, but if there was a distraction or people weren't listening then it was better. I'd get through the first part of the gig somehow and as we got nearer the end of the song called 'Twilight Alehouse', a bit of a knockabout track which was the penultimate number, and were about to start 'The Knife' to finish the set, I'd have a feeling of exquisite relief: I was safe, I was through, I'd made it again. I've never taken heroin but I imagine it must be a similar experience. And afterwards I'd feel fantastic. But then the following morning the whole cycle would start up again. I had probably been the keenest from day one, consistently in groups from the age of eleven or twelve, absolutely determined to be like the Beatles or the Stones, so it was a terrible shock to have lost this dream. And I was completely losing it. I was no use to the group.

PETER: Ant was going though some nightmare stuff. We were aware he was experiencing some kind of tension, which was unnerving, but we didn't know what it was, and none of us were good at externalizing feelings. There was one part of Ant which was a completely natural performer but there's also a drama within Ant, I think, which was counteracting his natural enjoyment and enthusiasm for performing and being on stage.

STAGE FRIGHT IS SUCH A TERRIFYING THING BECAUSE IT COMES FROM NOWHERE AND GRIPS YOU TIGHT. IT'S COMPLETELY IRRATIONAL, BECAUSE YOU'VE PLAYED THE SONGS A THOUSAND TIMES BEFORE. ANTHONY PHILLIPS

ANT: Somehow I got through it mentally, but physically I cracked. I contracted bronchial pneumonia, which sounds a lot worse than it was. It actually wasn't as bad as the glandular fever I'd had. I'd wake up with a really, really heavy cold on my chest. I got over it quite quickly, but I felt awful because the others couldn't work for three or four weeks while I was out of action. Then I recovered and we were able to record *Trespass*.

Overleaf: Tony Stratton Smith had been a sports journalist originally. Legend has it that when he was working for the *Manchester Evening News*, he was due to be flying with the Manchester Utd team on the plane involved in the Munich Air Disaster, but he missed the flight because he was congenitally late – and thereafter decided that fate intended him to be late for the rest of his life.

FOR SIGNATURE AND IMMEDIATE RETURN PLEASE

LICENSED ANNUALLY BY THE WESTMINSTER CITY COUNCIL

TC/8022

TERRY KING ASSOCIATES.

Panton House, 25, Haymarket, London, S.W.1. Tel. 01.930.1771

This Agency is not responsible for any non-fulfilment of Contracts by Proprietors, Managers or Artistes, but every reasonable safeguard is assured.

An Agreement made .... 21st. .... day of ... APRIL .... 19.70.

between .... DAVID STOPPS .... hereinafter called the Management

of the one part, and .... PETER GABRIEL ....
hereinafter called the Artiste, of the other part.

Witnesseth that the Management hereby engages the Artiste and the Artiste accepts

an engagement to { present ...... GENESIS ......
to appear as ... KNOWN ......

at the Venue on the dates for the periods and at the salaries stated in the Schedule hereto.

SCHEDULE

The Artiste agrees to appear for a salary of (a) £.... 30. net ~~per~~ ~~over £25.~~ DR

or (b) £ .... or ....

of the gross door and advance receipts whichever is the greater

Minimum admission prices .... (members) .... (guests).

for .... 2 .... performances(s) of ...... 45 mins. ...... duration

between the hours of 7.30.pm. and .... and .... and .... 11.00.pm.

......1....Day(s) at Friars New Friarage on MON 15th. JUNE ...... 19.70.

...........Day(s) at Walton St., ... on .... 19.....

...........Day(s) at Aylesbury ...... on .... 19.....

...........Day(s) at ...... on .... 19.....

SPECIAL CLAUSES

1.   The Artiste shall not, without the written consent of the Management, appear at any place of public entertainment within a radius of .... miles of any of the Venues mentioned herein, for .... weeks prior to and during this Engagement.

2.   Where musicians are booked through this Agency, the Management agrees that any other band performing the Engagement(s) described in this agreement shall be composed of members of the Musicians' Union, and in the event of Musicians' Union action arising from the engagement of non-unionists, the management shall be responsible for payment of the full fees or percentages as stated in this agreement.

3.   In the case of percentage engagements, the Management must provide the Artiste or his representative with a written statement of the full details of ticket numbers, admission prices and number of patrons and provide full facilities for the checking of the same.

4.   Salary payable by Cash/~~Cheque~~ to Artiste/~~xxxxxxxxxxxxx~~ on completion of performance, ~~within~~ .... ~~xxxxxxxxxxxxxxxxxxxxxxxx~~.

5.   The Artiste shall arrive by .... 6.30.pm.

ADDITIONAL CLAUSES

Above: an early booking for
Genesis at Friars in June 1970 –
note the fee: £30 net.

We literally recorded the live set. There wasn't any time to go back and dig out some of those nice acoustic numbers which had died out on the road when we were trying to play them with two little lads shouting over them.

I was OK recording. I remember having a bit of a battle with the engineer, Robin Cable, over the sound of the twelve-string. Twelve-string guitar was still thought of as a kind of percussion instrument, a Roger Whittaker strumalong, whereas Mike and I were using it as a very colourful instrument with layers of complicated textures. It was a bit like Pete and the PA system: Robin Cable kept moving the mikes and I kept moving them back again; he would say, 'That doesn't sound like a twelve-string' and I'd say, 'It does.' It was a bit difficult.

TONY: There was a massive development between *From Genesis To Revelation* and *Trespass*. Having made the decision to play live, we had become a working band and so had been able to get a direct response to the songs. We had two really long, loud tracks, 'The Knife' and 'Going Out To Get You', which at one point were both something like twenty minutes long, and from playing them live we slowly realized that we couldn't do that in front of an audience. Some of our songs were difficult and wouldn't get an immediate response, but we learned to construct a show to try to build up to them.

I always feel with *Trespass* that we were still writing very much in the two pairs, myself and Peter, and Mike and Ant, and then coming together, and I felt that I contributed less to that album than most of the other albums. Peter and I had written 'The Knife' together; the organ sounds a bit more like the Nice, and the song was originally called 'The Nice'. 'Stagnation' was something we very much worked on all together, and there was an extended instrumental section at the end of 'Looking For Someone' that predicted a lot of what happened in the later albums, which was also a group-written piece. But 'Dusk' and 'White Mountain' were really Ant and Mike's work, and 'Visions Of Angels' was very much Ant's song, which had originally been intended for *From Genesis To Revelation*.

'Stagnation' is probably the best track on the album, because it showed the way we were developing. I particularly like the way there wasn't much repetition: we went to a section, developed it, and moved onto the next section, which became a characteristic element of Genesis, a kind of storytelling with music.

I also had to write a solo for 'Stagnation', which was a totally novel thing for me. I'd never done a solo. It always used to be the thing when we were playing with school groups, jamming on a twelve-bar blues: at some point you'd have to play a solo and I couldn't do it. On this track I liked the idea of deliberately constructing a solo as opposed to trying to improvise one, so that it became more of an instrumental, and I found I was comfortable with that.

PETER: The album was produced by John Anthony. He was a great morale booster, particularly in trying to get the performances out of us, but I don't think, largely because of our own anxieties, that we gave him our best performances. And I don't think the album was exactly what Charisma wanted. It was always hard to tell. Strat would sometimes like the most unlikely things; you could never really be sure what he was going to like until he heard it.

I think he knew that live we had something and that those performances were getting stronger and more confident. There was one time when we played the Olympia Theatre in Paris, Edith Piaf's spiritual home. The guy who ran it had a church in northern France and was so moved by our performance that he invited us to play in the church. Although we never did, it was one of those moments that I believe reinforced Strat in his thinking that he was pushing something special here.

ANT: After the recording sessions, I felt like a bit of a zombie, and then we started again on the road and I was nowhere, absolutely nowhere. By now I wasn't paralytically nervous,

but my heart had gone out of it, I just couldn't get back into it. I was still trying to disguise it, turning my volume down to hide any wrong notes. It wasn't very good and the truth of it is that it wasn't good for the others. In the end I talked to Mike a bit about what was happening, and I think Pete knew, but it was most extraordinary, because even years later Tony Banks' wife Margaret would ask me, 'Well, Ant, why did you leave?' We did a few more gigs and then I said to Mike, 'I just can't do it, there's no point'. I remember he went and poured himself a Scotch.

MIKE: It was an incredible surprise to me because I hadn't really clocked it, despite being close to Ant. I had a girlfriend by then and at the time we were living in a flat in London and Ant was living at home. It made me realize how far we'd drifted apart as friends between the Christmas Cottage days and the time when he said he wanted to leave.

Ant looked troubled about everything in life. The glandular fever had got him down and he'd had this terrible stage fright. I think we were all tired at the time. We'd been working pretty hard, driving a lot, gigging a lot, probably all at a bit of a low ebb physically.

It was Richmond Rugby Club, some kind of bash. Richard Macphail took the three of us into the middle of the rugby pitch and said, 'Ant wants a word', and he told me. At the time we thought the four of us were indispensable, in a young, intense way, and that if one of us left we couldn't carry on, so I thought that was it. We were probably closer to stopping then than at any other time.

I suppose I should have said something, tried to change Ant's mind, but I never did. I'm funny that way. I've always had this feeling that if someone doesn't want to be involved in the band, then they shouldn't be. If he didn't want to do it any more, that was fine.

TONY: The stage fright took me by surprise. I'm not a natural showman. I hate putting my head above the parapet; I'm an introvert. Particularly in those early days I was always very nervous about going on stage but never frightened in the sense that I couldn't play. I had a confidence about what I was doing, and confidence in the other people around me. And Ant seemed to enjoy performing – he was the biggest show-off in a way: he used to wear funny hats, used to dress up and had the right colour guitar, so I found it very strange, and when it came up I initially thought he was just being bloody-minded. It pissed me off to some extent. I felt, 'We've done all this, and now he's throwing it all away', because I thought that we would probably have to split up as a result.

PETER: In some ways I think Ant allowed himself the luxury of quitting, because it's a tough thing when you've got to stand up and be counted and you have to face real critics, audiences and reviews that hate you sometimes, not just disliking you, but really disliking you. You have to have a solid enough persona to somehow be comfortable with the pain of being called 'shit' and I don't think Ant was very good at that. In fact, I thought Ant was being a wuss, because I knew he loved performing and I think he had the power to decide whether he was going to enjoy it or be beaten down by it. I'm sure he didn't see it like that, but that's how it felt to me at the time. So I was pissed off, probably much the same way the others were pissed off with me when I decided to leave.

ANT: The others had every right to feel disappointed and irritated with me, because I probably should have made the decision the first time round, before going out on the road after we'd recorded *Trespass*. But I felt I had to try and give it one more shot.

PETER: We talked about ways to keep Ant involved in the writing, but he seemed pretty resolute. It was a shame that he didn't carry on with it, because he was one of the most gifted of all the band.

WHEN ANT LEFT HE PROBABLY THOUGHT THE BAND WOULDN'T CARRY ON WITHOUT HIM. WHICH WAS A PERFECTLY REASONABLE THING TO THINK. Tony Banks

TONY: It hadn't really occurred to me that we had enough strength to continue. I probably underestimated just how good some of the elements we had were, particularly Peter as a front man and vocalist. Because he was such a close friend, I never viewed him as an outsider might. And so we were facing the prospect that it was all going to end in Haywards Heath, a kind of non-event gig, goodbye, last Genesis gig ever, 'Was that it?' We could have ended up along with all those other groups we used to play with at the time who didn't survive the era.

MIKE: The night of our final gig with Ant, we were driving back, myself and Pete, in Pete's Hillman Imp. We hadn't really spoken about whether we should carry on; and we sort of chatted ourselves through it. Somewhere between the start of the journey and the end, I'd gone from 'Well, that's it' to 'Let's carry on'. That's how I remember it. And I spoke to Tony afterwards, who said, 'If we are going to carry on and if we're going to go through the painful process of finding a new guitarist, we should get a new drummer'.

TONY: We had one conversation in the aftermath of Ant's decision when Richard Macphail said, 'You can't not do this. This is special. You've got to keep it going'. Peter and Mike felt the same way and were very keen, so I said, 'OK, let's give it a go,' but I did say we should get ourselves a new drummer at the same time.

I'm not a terrifically rhythmically conscious person, but I do know when something doesn't really work. John Mayhew was fine, a perfectly solid drummer, but I felt he just didn't have the kind of spark of inspiration we wanted, and a lot of his parts had tended to end up being written by Ant, who had a good drumming mind. I think John himself got a bit frustrated by it all.

MIKE: It wasn't John's technique, more his view on how to understand the music. What we wanted him to play he could play quite easily, but he often couldn't get it until Ant or Peter showed him on the drums. Running him down is unfair – gosh, we must have been a funny bunch to him, four public school boys and this guy who used to be a carpenter. It had been a strange marriage.

PETER: John had lifted our music up without question, but it needed to move to another level, and I think I and everyone else in the band believed that a band is only as good as its drummer, which is tough on the drummer. You can't transcend the spine of the music, which determines the shape of the body that forms around it – and that's what rhythm is, I think.

I was dispatched to drop the bad news; I felt terrible because John was having a tough time with his marriage, but I've always tried to be straightforward about these things and there was a real sense of relief once I'd done the nasty deed.

TONY: Charisma didn't seem to have a problem with the personnel changes. I think it was us who felt that there was some sort of special magic with the four of us. I don't think Charisma thought of it that way at all. They were a bit more realistic.

PETER: We advertised for a new drummer in the back of *Melody Maker*. I'd been taking a lot of phone calls off the ad, and then I spoke to Phil Collins, who said he'd played percussion with George Harrison. I remember that stuck out. I think Phil was on second tambourine somewhere but he was there... However, we weren't great fans of Flaming Youth, the band Phil was in; it was a pop package, an early boy band in a way, with aspirations of albums about the stars.

Overleaf: An exuberant Tony Stratton Smith in the offices of Charisma with Glen Colson (left). A poster for the Six Bob Tour on which Genesis supported Van Der Graaf Generator and Lindisfarne is top middle. Mike remembers, 'Strat was an inspirational person, but he was also very proactive. Bands like Rare Bird and Lindisfarne would be playing gigs all the time and they always had brand-new PAs, and new gear, so he was not just talk, he was the real thing.'

ANT'S TALE: ANTHONY PHILLIPS

Even though I was no longer a part of Genesis, I found it was completely impossible to escape from the band. I had not left them 'because of musical differences'. I still had enormous respect for the others. We'd had our moments of musical friction and differences of opinion, of course, but we had all had very similar and positive views about each of the albums at the time we were making them. There had been some good times, very good times. I could just have done without those few dodgy months towards the end.

So although I was out of it, there was a part of me, an umbilical cord, that could not be cut. Part of my being had gone right into the very fabric of the band because all the twelve-string guitar work that Mike and I had created together was very much a child born of both of us, and that child carried on developing even though I was no longer in loco parentis as it were.

A couple of years later, in about 1972, Mike was staying with me at my parents' place. There was a twelve-string guitar sitting in the kitchen, and Mike came in and started improvising on the guitar. Shortly afterwards I also went into the kitchen and played some improvisations. Somebody who heard both of us said later that they were absolutely amazed by the similarity of what we were both playing. And that was the trouble. People would say about my music, 'It sounds like

Genesis', and my reaction was, 'Well, yeah. What do you want me to do, suddenly start performing Norwegian carpenters' songs? This is me as well.' That aspect was particularly difficult; I could never get away from it.

I decided to move on by heading in a different direction. There had been some very well-intentioned masters at Charterhouse who had tried to get us to listen to classical music, but at the time our ears – clamouring for the Beatles or the Stones – were closed. We had an attitude that this was something for a later time in our lives. Quite soon after leaving Genesis I heard Sibelius's 'Karelia Suite', which struck me as a wonderful piece of music. Although it is a piece of 'classical music', it struck me forcibly how tuneful and varied it was, and not at all predictable in the way – and I know this will be heresy to some people – that some music from the definitive classical period can be in terms of harmony and structure. I found the music absolutely riveting. It really was a road to Damascus moment: 'Oh, come on, it's incredible that just one guy could create all this music'. Because, remember, we had had that unfortunate experience on From Genesis To Revelation with the string orchestrator who, through no fault of his – he was told what to do and there was a limited budget – had created these high-wheeling string arrangements. At the time I had thought, 'I don't ever want

to let anybody else muck about with our work without us having any say', and I felt determined to learn how to do that for myself, although it was an impossible enterprise at the age of eighteen because I was completely untrained in musical theory. However, from the moment I heard Sibelius in 1970 I embarked on the long road to learn all about it.

I started studying classical music, which was hugely exciting at times, but there was an awful lot of drudgery involved in learning keyboard techniques. I could play piano by ear, but I'm not a very good sight reader. I'm not a good pianist at all, in fact, so it was a battle to try and achieve my aim of mastering arrangements and orchestrations. Meanwhile Genesis were motoring ahead, although they hadn't yet achieved the global success. That didn't come until the release of 'Follow You Follow Me', but they were picking up a huge following. And I thought the music they were making was fantastic.

It reached the point where it became painful for me to listen to a Genesis album because I'd be thinking, 'Oh God, I could have been involved in that'. It grew slightly easier later on when the band became more commercial because, whilst I respected what they were writing, it wasn't so much my kind of area. I could see that the music was very good, but for me it wasn't breaking new ground musically in the way that Selling England By The Pound, a fantastic album, had been. That was one record that especially made me think, 'Ooh dear'. It was flattering being associated with the music up to a point, but then, naturally, there was the flip side which was that Genesis were being incredibly successful and I wasn't. I started getting a few comments along the lines of 'Pete Best and the Beatles' but mine was a different situation. I think if I had walked away for musical differences, I would have felt a right prat, but as such it was one of those things that happens in life. And to be honest, apart from improving my own personal health, my decision to leave was better for the group as a whole, because at the end of my time with them they were essentially carrying a passenger.

I also don't believe that the group could have gone on as it was. There were too many composers within Genesis, too many strong minds, too many talented people vying for a limited amount of territory. You can't go on compromising for ever. Otherwise you end up with people who are rather dissatisfied with the finished product. Ask Steve Hackett. I think the band eventually got the personnel down to a manageable number with each of the separate power blocks clearly delineated. There was nobody treading on anybody else's toes when it consisted of Mike, Phil and Tony.

I worked with Phil and Mike on The Geese And The Ghost, my first solo album, and before that on a project to write a modern hymn. That was really tricky because we worked so well together. Phil was such a good guy and we got on; he's a naturally easy guy to get on with. He likes sport as

I do, which none of the others did, so we had something else in common. He was a very positive influence. He persuaded a group of his friends to come over and help us produce a demo for the project. After this hands-on experience of actually playing with Phil, I definitely had the feeling, 'Wouldn't it have been phenomenal if we had been in Genesis together?' I could see – and no disrespect to John Mayhew – how Phil's buoyancy would have lifted the group and psychologically made a big difference to the atmosphere.

Having said I was never a very talented keyboard player – which is true – when Peter came back into the business after taking his sabbatical he put together some demos at Trident studios for his first solo album. Peter had been out of Genesis for about a year. So who did he get on piano? A. Phillips. Yes, I was the keyboard player – which is really weird and I was very flattered. I imagine Peter's thinking was that while I'm very far from being a virtuoso, I did understand his music. I could play his material with a few extra frills, but I probably wouldn't put too much of myself into the arrangement or constantly argue back at him, simply because the piano was not my home turf.

I didn't have a piano at the time and had to go over to somebody else's house and practise. We played 'Here Comes The Flood' and a number of the other tracks from the album. Mike and Phil were also involved along with John Goodsall, the guitarist from Brand X. I think it was nice for Peter because it gave him the opportunity to dip his toes in the water in an environment that was harmonious and fun. It was the only time I've ever played with Mike and Phil together as a proper bass and drums rhythm section – on the earlier occasion Mike and I had both been playing acoustic guitars. That was another moment that made me think, 'What have I missed here?', because Phil and Mike were so solid and yet so relaxed together, the kind of relaxation that only comes from confidence and empathy and years of understanding. It was an absolute dream in fact. I just played a few chords and sat and listened to the two of them. They were so good.

In the years after his decision to leave Genesis, Anthony Phillips concentrated on his classical guitar and piano technique, and studied harmony and composition at the Guildhall School of Music and Drama in London. He worked with Mike Rutherford, Phil Collins and Harry Williamson, and evolved his solo writing and recording, the first fruit of which was 1977's *The Geese And The Ghost* (named after two sounds he produced on an ARP Pro-Soloist synth). He has since had a consistent stream of solo releases, including the *Private Parts & Pieces* series of albums – currently up to number X – also composing soundtracks and advertising music. Ant has not performed live since 1970, but says the prospect of him ever doing so is 'not impossible'.

THE DRUMMERS' TALE, PART III: JOHN MAYHEW

One afternoon in the summer of 1969 I got home after doing the shopfitting on a boutique and my girlfiend Nicky said, 'A guy called Mike Rutherford phoned, and he's going to call back at six o'clock. He wants you to join his band. They're called Genesis.' As soon as I heard that name, Genesis, something clicked; it sounded right. Some things just go like a dream. Well, more or less. Mike did ring back, and set about trying to convince me to join Genesis. He was really selling the band to me, and I remember thinking that this was going to be quite something.

I'd just left a band called Milton's Fingers, come back to London and been giving my telephone number out to all and sundry. For four or five years I'd been drumming in various bands, initially in Suffolk, playing the American Air Force bases, country clubs, parties, pubs. When I was 19 or so, my family split up and I went to London and joined a couple more bands – there was a virile music scene at the time – and juggled the music with specialized carpentry work, mainly as a shopfitter, which I really enjoyed.

I'd met Milton's Fingers one Easter. I was hitching back to Ipswich with my girlfriend, and a red van with clouds painted all over it came past us. Normally a band wouldn't pick up hitch-hikers, because all the space was taken up with equipment. But this van did slow down, and they said, 'Get in.' We started talking, and I told them I played drums. They said, 'Oh, do you now?', because their drummer, a guy called Frog, was leaving to play on the cruise ships. They came from Scotland, a tight four-part harmony group, led by a guy called Milton McLoughlin. We got onto the university circuit, were very professional, worked hard. We were living in a house out in the country, but my girlfriend was a fast city girl and although she stuck it for quite a long time, in the end she left to go back to London. I followed her and left Milton's Fingers. What was I supposed to do? I was madly in love with her.

So I was at something of a loose end when Mike invited me down to meet Genesis at Anthony Phillips' parents' place. I duly headed down there, taking all my drums on the train, and was standing there outside the station with the cases all piled up. This black London taxi turned up, with Peter Gabriel and Richard Macphail and maybe one of the others as well; I think they'd forgotten I had a drum kit with me. When I got in Peter was sitting on the little dicky seat with loads of little scraps of paper, scribbling away, writing lines, bits and pieces of lyrics. It made quite an impression on me. I've been a notetaker and scribbler ever since.

They were very welcoming. We came from very different backgrounds, but they never made me feel awkward. I didn't see them as toffs; they were just four guys. We were all musicians, working, living and playing music together. They were very serious, they held their music in high regard and had great confidence about it. I remember Tony saying one day something to the effect that if we weren't in America within a year he was going to leave.

This music was like nothing I'd heard before. From the off I was casting around in my head to find a style that suited them, because it was so unlike any band I'd played in. It was a challenge, because I was self-taught, had never had a lesson in my life. I'd only started playing drums at sixteen, when a friend in Ipswich asked me if I wanted to join his band. I'd said, 'Yup, sure,' even though I'd never picked up a pair of drum sticks in my life. I borrowed a few bits and pieces, and then bought my first drum kit from a guy I knew who lived on a boat. I brought it home, into the backyard, not sure where all these tubes and screws went. My father, who was a painter and decorator, took one look at the kit, which was a bit tatty, and said, 'I'll paint that for you', so I had this lovely white drum kit to start with. A week later I was playing at a wedding, keeping some simple pattern going all night, whatever the song. I think I earned a quid.

I loved playing drums, but I was not a natural. Drumming never seemed to fall on me comfortably. I was forever adjusting the kit, twiddling with the levers or moving the cymbals and drums up and down, anything to make it feel easier and smoother, but it never quite came off. The sticks always felt heavy and ungainly. My main strength was that I was solid, and I'd learnt to be a good timekeeper, after a few terse reminders to slow down or speed up. I think that was one quality I was able to add to Genesis at the time I joined them. Plus I had the experience of playing hundreds of gigs in every kind of venue, and they really weren't used to playing live.

I moved down with the others into Christmas Cottage. I've often been asked if there were any fireworks or tantrums. There never were. If there had been, I'd say so; I'm not trying to protect the good name of the band. I never saw anyone lose their temper or storm out, never to return. It was all happening underneath, the stresses and the fears and the worries.

Here they were putting a year of their precious young lives into this music. I can imagine their parents might have worried about

them turning into drug-smoking layabouts and drinkers, but in that cottage we lived like monks, never went to the pub or out to a restaurant. Richard Macphail and I had an occasional joint, but I felt guilty as hell about it the first time we did, because I thought the others would think I was a druggy, which I wasn't.

We did work hard. We'd get going early, stop for some lunch, chat, go back for the afternoon, stop for supper – 'Supper's ready', probably where that came from – lots of bread and yogurt and cauliflower cheese. Richard had taken on all the domestic duties. I can remember rehearsing in the living room and seeing, out of the corner of my eye, the washing machine filled to overflowing with this grey soapy soup starting to bubble up out of it.

We travelled to gigs in Richard's bread van. He asked me to put a partition in it and although I'd never done anything like that, I had a go. I also made a cover for the organ keyboard and built a reverb Leslie cabinet. At one gig, when the organ was being taken in, one of the keys caught on something and got smashed off. Disaster. I quickly found a screw from somewhere and a piece of wood like a lolly stick and screwed this dummy key onto the keyboard so Tony had something to play on that night.

Peter used to have his bass drum on stage. Fortunately it was pitched so low and there was so much other noise going on all around, I didn't really notice when he was banging it, though obviously a rogue bass drum beat wasn't going to help anything. Ant and Peter used to have ideas about what the rhythm patterns should be, and I would follow them as best I could. They were always good ideas, always had a reason behind them.

I can't really remember much about recording Trespass. After all the rehearsing and the gigs, the material was pretty honed. Ant said we were on autopilot, it was so practised. We weren't having to struggle to create anything, we were note perfect. We played the songs as we'd always played them; and the album is pretty much a snapshot of what we were doing on stage.

There came a point when the others could see that my long hair and smart black fibre drum cases weren't going to be enough. Their music needed a new vocabulary. In King Crimson, Mike Giles, the drummer on The Court Of The Crimson King, had a beautiful style. He avoided clichés, played lovely drum breaks. We listened to that album a lot when we were in the cottage, and I often wonder whether the band were thinking, 'Is it possible to have a drummer like this rather than a drummer like John?'

I realized I didn't have the technical skills to carry me onwards and upwards, so it didn't come as any surprise to me when I was asked to leave. I think even at the time of recording Trespass I knew I'd be leaving soon, but I was still not looking forward to that moment: I had really grown to love the band's music.

Peter told me in a coffee shop in London's West End somewhere; Mike was there with him. We'd met up casually, but I knew what it was about. Peter delivered the news in his usual stuttering way, but he did it with a lot of dignity. I don't think he went to great lengths, but quietly said, 'John, I think it's time you left the band.' He said he was very sorry, but they were looking for a new drummer and a new lease of life. I was hurt all right. Tears came along. After putting your guts into something for a year, of course it hurts. What I'd never told them was that I'd been feeling quite depressed all the time I was with them. I have suffered with anxiety and depression for many years, and was actually in the middle of a breakdown when I was with Genesis. I was clinically depressed. I'd had quite a funny upbringing, and it had all impacted on me. That's why I didn't smile very much. I've been in other situations where I've been the joker, provided the light relief, deliberately so because I like that kind of atmosphere. But when I was with Genesis it just didn't happen, because I was too unhappy – not with them, but with the rest of my life.

I went back to Suffolk. I'd had enough of London. Genesis was finished; there didn't seem much point in staying. In Ipswich someone was playing Trespass on a sound system. I told them, 'That's me playing', and they said, 'No, pull the other one.' It already seemed a long way away. I continued playing in bands throughout the rest of the decade, even after I left to go to New Zealand in 1977, and on to Australia. It was an adventure right up to the very end. The day I stopped playing music I was in Sydney, living in a suburb called Neutral Bay, in 1982. On the way to a gig I had said to myself, 'If this is same old same old, I'm packing it in.' It was. I found myself driving home at one in the morning. It was pissing down with rain, I was sweaty, wet, clammy, cold, just fifty dollars in my pocket. I think I knew before I went out that night that it was going to be the last gig, which was fine with me. I wanted something new in my life. It turned out to be scenic painting. I went off to college for three years, got myself a diploma and changed my whole life again.

I met Ant in 2006 at a Genesis fan convention in London. After twenty-five years in New Zealand and Australia, I was back in the UK, living in Scotland. He was the band member I was most nervous about meeting again, but he was not at all judgmental the way I had thought he might be. I had spent the intervening years thinking that in some way I'd been responsible for holding Genesis back, to my chagrin, but he told me I hadn't.

And I realized that what I had been able to do was to provide a solid platform on which they could set up a repertoire and sort themselves out for a move into the professional world. And if I was that steadying force, then I'm glad that's what happened.

After he stopped performing in 1982, John Mayhew worked as a scenic artist and furniture craftsman, and dropped off the radar as far as Genesis fans were concerned – even the band didn't know where to find him. When John did resurface in Scotland in the early 2000s, Dave Burgess, a fellow student at a Charles Rennie Macintosh workshop (and a Genesis fan) put him in touch with the band's management, who were finally able to pay him the back royalties they had been setting aside for him over the years.

THE CHARISMATIC'S TALE: GAIL COLSON

I used to work for Shel Talmy, an American record producer based in London, who produced the Kinks, the Who and Manfred Mann; he was 'the' producer at the time. I'd started in the music industry in 1966 working as a secretary for a PR man who shared an office with Shel. When he left, Shel told me he'd actually been paying my salary for six months, so I should stay with him, which I did: Shel was blind and I became his eyes. He was going to produce a band called the Creation, who were managed by Tony Stratton Smith. The music business was a very small industry in those days, and much of the activity was centred around the Ship pub and then the Le Chasse club. Somewhere along the way, Tony and I got to know each other and became friends.

Strat was an ex-journalist, charming, and totally committed to the bands he worked with. He put whatever money he had into the business and into the bands, because he absolutely lived and breathed them. At some point he was so broke he used to come into Shel's office and I would lend him £15 on a Thursday afternoon or a Friday morning and he would pay me back the following Wednesday, and then borrow it again. I was only earning £20 or so a week and to me it was the same £15 he was using to pay his secretary. So as he couldn't pay her I started doing his work on the side.

I stopped working for Shel, by which point Strat was managing the Nice and the Bonzo Dog Doo-Dah Band, and went to work for Tony Secunda, a PR man who looked after the Move and Procol Harum. I lasted five weeks there. I'd be taking dictation and he'd be smoking dope all day long, out of his head. I realize I was quite straight then. I actually left him a letter on the typewriter, saying 'Sorry, I can't deal with this'; he was a total lunatic. I worked for the Bonzos for six months or so, in the meantime sitting with Strat in the Ship every night or Le Chasse drinking and bemoaning record companies and saying how useless they were. This was 1969 and both the Nice and the Bonzos had gone over to America; the Nice were with Immediate Records and had done a tour of America where the record company was on answerphone for the entire three weeks they were there. We thought we could do better.

Shel Talmy had had an independent label called Planet Records which the Creation were on. So Strat decided I must know what to do, how to start a record label. The truth was I knew what MCPS and PRS were and that was about it. And that's how we began Charisma. Strat came up with the name: he had originally come up with it as a name for the band Ashton, Gardener & Dyke but they didn't like it, so he used it for the label instead. At the time nobody knew what 'charisma' meant — now everybody uses the word, but at the time people would say, 'What?' In fact when we wrote the press release we had to explain that it came from a Greek verb 'charizesthai', 'to favour', and that it meant to give off light.

We started off in Strat's flat in Dean Street. I'd head over to the flat in the morning, go in with the milk, wake him up. And then he'd be in the bath for a long time. I remember we used to pass the phone through to the bathroom for hours on end. My brother Glen was lying at home in bed doing nothing, so he joined us and became the press officer, Terry the Pill, who was the poster king and had been Jimi Hendrix's roadie at some point, got involved, along with his wife Eve Slater. We all knew each other from drinking together. And my husband Fred Munt — who'd been the Bonzos' road manager — later ran the management company. It was all very incestuous. It was like a family, when I think of it.

The work was 24/7, long hours into the night, but it didn't seem like hard work because it carried on in the Marquee bar or the Ship, where Strat would hold court. We never saw him in the office until about five minutes before lunch, if that. He did drink a lot: vodka and tonics in the pub, or lunch would be a couple of bottles of wine, some brandies, back in the office for an hour and then back to the Marquee. He used to dry out at the weekends occasionally, but Monday through Friday was drink. He was actually able to operate successfully, as some people can, while he was

drinking; it didn't hamper him – although of course he died at the age of fifty-three.

At some point Strat rented a house in Sussex – Lord Beaverbrook's old house, Luxford, in Crowborough – and we all used to go down there at the weekends. Some of the bands, including Genesis, used to rehearse there in the week, and Van Der Graaf Generator made an album down there. We carried on like we had during the week: the only difference was Strat would be sober. The rest of us would be stoned or drunk, and betting on this card game called kalooki that I used to beat everybody at.

Rare Bird was the first record release on Charisma: 10 December 1969, CAS 1005, it's imprinted on my brain. The single was called 'Sympathy'; it sold a million in France. It kind of went downhill from there... We never had a million seller after that, certainly not of a single. Graham Field, the keyboard player with Rare Bird, came in one day after Genesis had supported them at a gig and said, 'You need to listen to this band'.

We put them on Upstairs at Ronnie Scott's, and there were more of them on stage then there were down in the audience, which was me, Tony, my brother Glen, and John Anthony, who produced Rare Bird; apart from effectively being the house A&R, he was another of this little clique. I remember later Rare Bird obviously regretted telling us about Genesis because they kind of went by the board, and Strat loved Genesis, though not quite as much as he loved Van Der Graaf Generator and Peter Hammill. He thought Peter Hammill was an absolute genius, which I can't disagree with, although he was an uncommercial genius.

I think most of the acts we ever signed were flukes. Genesis were brought in by Rare Bird. When the Nice split up, Keith Emerson went on to Emerson, Lake & Palmer, Brian Davison, the drummer, put together a band called Every Which Way, and Lee Jackson, the bass player, formed the Jackson Heights. Lee wanted to use a particular musician from Newcastle, which is where he was from, but that guy was already in another band, whose manager said, 'I'll release him to play with Lee if you sign this other band' – and that was Lindisfarne. Talk about more luck than judgment.

Genesis struck us as posh little public schoolboys, not that that was anything unusual. Van Der Graaf were all public schoolboys. Audience, another band we had, were all university-educated. And they all had long hair, so Genesis weren't that different to anybody else. It was Lindisfarne who really stuck out because of their Geordie accents.

We didn't have any money to start with, none whatsoever. Strat had found B&C Records to distribute us, and they advanced us the money. We had to cover all the recording and equipment costs, and Genesis were on a salary: most probably £5 or £10 a week. It sounds like we were really ripping them off but at the time we weren't – they wouldn't have got a better deal anywhere else. Tony Smith still shivers and says to me, 'Ooh, those contracts', but that's what everyone got. Absolutely standard.

We lived off the record company and distribution advances. This is a terrible thing to admit but when Genesis were playing the Lyceum, we did a run of lunchtime concerts at the venue around Christmas: they were free concerts and we asked people to contribute to one of Strat's charities in Brazil. And once it actually went on our salaries because we had no money to pay the staff. I was trying to hold the whole thing together and stop Strat from spending what money we did have. It would either go on drink or horses, once he got into owning horses.

Later, we were working with Phonogram International, who were based in Baarn, Holland. I was just a young girl, as far as they were concerned, so Strat and I used to have to go over every three months to present our budget. On the plane going over I would tell Strat what was going on, what was coming out, what the sales predictons were, etc., and he would go in and talk because I wasn't allowed to. He could blind them with science and he could talk about horses, incredibly eloquent, very well-read. He was a brilliant writer. He wrote a book called The Rebel Nun which has been translated into God knows how many languages, and he used to write fantastic letters to the bands.

My brother Glen handled the press for the company. He was very popular with the journalists – they would rather not review a release from Charisma than give him a bad review. It was unbelievable, because he'd never done anything like that before he joined Charisma and within a year he'd been voted PR man of the year. We'd started him off as a plugger at Radio One but he didn't like that. His forte was PR. I think the journalists liked his honesty, because he'd tell them, 'Look, I don't fucking like this, but Strat loves it and, you know, it's my job'.

One day Genesis were moaning at Glen about why he couldn't get them any press and he was saying, 'Because you're boring fuckers, and there's nothing going on.' And the next minute Peter put on a fox's head, wore one of Jill, his wife's dresses and at one fell swoop, there they were on the front cover of Melody Maker...

Gail Colson, part of Charisma Records since its inception, started out as Tony Stratton Smith's assistant, then became label manager and later the company's joint managing director. In the late 1970s, she left Charisma to set up her own management company, Gailforce, which she continues to run. Her clients have included Peter Gabriel, Morrissey, Peter Hammill, the Pretenders and Chrissie Hynde.

CHAPTER FIVE

INTRODUCING... MR PHIL COLLINS

PHIL COLLINS: I was given my first drum when I was three, and I started playing when I was five. From then on, much of my family's social life revolved at the Richmond Yacht Club: everybody was there – my mum and dad, and my uncles, who assembled my first drum kit when I was five.

We used to participate in the club's concerts and pantomimes, playing accordion, piano, drums and acoustic guitar to accompany the people in the club who liked to get up and sing. In the Yacht Club everybody mucked in. 'You can cook, what can you do?' 'Oh, I can sing a song'; everyone found their role. And so for me that was just normal life. Being up on a stage or in front of people was not alien to me. I'm now at a point where the 'show business' awareness I had as a child has paid off, whereas Tony and Mike, for example, did not come from that kind of background.

My mother had been managing a toy shop for a friend of hers, and when that closed she had nothing to do. In the meantime she had sent me to elocution lessons, for some reason, and had befriended the person who ran the dancing school associated with the elocution lessons. That friend wanted to set up a children's theatrical and TV agency, which was the big thing at the time, and as my mum was at a loose end, she said that she would start answering the phone for the agency; they used our home number.

Eventually a call came along about the role of the Artful Dodger in *Oliver!*; this was three or four years into the musical's West End run. I went along for the audition and got the part. At the time I was at Chiswick County Grammar School, and after I'd been given the role, my headmaster at the school told me, 'Well, congratulations, but you'll have to leave, because you can't do nine months of appearing on stage every evening and still have a grammar school education.' I guess my mum and dad made a decision that I should leave, and so I went to drama school.

I finished my stint as the Artful Dodger, my voice broke, and I did some other TV and film bits, including *Chitty Chitty Bang Bang* and *A Hard Day's Night*. But playing drums was what I really wanted to do. I was checking my watch, just waiting to grow up so I could drum full-time. At drama school I'd continued keeping my hand in, playing in a band with my future first wife among the backing singers. We'd go to the Marquee to watch the bands playing. We were very professional even as a school band. Finally I decided to stop being an actor and become a professional musician. And that's when my father 'sent me to Coventry'.

My father worked in the City, at Sun Alliance Insurance, and wanted his children to follow in his footsteps, but the world was changing. My brother went into insurance and then escaped to go to art school; my sister was also in the business and left to become a professional ice skater. My father thought I would move into insurance too. He certainly didn't approve of me becoming a musician. I imagine that in his office they had started off saying, 'What's young Philip doing?' and my father would have told them, 'He's on stage in the West End in *Oliver!*' 'Really? You must be so proud.' And then it was suddenly, 'And what's young Philip up to now?' 'He's in a pop band.' Oh, how terrible for you.'

I always thought that my dad had been destined to do his forty years in the City, but I found out much, much later, from my brother, that my father had actually been stopped from doing what he wanted to do by his father. He had run away to go to sea – he wanted to work on the boats – but my grandfather had brought him back to be in the Sun Alliance office just like he was. So my father became this Basil Fawlty repressed character, thinking, 'If I can't have fun, why should anybody else?' It suddenly all made sense.

My mum was very supportive. She helped fund me when I started out as a musician. I was earning no money. Even when I joined Genesis I was only getting a tenner a week. But she bought one of the bands I was in a van so we could get work. She knew the people who ran the Eel Pie Island Hotel near the Yacht Club. I remember walking past the hotel one Thursday night on the way back from the Yacht Club to the mainland and I heard this noise, this extraordinary voice. I said, 'What's that?' and my brother said. 'I don't know. It's some beatnik thing.' It was actually the Rolling Stones and Howlin' Wolf. And because of my mum's connections that hotel became our rehearsal space. My mum kept us afloat.

Opposite: The new boy, Phil Collins, came from a stage-school background and had been playing drums in a band since childhood.

Tony Stratton Smith was a friend. I had joined a band whose manager, Rodney Inge, lived at the Russell Hotel, which the bass player's aunt owned, and we used to meet up there to go to gigs. Amongst the people that stayed in the hotel were Tony Stratton Smith, Jimmy Savile – it was his base when he was in London doing *Top Of The Pops* – and various members of and roadies for the Koobas, the Nice and the Jimi Hendrix Experience. It was an interesting mix of people and sometimes if we came back late I'd stay there as well. I guess that's where I first met Strat, although it feels like I've known him all my life. And we used to bump into him at the Marquee bar or at Le Chasse.

Le Chasse was a musician's club, on the first floor above a betting office on Wardour Street. You couldn't really get in there unless you knew somebody on the staff – I knew the barman. All the bands, roadies, managers, musicians used to drink there and Keith Moon occasionally served behind the bar. He once served me and gave me eighteen bob back out of a quid for a huge round of drinks, so he wasn't the kind of guy you really wanted working for you...

Strat's friends at the Chasse included Ken Howard and Alan Blaikley who managed the Herd and Dave Dee. Brian Chatton, our keyboard player, got to know them all. Brian was a pretty boy – not gay, but they were and he got on well enough with them that they took him under their wing. They were looking for a band to replace the Herd and Dave Dee, who had reached a peak, and they took our band, which was called Hickory at the time, and turned us into Flaming Youth. We did quite a few gigs but nothing like we wanted to do, and we had a record called *Ark 2* out which was album of the month for October 1969 in *Melody Maker*, above *Led Zeppelin II*... But that was the peak of our career, and in the end I got frustrated in this band never really working enough.

So I started auditioning for loads of people, including Manfred Mann's Chapter Three, and Dada, who became Vinegar Joe. I used to get all the music papers delivered – *Melody Maker*, *Sounds*, *NME*, *Disc And Music Echo*, *Record Mirror* – and in the back of the *Melody Maker* one week I saw this advert with a box around it, which was always worth the extra money, which mentioned 'Tony Stratton Smith', who of course I knew, but it didn't say who the band were... I made a point of going over to the Marquee, and lo and behold found Strat. I said, 'I saw your advert this week; any chance of getting a recommendation?' and Strat said, 'Oh no, these guys are pretty fussy. I don't think I can steamroller this. You're going to have to go for the audition'.

My only knowledge of Genesis was through seeing the ads for their gigs. It seemed like they were constantly working. They and Quintessence were my two bugbears. I was always saying to Flaming Youth's managers, 'How the fuck are they working and we're not? We're doing like

Opposite, from left: Young Phil with his father, who had a career mapped out for him in insurance; as the Artful Dodger in *Oliver!* This page, top left: Phil with his father, mother, sister Carole and family friend Len Tungay outside Dick Waite's Boathouse in Twickenham – now Pete Townshend's Oceanic Studios. The young Phil used to spend every weekend there on the Tungays' boat, and grew up performing for Richmond Yacht Club members at their regular shows and pantomimes. This page, top right: Phil drumming on a double bass drum kit with his school band, The Real Thing, at Richmond Yacht Club. It was Phil's birthday, and he remembers vividly that actress Olivia Hussey was there that night. Below: Phil with Flaming Youth – clockwise from left: Phil, Ronnie Caryl (the guitarist who came with Phil to Peter's house to audition for Genesis), 'Flash' Gordon Smith (guitar and bass) and Brian Chatton (keyboards). Ronnie Caryl still plays with Phil on his solo tours.

three gigs every three or four months'. So when I found out that the audition was for Genesis I thought, 'At least I'm going to be working if I get the gig'. They were looking for a guitar player to replace Ant as well as a drummer, so I went down to the audition with my friend Ronnie Caryl from Flaming Youth, who I'd known since we were thirteen or fourteen and had formed a band together when we were both at drama school.

PETER: The auditions were at my parents' house in Chobham. We needed to see a dozen people or so, and we couldn't afford to sit and jam and take a couple of hours with each of them, so we devised a test of a few pieces. Part of the problem with John Mayhew had been that he was slow learning things and when we had intricate patterns on songs it would take John a long time to learn them. So we wanted someone we could throw a difficult pattern to and who could pick it up quickly, someone who could get a groove going, who could do a few flourishes.

PHIL: We drove there in Ronnie's Morris Minor, drums in the back, heading down to Chobham through all these tree-lined drives. Of course, coming from Hounslow, it was like suddenly cruising along Fifth Avenue if you'd been living in Harlem. We arrived early. Peter met us and said, 'Would you like to go for a swim in the pool while we're auditioning people ahead of you?' This I hadn't expected. We went into the back garden, where there was a beautiful open air pool, the grand piano on the patio and a big umbrella for the drums to be set up under. Mike Rutherford was there in a smoking jacket like Noël Coward – he says it's not true, but he did have a kind of red dressing gown and slippers – and Ronnie and I thought, 'This is another world'. So we went for a swim and I heard all the other drummers ahead of me...

MIKE: Phil claims that I was wearing a kind of smoking jacket. It makes me sound terribly like, 'Bring on the next drummer...' I'm not sure it was a smoking jacket, but a dressing gown, that's possible...

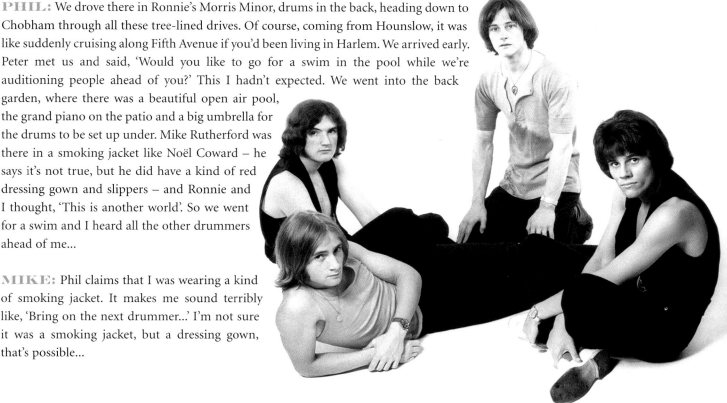

PHIL: There was a break in the auditions, when all the drummers who were auditioning that day spent some time sitting with the guys in the living room. They put on *Trespass*, and my initial impression was of a very soft and round music, not edgy, with vocal harmonies and I came away thinking Crosby, Stills and Nash, maybe because the sun was shining, and it felt like a day in the country. By this point I knew all the music, because I'd got big ears anyway. One or two of the other drummers had soloed before they had the audition, presumably thinking that if the audition didn't impress the band, then their soloing would, which I thought was not the right move. I went in knowing the material and I was really good, I have to say. Whatever else I might not be good at, I was a good drummer.

LISTENING TO THE OTHER DRUMMERS, THERE WAS NOTHING THERE TO SCARE ME. I WASN'T ARROGANT, I WAS JUST CONFIDENT. Phil Collins

PHIL: At some point I remember seeing Mike and Ronnie hunched over twelve-string guitars learning things, but Ronnie was always more of a blues player. He was into John Mayall at the time, the Bluesbreakers with Eric Clapton on the 'Beano' album, and we used to play Cream numbers together. Genesis was a little outside his range, whereas I was already into arrangements, listening to big bands, some jazz, early Yes.

MIKE: Ronnie was fine but I didn't feel he was right, probably because my frame of mind was to try and find Ant Mk II. They drove back in the car and Ronnie turned to Phil: 'Sorry, mate, yours didn't go very well, but mine was good', and of course Phil got the job and Ronnie didn't.

Right: Phil and his left-handed drum kit. Mike says, 'By the time Phil sat down to audition, I knew immediately he was the one, He was very proficient and sounded great, but he also got the parts straight away. We didn't realize he'd been listening to all the other drummers while he was sitting round the swimming pool...'

PHIL: Ronnie was OK about it. It was just another job he hadn't got. The others were unanimous that I was the right choice, but Mike was the disbeliever, not entirely sure whether I was the best: we've always had a little joke about that.

TONY: I think we would have levelled out with the line-up we had and by finding Phil, we ended up bringing in someone who gave us so much more than just being a drummer, which was obviously a totally unknown factor at the time.

Of course everyone's going to say 'Oh, I thought Phil was the best', but Pete and I definitely thought he was. Phil had something about him that was kind of special. It was a combination of things. He could make it swing a little bit, he could also tell good jokes and make us laugh, which was very important. He was able to fit in, but he brought a lighter, breezier personality than the rest of us. We were all a bit heavy, quite intense. He had some knowledge of the music business from his time with Flaming Youth. And he could sing, which was an advantage because Mike and I were not very good at back-up vocals.

MIKE: The weird thing is that when a drummer sits down at a kit, it's the way he sits down and the first few rolls he does: you pick up on the confidence. The whole thing about drums is that they should give a musical band a huge lift, energy and power and that's what Phil did straight away. You could sense it at the audition.

PETER: I was convinced from the first moment. I knew when Phil sat down on the kit, before he'd played a note, that this was a guy who really was in command of what he was doing, because he was so confident. It's like watching a jockey sit on a horse.

The only other person we were considering talking to, and who John Anthony was pushing hard, was Roger Taylor, because apparently Queen were on the verge of giving up at that point, and John was saying, 'Well, Roger is a really good drummer'. He is, of course, and quite similar to Phil, but he never came to audition.

ANT: There was a huge silver lining for Genesis which was that me leaving meant they had to have a time of reassessment. They got Phil. I mean, come on, it's got to have been worth it to have got Phil. I feel sorry for John Mayhew, saying that, because John was a decent drummer, but what an impossible act to have preceded, if you like.

MIKE: We took a holiday and reconvened in Farnham, where my parents had a house. There was an old deserted maltings in the town, which is now an arts and crafts centre, but at the time was just bare floorboards and pigeon shit. We moved in there and started to write as a four-piece.

PHIL HAD THE LOVELY CHEMISTRY OF A DRUMMER: BIG SMILE, A JOKER, SOMEONE WHO WAS A LITTLE BIT MORE RELAXED ABOUT LIFE, A GOOD INFLUENCE ON THE REST OF US.
MIKE RUTHERFORD

PETER: When Phil came on board, there was a sense of lightness restored, a new lease of life. It was fun to play, exciting to jam. We could throw ideas out and he knew how to make them sound good and lift them up. Without a guitarist Tony was playing twice as many solos and covering the guitar parts on fuzz electric piano. And Mike, too, expanded to fill some of the space Ant had left, creating interesting chords. I was a big Who fan, so I remember on 'The Musical Box' pushing him hard to add these crashing chords.

TONY: I took over all the lead guitar parts; fortunately it was possible to do, although I'm not the kind of person who can rub his stomach and pat his head at the same time. Obviously it didn't sound as good as it did with a guitarist, but it sounded similar. We ended up performing as a four-piece for the period while we couldn't find a guitarist. It made me develop incredibly as a musician, but it was tough.

PHIL: During the rehearsals at the Maltings, suddenly someone would leave, someone would walk out, or a guitar would be thrown down, and unbeknownst to me at the time, somebody had offended someone else or said something, transgressed an unwritten rule. I'd think, 'Where's he gone?' And one of the others would say, 'He'll be back in a minute' and so we'd carry on with something else. I hadn't understood Ant's importance in the group and that the dynamic I was entering was far more fragile than I had anticipated; it was very highly strung. Slowly I found that my job became the diffuser of tension. It's still my job in some respects.

TONY: I was subject to tantrums in those days, and I remember having some shouting match about some chord sequence or other and storming out of the rehearsal room. I did feel, 'poor Phil', because he was used to having fun playing, and was a bit shellshocked by the stuff going on, particularly between me and Pete. But sometimes we needed a bit of violent disagreement to produce results.

MIKE: We did a lot of writing there. 'The Return Of The Giant Hogweed' emerged. 'Musical Box' started there and we just managed to make it work as a four-piece, me using bass pedals and rhythm guitar, Tony playing lead on a fuzz box on his Pianet. We had been forced to adjust and create a sound that worked quite well. And we probably could have found a way forward had that been the route we took.

PETER: Tony was able to cover a lot of the parts and Mike also filled up quite a lot of space, but there just wasn't enough variation. One long Tony solo per song was as much as I felt we could tolerate!

TONY: We were still trying to replace Ant. We played a lot at Friars in Aylesbury, which was a great venue for us throughout this period, and we were friendly with Dave Stopps who ran it. He suggested we try Mick Barnard, who was a guitarist in a local group called the Farm.

We auditioned Mick and liked his style. The echo on his guitar was really effective, and if he'd been a little more assertive, it might have gone somewhere. But I think we found we couldn't get enough out of him; he was too reserved.

We also tried Ronnie Caryl again because we were desperate for a guitarist and Phil asked us to give him another shot. And although we thought he was good he wasn't right either. Ronnie was much more of a bluesy guitarist and it didn't feel like that fitted in with us.

PHIL: There was always some underlying issue about the fact that although he was a great player we were looking for someone who added some originality to the writing, which Ant obviously had done. Being a good guitar player wasn't enough. And that's why Ronnie and Mick didn't get it. I was less sensitive to that because I was still a player rather than a writer.

TONY: Some of the guitarists we auditioned had no idea: I remember one guy saying 'I can do better than this' and soloing all the way through 'Stagnation'. The nature of the guitar is that it tends to attract people who like to be flamboyant and out there making a lot of noise as the centre of attention. We were looking for exactly the opposite of that. We wanted an ensemble performer.

PETER: After a while we felt that there weren't enough colours and variety in the guitarists we were seeing. I noticed an ad in *Melody Maker* that Steve Hackett had put in. The wording he used attracted me. It was something to do with being adventurous or unconventional or experimental.

MIKE: I had got a stomach thing, the start of an ulcer, God knows why, probably not living a very healthy lifestyle, and was in bed for a couple of weeks at home. And while I was laid up, Peter and Tony discovered Steve through an advert in the *Melody Maker*. I think it was no coincidence that I wasn't around to say 'Oh, no, no'. I was still looking for 'son of Ant'. They were much more open to a different approach.

PETER: We found Steve and his brother John playing this weird music on an estate near Victoria Station. It was a very enclosed world in some ways but there was a real mood around his playing. We thought Steve was very musical and although he wasn't as natural a fit as Ant, he was definitely adding moods and colours.

Opposite: Tony with a twelve-string guitar. He says he always liked playing guitar because it allowed him to surprise himself in a way he couldn't always do with the keyboard. 'Half the time I didn't know what I was playing', he says, but it led to the creation of crucial chord sequences, like the opening of 'Supper's Ready'. Below: Steve with a bass guitar. Overleaf: The new line-up poses for a photo: including Phil Collins (second from left) and Steve Hackett (far right)

STEVE WAS AN ORIGINAL GUITARIST, VERY ELECTRONIC WITH WEIRD, FUZZ SOUNDS. AND NOT ONLY DID HE WEAR BLACK, HE EVEN SOUNDED A LITTLE DARKER, WHICH WAS GOOD FOR US.

MIKE RUTHERFORD

STEVE HACKETT: I had been working and recording with a band called the Heath Brothers, three South Africans. The brothers wanted to control and produce everything themselves. There was this one piece of work that I was very proud of, but when I heard what they had done with it on the mix, I didn't like the sound at all, and asked them to rework it. They said 'Tough', and I told them, 'If you don't remix it, I'm off'. They wouldn't, so I left. And went back to placing ads in the back of *Melody Maker*. I obviously hit the right tone, because Peter Gabriel phoned me up.

Peter and Tony came round to the flat we had. I was twenty, living at home, in Pimlico, Ebury Bridge, overlooking the trains. If the trains didn't drown you out, the brass band that used to march every day up to Buckingham Palace and back would. Many was the quiet tinkly moment that I was trying to perfect and then boom, boom, boom, Sergeant Pepper would come marching up the road; my God, I used to get exasperated.

I hadn't been entirely sure who Genesis were. I had two bands in my mind, Genesis and another group called Quintessence and I wasn't quite sure which one of them Genesis was. Peter had suggested I go and listen to *Trespass*, especially 'Stagnation'. I went down to the local WH Smith in Sloane Square and because I had no money to buy the album my brother John and I listened to the tracks there, trying to work out if we were listening to guitar or keyboard. Peter and Tony explained that it was a lot of twelve-strings. I'd bought and sold twelve-strings in the past and was just about to get another one, so I thought 'I must make this investment because obviously the band are interested in this'.

These pages: Peter's still standing – a performance for Belgian TV in February 1972. Steve Hackett says he always thought of himself and the rest of the band sitting down as Peter's 'pit orchestra'.

I remember them as a couple of guys in dark overcoats, one far more verbose than the other. Tony was quiet, extremely reticent – I think it wasn't until six months after I joined the band that he said, 'Oh, I really liked what you played that day'. I'd played a few melodic flute and guitar pieces with John, and then some atonal electric stuff and some blues on my own. And they responded more to the melodic material than the dissonant pieces or the blues, and I realized that they were really a non-blues based group, exploring European roots more than American, which brought something precious to the band.

PHIL: We had an audition with Steve at Tony's basement flat in Earls Court. Steve came down all dressed in black, the Robert Fripp look, with some very strange fuzz boxes and it was the fact that he was doing things that nobody else was doing that appealed to everybody.

STEVE: I'm not surprised that Mike was fussy. They wanted less of a guitar hero and more someone who might have a love of chords. When I met Mike he was sitting in bed in a pair of pyjamas and I didn't realize that this was probably the important part of the audition, because Tony and Peter must have thought, 'We liked what we heard, but Mike is our other guitarist so you really need to hit it off with him'. Fortunately I was young and stupid enough not to get nervous. What was interesting was that straightaway we began swapping chord shapes like a pair of stamp collectors, and found out that we shared a love of first inversion chords, in other words

if you play a C you've an E bass note and if you're playing a D you've got an F sharp bass note: the kind of chords that are part of the stirring work of Holst and all those English hymns.

I remember Tony telling me once that school had been pretty grim but everything was made right at Evensong. I loved hymns and classical music, so we always hit it off in that area. When I first met Phil I'd said, 'Do you think we'll make a go of this together?' He replied, 'Oh yes, sure. And we're bound to influence each other', and it had never dawned on me that I could be influenced by other musicians.

STEVE: My first gig with Genesis was at University College, London. It was an absolute disaster. For some reason I wasn't able to use the fuzz box I normally did. Suddenly I found myself with a Shaftesbury Duo Fuzz, which is usually a good fuzz box, but that night it fed back the whole time, which completely threw me, and I wasn't able to give it my best. That was the changeover from semi-pro thinking to professional thinking. I felt so humiliated doing that gig. I just wanted to die. I think dying would have been easier. I'll let you know once I've died.

MIKE: At Steve's first gig Phil seemed drunk, and did a drum fill about four inches away from the drum he was aiming for. The audience wouldn't have noticed it, but I remember thinking it was a bit tough for Steve.

PHIL: At those university gigs, you'd arrive, do a sound check at five o'clock and not play till midnight, so what do you do: you have some food and you have a beer and then another. I remember thinking that night that I'd had a couple of beers too many, and in the strobe lights I was playing two inches to the left of the drums on occasion. I could have been a lot more rock-steady than I was. It was probably nerve-wracking for Steve on the first gig: we all think we're not good enough at that point.

STEVE: There was a blazing row afterwards, but I didn't seem to be in the line of fire. I felt it was my fault, but Phil claimed to have been drunk. I don't know whether he was or whether he was kindly taking the blame for my own personal failings. I felt I'd blown everything, that I wasn't going to be given a second chance. But luckily we were coming up to one of the biggest gigs you could play at the time: the Lyceum in London. Thankfully, there was another gig first, at a teacher's training college in Bangor, with about three people in the audience, where we played in what was not much more than a classroom, a bit like doing a rehearsal with a few stragglers in attendance – but at least it meant that I got through the set.

Before the show at the Lyceum I was still terrified, wondering which way it was going to go: my mother told me afterwards, 'You were green, your face was green'. I did the gig, apparently to everyone's satisfaction, and when it was over Richard Macphail, who had been mixing the sound upfront, came up onto the stage, took me gently by the arm and told me, 'It's over, Steve, you can leave the stage now'. I hadn't realized it had finished. The moment of danger had passed. But it had been touch and go...

TONY: I don't think Steve had had much live experience. He wasn't a natural showman. He would sit down to play guitar, because he had all these pedals, at a time when most guitarists were up there on stage with their head thrown back, turning out endless solos, using their teeth. Steve had a serious disposition, but that suited the way we wanted to go about things.

PETER: Steve wasn't a full frontal guitarist flashing his crotch. He was a more introverted guy who dug his particular vein with a trowel rather than a spade. What had attracted me to his playing was that it was about mood and sound and colour and added a slightly darker element, more brown than black.

STEVE: Before I joined Genesis formally I had been to see them playing another gig at the Lyceum; I remember a hairy student-looking type called Richard Branson drove us back afterwards in his little Austin Healey: another very low-key character.

The band had started the set like an acoustic folk outfit, with a song called 'Happy The Man' that had something of a Cat Stevens feel. They were quieter than most bands I'd seen. They weren't trying to beat you over the head with volume. There was no bluster. They gradually built the energy up and I felt there wasn't a substantial rock tune until they played 'The Knife' at the end, a rousing finish which got the whole crowd going. Both then and during my time with Genesis in the early days, I used to long for that rock number at the end of the show, because many of the more subtle moments were lost on most audiences, who really wanted to bop or headbang. I personally would have been happy if the set had been full of those types of numbers and increasingly that's what happened: the band got louder and we gradually ditched the more acoustic moments, but here's me all these years later playing nylon guitar at least as much as I play electric, and I'm very glad for the time we spent tinkling away.

I felt I could bring a certain energy to the band and I imagined it might be easy. But despite having thought of them as a quiet band, I found once I joined that I'd never worked with a band playing at that volume before. The volume of Phil's drums in the rehearsal room was absolutely terrifying – incredibly loud with an extraordinary amount of fire coming off his kit – and I realized that my little amp wasn't going to cut it. So straight away I decided I needed new gear and luckily the band, or rather Charisma Records, were bankrolling that, which meant I had the opportunity to buy a 100 watt amp and a Les Paul, the guitarist's equivalent of a Maserati. 'I've just got to have one, old chap, I've just got to have one'.

PHIL: With Tony, Mike and Steve at this point I was desperately trying to get some kind of groove going, and sometimes it was very difficult because the parts were more important, the sound was more important than the groove, and of course that for a drummer is the wrong way round.

PETER: Rhythmically, things were feeling better. Phil is a very gifted musician. He's someone who can pick up any sort of instrument and instantly produce something that feels good. People in the world at large see him through his songs now, which appeal to a particular audience, but he can fit into almost any type of music very comfortably. He was a real musician, whereas most of us were feeling like we were faking it.

TONY: We marked time from *Trespass* through to *Nursery Cryme* in terms of our commercial success, but we were re-grouping and integrating Steve and Phil, and we became a much stronger group as a result. It was more difficult to assimilate Steve in the band than it was with Phil, and Steve would probably agree that there were a couple of sides to him that the rest of us weren't really interested in. But where we did coincide it was fantastic. I did an awful lot of duet playing with him, the two of us playing lead together or in harmony, swapping parts.

Everything we did then was very structured, and Steve took the same approach. At the time we did get a fair amount of criticism for it. People would complain, 'You always play the same thing every night' and I'd say, 'But don't you understand that when people improvise, they tend to play the same things every night but just in a different order?'

STEVE WAS MORE SOLITARY WITHIN THE LANDSCAPE OF THE MUSIC. IT WAS PROBABLY HARD FOR HIM JOINING A BAND WITH ALL THESE BIG PERSONALITIES. HE QUIETLY CAME IN AND I ENJOYED HIS PLAYING STRAIGHT AWAY. Mike Rutherford

TONY: Shortly after Steve joined, the Six Bob Tour started; this was an idea that Strat had had: three bands on tour together and six shillings to see the whole show. The three groups – all on Charisma, of course – were Van Der Graaf Generator, Lindisfarne and ourselves, and the first show was the one at the Lyceum, Steve's third gig with us, in the January of '71. Because we were third on the bill, and so first onstage, we had no real pressure because we had nothing to lose. We'd start off the show, and sometimes it went amazingly well: people got very captured by the atmosphere.

Lindisfarne would follow us, and were the real crowd-pleasers. They'd always play 'We Can Swing Together' and the theme from *Z Cars*, which went down a complete storm. And finally Van Der Graaf would come on with music that was both heavy and difficult. I felt so sorry for them.

PHIL: On stage, you knew you were on a hiding to nothing with Lindisfarne. They were a good time band, and they always got the crowd on their side; no one wanted to follow Lindisfarne. Van Der Graaf, who normally closed the show, were very intense. We were kind of in the middle: entertaining with intensity. Van Der Graaf were pretty uncompromising, and I always respected that. They did what they did and there was no quarter given.

MIKE: For the first time we found ourselves surrounded by more professional people. Van Der Graaf taught me how not to structure a set. They put all their heavy, dark songs together and the other faster, lighter ones together, so there was no flow. We learnt how to improve our sound, watching how the other bands' roadies operated. We were out there in the real world.

TONY: We suddenly found ourselves going down very well, particularly in places like Manchester, Newcastle, Glasgow, where we might have previously played the odd show but had no great success. As has often proved to be the case with Genesis, it is often the more industrial cities that tend to like us. We never did well in colleges, for example. We were too clever for them. The students wanted something more down-to-earth, whereas the guys who perhaps were having a slightly more mundane existence were very happy to embrace this music which was very escapist and quite elaborate.

PETER: The Six Bob Tour was a wonderful thing, great memories of life on the bus. Gail Colson, Strat's right-hand woman, was either going out with or already married to Fred Munt, who had been the Bonzo Dog Doo-Dah Band's tour manager. Fred enjoyed the high life of rock'n'roll excitement and one time – although the only people generating any fan excitement at that time were Lindisfarne – he had everyone crawl out of a bathroom window to get to the tour bus. We reached the front of the building where all these thousands of fans were supposed to mob us and I think we found two tired-looking grandmothers. But the whole operation was carried out with military precision and urgency.

I used to hang out with Dave Jackson of Van Der Graaf a fair amount, as well as Rod Clements from Lindisfarne. In fact, when I couldn't get a mortgage for my first house when I moved to the West country in 1974, it was actually Rod Clements' dad who got us a mortgage with a Newcastle building society, so there were practical gains as well...

STEVE: We'd be travelling up and down the motorway in a large coach. Genesis would be in the middle with Lindisfarne at the back and Van Der Graaf in the front. My abiding memory of the Genesis section is of people doing the *Times* crossword. If you wanted to talk about the meaning of the universe, life and death, you went up front and spoke to Dave Jackson, Peter Hammill, Guy Evans and Hugh Banton. And if you wanted to have a drink at lunch time you went to the back, sat down with Lindisfarne and discussed the merits of Guinness versus Newcastle Brown Ale.

> **YOU COULD SIT WITH LINDISFARNE WHO WERE THE DRINKERS, OR VAN DER GRAAF WHO WERE THE SMOKERS. I USED TO FLUCTUATE BETWEEN BOTH BANDS BECAUSE I WAS A SMOKER AND A DRINKER. I FELT VERY WELCOME.** Phil Collins

STEVE: As well as touring the UK, we were off to the country to write *Nursery Cryme*, living at Strat's place in Crowborough. He had rented this house that was called a 'cottage'; it did have a thatched roof, but it was a palatial mansion to me, with a large garden and an

Opposite: Paul Korczak, one of the road crew, helping smuggle a stash of Italian wine hidden inside one of the speaker cabinets.

outbuilding that we christened 'Toad Hall', where we would sometimes rehearse up to midnight, absolutely lovely and idyllic. I'd never been in a facility like that, although I realize it might have seemed small beer to the guys who'd been to Charterhouse. I visited Charterhouse only recently because my brother's band was playing there and I was going to do a guest spot with him. It was the first time I'd been to the school, and glimpsing the lush playing fields of Charterhouse I would imagine that Strat's place might have just seemed like another day in the life for them.

TONY: Tony kindly let us use the house for a month or two. We were finding our feet to a certain extent, but listening back to the album now, I think there are two or three really strong moments on it. In terms of sales, of course, it didn't go up at all from the previous one.

PHIL: Charisma was a family, a close group of people, and we used to have fantastic dinners down at Crowborough. It was a melting pot: old roadies from Van Der Graaf Generator would turn up.

STEVE: We often sat outside, which the band liked doing, sitting around out on the lawn with our guitars. We had all the time in the world to rehearse. And we were producing, to my mind, wonderful material. Of course, I have no doubt that if we were recording it all again tomorrow, we could do it much better now – in time and in tune and all at the same time... but then 1971 was a long time ago. I felt very proud of the band; I felt we were hot at that time.

As far as writing was concerned, I hadn't really written any tunes: I'd written more riffs than tunes. I felt that was the way to go, just be a guitarist; I thought the others were much more developed songwriters. I didn't know the difference between a chorus and a verse. Therefore I was incapable of coming up with anything formulaic because I didn't know the formula. I was a slow dog to start.

PETER: We were always slow developers. King Crimson, who of course were a huge influence on us, a band we aspired to, blossomed on their very first album in a way that caught everyone's attention and got the Stones to invite them to support them in Hyde Park in 1969; there was all this glamour and excitement. Later Francis Monkman came to see us at one of the gigs in London and mentioned he had a band, and we thought 'Yep, there's another chap with a band, great.' It turned out his band was Curved Air, who also shot past us in visibility and achievement. We were always the tortoise in most of the races, but we were getting used to the slow pace of our evolution and success, and in the long run I think it served us much better because it was a slower build and slower decay.

MIKE: John Anthony was the producer again on *Nursery Cryme*. The difference was that *Trespass* had been an album whose songs we had played live for a long time. We had arrived in the studio with the songs very much formed, 'This is how they are, mate, don't bugger it around'. On *Nursery Cryme*, the songs were still taking shape, slightly less established in their arrangements and their sounds.

PETER: Steve and Phil at that time were not prepared to get into the front-line squabbles. Tony was quite used to getting his way and I was probably the only person who would take him on, on any issue. We were best men at each other's weddings and best friends and worst enemies at the same time... When there was a discussion about whether a solo should last for twenty minutes, if you said, 'No', you had to decide whether you were prepared to take the next four days of argument to justify your position. Yet there were many areas where we were in agreement and working together well as a band, and there was a character emerging that was different from the rest of the prog rock field. Not necessarily better but different.

PHIL: There were probably plenty of tense moments during the writing of *Nursery Cryme* which I wasn't aware of, things going on that I surfed through. To me it seemed to be a pretty normal band. The problem for me was in the recording. We always sounded really edgy live, and bright, and then when we went into the studio it all seemed to get rounded off. There was the classic moment on 'The Fountain Of Salmacis' – take thirty-one. A drummer's best take is usually the second or third take, and I never go past that on my own records. So on take thirty-one you're playing everything safe because you don't want to fuck it up and then at the end of the take everyone says 'That's the one, that's the best take'. And then they all go off and replace their own parts, and suddenly I'm the only one who's left with my thirty-first tired take! So I never thought we ever sounded good on record, to be honest, until *The Lamb*, because it was recorded live at a farm in Glaspant in Wales with the Island mobile studio.

TONY: *Nursery Cryme* was a definite improvement on *Trespass* as far as I was concerned. 'The Musical Box' developed out of the kind of things we'd been doing a bit around the time of *Trespass*. The part I was most happy with on that particular song was the final section, where Mike had this little chord sequence and I started playing these very simple major chords on top of it so that it became almost like a fugue, quite quietly, before developing into something that was really, really exciting. I remember a bit of an argument at the time about whether there should be vocals on it or not. I felt there shouldn't because I thought, 'It's such great piece of organ playing'! But Pete started singing and although I initially felt, 'Oh no, no, shut up', then I stopped myself: 'Hang on, this sounds really good'. The combination moved it onto another level, a big high, which always got a great response from audiences.

'The Fountain Of Salmacis' was the first significant use of the Mellotron, which we'd actually bought by this stage. I'd written this main part when I was at university but we'd never used it; perhaps on *Trespass* I still wasn't sure whether the kind of pieces I was writing on my own were suitable for the group, so I never suggested it, and Steve was now an ally in these kind of areas. I had a chord sequence which became very much a Genesis trademark, where we would be in E minor and go to the chords C and D, often keeping the bass note down on E. Over the years I've done something similar a great number of times. Taking this little sequence and then adding the Mellotron sounded really good and made me realize that you could take what was almost a classical piece and make it sound very exciting, which was a significant realization for me. The rest of the song was built around that introduction. Peter had this idea of writing a song about the tale of Hermaphroditus, and we wrote the lyric together.

Above: Peter and Phil at the Great Western Express Festival, Lincoln, May 1972, a four-day extravaganza also featuring the Beach Boys, Lindisfarne, Humble Pie, the Faces and the Groundhogs. It was the Spring Bank Holiday, and in traditional fashion, it rained. Overleaf: Group portrait by Armando Gallo.

I FELT IT WAS GOOD TO JOIN UP WITH PHIL AS THE OTHER NEW BOY: COLLINS MINOR AND HACKETT JUNIOR, GOING OFF TO A CORNER SOMEWHERE AND PRESENTING THE SENIOR BOYS, THE PREFECTS, WITH OUR HUMBLE EFFORTS.

STEVE HACKETT

STEVE: Phil and I wrote one track on that album: 'Absent Friends' – it was the first song Phil sang with Genesis; I had written the song and then he and I wrote the lyrics together. We were trying to devise a song where the cast of players would have a different relationship to the traditional one of boy/girl so we dreamt up the idea of a couple of old ladies whose husbands had passed on, and concentrated on very English imagery, a park with padlocked swings and generally the kind of 'keep off the grass' feel that I was to explore with future songs. I guess it was our idea of producing a lyric that was quintessentially – and there's a pretentious word for you – quintessentially English.

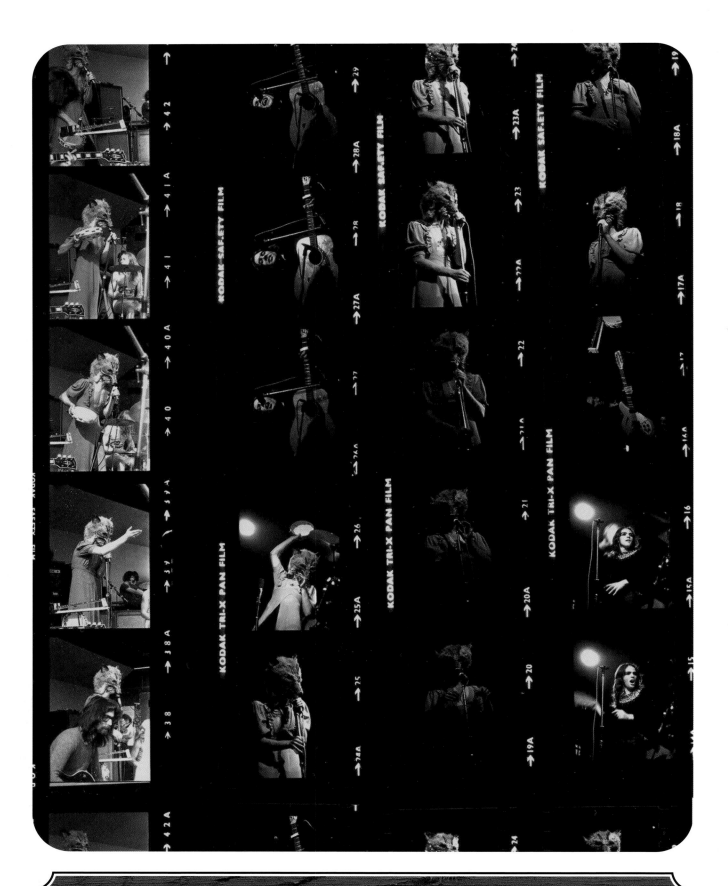

CHAPTER SIX

THE FOX'S HEAD

PETER: In live performances I was still blasting away on the bass drum. Part of the problem was that during solos I didn't feel I was the world's most gifted dancer and people seemed to view it as a negative thing if I went offstage and had a cup of tea, so I needed something physical to do. I waved my hands around, shook the tambourine and whacked my kick drum, much to Phil's disgust.

PHIL: I've never heard Pete play drums so I only have his word for it that he's a drummer... I guess that fear of having his security blanket taken away meant he used to hide behind his flute and his tambourine and his bass drum, but that bass drum was as loud as mine. This was before the days of miked-up drums, so I was supplying my own dynamics. Of course, with another drummer on my right using his own bass drum, a drummer who was quite excited and standing up, it was never going to be quite as tight as it should be, so we started to stuff things into Pete's drum to make it quieter, and eventually you could see it moving but you couldn't hear it.

Peter was also starting with his stories. I would help out by doing a one-handed drum solo whenever the gaps between songs got too long while everyone was tuning or getting the Mellotron ready for the next tune. That left Peter with dead air, which he filled with stories. I became his stooge. He would say, 'Look at Phil Collins with his one-handed drum solo, notice how the other hand isn't moving at all...'

PETER: The storytelling had emerged as a means of filling in the gaps when we had thirty-six strings being tuned by people who weren't very good at tuning them, and during long debates about which strings were in or out of tune. It was out of pure necessity, because during those moments everyone looks at the singer to fill in the gaps. I never really worried much about what the song was saying, I just made up my stories and plugged them in occasionally.

TONY: During the writing and recording of *Nursery Cryme*, we were playing at Friars in Aylesbury, one of our favourite venues. Pete got carried away and leapt off the stage into the audience, assuming they would catch him, and of course they all ran away...

PETER: I was still trying to work out how to break the gap between stage and audience. Very often I felt I was a filter between the audience and the band, because sometimes they thought that they could play behind a black curtain and it wouldn't matter. I knew that it did matter and we had to make those connections. So at Friars I wanted to jump out in the audience, which would have been fine, except that a dancer doing some early headbanging, and probably well pissed, changed direction at the crucial moment and broke my fall as I jumped off the stage. Consequently I landed badly and broke a bone in my leg, but because it was 'The Knife', an up number, I was pumped full of adrenalin. I knew something had gone but I couldn't feel any pain at all. I got some people from the audience to carry me back on stage, couldn't stand up and finished the number off on my knees. Eventually the rest of the band had gone off stage after taking their bows. I was still there on my knees and I could see them thinking 'You old ham, stop milking it'.

TONY: Mike and I were saying, 'Come on, we've got to do an encore, we've got to get back out there,' and Pete was saying, 'I don't know that I can do it', looking very pale. 'Oh come on, you've got to do it.' He was obviously in severe pain and it was then we realized he'd broken his ankle. It was a very stupid thing to do, I have to say.

PETER: At this point the pain was extraordinary. The others finally realized that something actually was wrong and I was dispatched to hospital. Mike turned up at the basement flat where I was staying with my wife and she thought he'd come to tell her that I'd died...

Opposite: Peter surprised the audience, and not least his fellow band members, during a show at the Dublin National Stadium on 28 September 1972, when he disappeared offstage during the instrumental interlude in 'The Musical Box' and re-emerged wearing a fox's head and a red dress. Paul Conroy, later head of Virgin Records, then working as a booker for Charisma, had suggested the idea as a way of promoting the release of *Foxtrot*, thinking of hiring in an actor, but Peter decided if anyone was going to be the centre of attention it ought to be him.

For the next few gigs, I quite enjoyed using a wheelchair and my plastered leg as props, until we played somewhere with a particularly raked stage. As I was getting carried away I forgot that there was a tendency to roll forward and I rolled off the front of the stage in my wheelchair.

STEVE: This was also a period where we started appearing at outdoor festivals. Rock festivals always sound glorious, but in fact the first five years of festivals we did in England or Europe it rained virtually every time. We used to groan at the very idea of them: 'Oh no, not another festival, not another mud bath'. And unfortunately lots of things tended to go wrong at festivals. The first time we were due to appear at the Reading Festival, the power was fluctuating so we couldn't get the organ in tune and if it was bad for the organ than it was going to be hell for the Mellotron, so we had to blow the gig. We also insisted on tuning the twelve-string guitars in the dressing rooms; by the time they'd been taken out to the stage the temperature would vary and they'd go out of tune. And as any guitarist will tell you, you had no hope of tuning a twelve string in front of a crowd in the days before digital tuners.

TONY: I don't think we were ever a good festival group. It's hard to build atmosphere in daylight. We would get up there and try to play some intricate music, going on a long time, with lots of chord changes, and let's say ninety per cent of the audience had no idea what we were on about. Plus the sound was always pretty rubbishy. That said, we were building a live following and it was getter bigger. So we had a certain reputation and were quite a good group to have on at these festivals but nothing really happened until we were closing the show, could play in the dark and had a number of our own audience there.

The good live response did not translate to album sales – which were quite static at five or six thousand. It was very difficult and without singles we had no promotion. There was no such thing as newspaper coverage. Nowadays you read more about pop music in a day than you could read in a year back then. There was no television to speak of, apart from *Top Of The Pops* and possibly *The Old Grey Whistle Test*, but we didn't go on either of those. Rock music was not part of the mainstream in the way it is now. It was a youth thing and most of the establishment totally ignored it. So you had no real promotion except your live shows and you could only play to so many people live.

However, we did start scoring some success in both Belgium and Italy, with *Trespass* in the case of Belgium and *Nursery Cryme* with Italy. We were very grateful for that, although inevitably it's not the same as your home country. We started visiting both countries, adventuring really. It was the start of our international touring.

PETER: When they couldn't get any work for us in the UK, there would always be some dodgy disco in Italy that would have us out in the summer. I think that's where I developed my love for all things Italian.

TONY: Later on we played the Palace of Sport in Rome, complete lunacy, 20,000 people standing there, it felt like a million people; they seemed to like all the romance. Perhaps it was the classical references in songs like 'Fountain Of Salmacis' that they liked.

MIKE: I think that enthusiasm for us in Belgium and Italy was very important for us, because England was slow, it was uphill, and suddenly we could go to a country where we were actually a bit more popular. Italy especially, which is a lovely country to go to anyway, was fun for us. It was quite tough work travelling around England, especially during the winter months; suddenly we'd be playing Rimini, a holiday resort full of pretty Italian people. They had a weird thing in Italy: on a Sunday afternoon you'd play the night clubs, a real out of town disco, with a two thirty or three o'clock show in the afternoon so the kids could get back home for the evening

These pages: Portraits of the band by Armando Gallo, Neal Preston and Andy Kent. Overleaf: From this point on, live performances by Genesis took on a life of their own.

on public transport, so a lot of young teenagers would come, loved the band, fantastic. The Italians by nature, if they like something there's a passion about it and they had this passion for our music which was a real boost for us.

STEVE: Tony Stratton Smith worked like an encouraging headmaster. Whenever we were off to Belgium, going over on the boat, no sleep that night and feeling like death on some TV show and they were making us do the third and fourth take of the same number because the cameras couldn't get it right, he would say, 'Marvellous, boys, yes, yes, yes. It's all heading the right way, keep it up, chaps'. He was able to buoy everyone's spirits, and we responded to that. Tony was very much a man of his passions and I miss him greatly. I wish I could press his hand warmly and tell him, 'You are the reason, more than any other person perhaps, that the band made it. You made it possible for us to survive as an outfit and develop'.

> THE STRONG MELODIES AND CHURCH INFLUENCES IN OUR MUSIC SEEMED TO APPEAL TO THE MEDITERRANEAN AREAS. WE GENERALLY FOUND THE FURTHER SOUTH WE GOT THE WARMER THE WELCOME, WITH A FEW EXCEPTIONS – GLASGOW BEING ONE.
>
> PETER GABRIEL

These pages: Festival fun, clockwise from above – performing at the 1972 Great Western Express Festival, wading to the stage at a Dutch event, and fans at Reading.

PETER: For the next album we were looking for a new producer; we thought we did sound better live and we weren't capturing that on the albums. Very early on we had had a brief encounter with Paul Samwell-Smith, the Yardbirds' bass player, who'd produced a session with us at the BBC, and ever since then we'd been looking for a producer who really understood us.

John Anthony was brilliant with people and I think, looking back on it, probably good with sound. He produced 'How Long' with Ace, a great song and really well recorded, so he obviously had chops in the right direction, but he wasn't particularly controlling and I think we wanted someone with more of a voice.

TONY: A producer called Bob Potter was brought in because Charisma thought he'd done a good job on Lindisfarne. He had also worked with a well-known American producer, Bob Johnson, including some Simon and Garfunkel albums which I'd really liked. But when he arrived he hated, for example – though some people might agree with him – the introduction to 'Watcher Of The Skies'. I thought this was one of the things we were all about so if he didn't like this, we were in trouble, and so we parted company.

PETER: Bob Potter just didn't connect with Tony and the keyboards, and although I quite liked the way he made it sound it wasn't worth fighting for. I don't think he particularly liked our material: his tastes were more towards the American songwriter folk-rock vibe and prog wouldn't have been what he played at home.

STEVE: I don't know whether there was some kind of culture clash with him. I suspect he may have been more rootsy, more streetwise, and the band were a bit more posh. He said after one or two numbers, 'I can't work with these guys.' I had managed to record 'Horizons' with him – an acoustic guitar piece – and I got it in about the fourth take. He said, 'I can work with you, but I can't work with the others'. I don't really know why – maybe he thought they had a too measured, too leisurely approach. I think he felt that everyone was working at a snail's pace.

TONY: Dave Hitchcock, who'd worked with Caravan, replaced Bob Potter, and we struck up a good relationship with the engineers, especially John Burns, and with *Foxtrot*, we started to get a little closer to how we sounded live, which developed through the next couple of albums.

STEVE: John Anthony had worked rather like an enthusiastic coach, keeping everyone laughing, wanting to bring out the best in people. And similarly on *Foxtrot*, John Burns took on that role. Dave remained quiet, while John was very hands on. We'd already recorded part of the backing track to 'Supper's Ready', the twelve-string stuff. And John immediately said, 'Oh, I think this sounds good, I don't get a bad vibe off this'. He said exactly the right thing, right manner, right time.

I had actually wanted to leave the band at the beginning of *Foxtrot*. I was very, very tired, and on the first day of recording I was thinking, 'I'm not really up for this. These guys are so good'. I thought when I'd joined them that it would be easy, that they would see how brilliant I was and everything would improve straight away. But in fact it was very different working within a band.

It seemed to be competitive and I wasn't prepared for that. I felt I hadn't really written anything for them, although I had this little piece called 'Horizons' that they were going to use, thankfully. I said, 'I don't think I'm really contributing much' but the others said, 'No, we really like your guitar playing'.

I'M NOT A PLAYER WHO CAN GET PEOPLE TO TAP THEIR FEET. I'M NOT THAT KIND OF PLAYER. IT'S AN EMOTIONAL THING WITH ME: IT CAN BE DONE WITH MOOD, IT CAN BE DONE WITH MELODY, IT CAN BE DONE WITH CHORDS. TONY BANKS

TONY: On *Foxtrot*, the one song we had written beforehand was 'Watcher Of The Skies' which had grown out of me fooling around with the Mellotron. We had hired in a Mellotron for *Trespass* and then went and bought one. In fact we bought one of the ex-King Crimson Mellotrons and Robert Fripp insisted it was the one they had used on *In The Court Of The Crimson King*: mind you, he had three Mellotrons and I'm sure he said that about all three of them when he was selling them.

The Mellotron used loops of tape to produce the sounds, great stretches of tape, and each of the sounds was on the same loop so that the whole machine would have to churn and churn until it found the starting point on all these tapes for thirty or forty different notes. And the tuning between the sounds was pretty bad. The left-hand keyboard had prerecorded loops and little riffs, but the only useful sounds for me were organ-based. It was the right-hand keyboard with the strings and brass that had the real impact on a track like 'Watcher Of The Skies' because people had never heard a big, big sound like that before. We had always had a tendency towards an orchestral sound, so the Mellotron was a natural addition to our work.

I had been searching for chords that actually sounded good on the Mellotron because of its tuning problems, and I happened to settle on these two chords that sounded great, even though they were way out of tune. There was an atmosphere about them that I really liked. Phil started playing a kind of riff in 6/4 underneath while we kept the chords going and tried to develop a song on top of it; Mike and I wrote a sort of sci-fi fantasy lyric, loosely based on Arthur C. Clarke's *Childhood's End*. I don't think the song ever quite lived up to the promise of the introduction, but it was a great beginning to a live show. We'd come on stage and – back in the days when these things weren't quite so much of a cliché – there would be smoke, UV lights and 'Watcher Of The Skies' would start up and you knew you were at a Genesis concert.

Above: Taking time out and (right) looning with Richard Macphail on the ferry to Belgium, January 1972, the band's first overseas trip.

Left: The band outside Headley Grange, the Hampshire house where Bad Company and Led Zeppelin, amongst others, recorded, including the famous 1970 Led Zep version of the old blues song 'Where The Levee Breaks', when producer Andy Johns placed John Bonham and his kit at the bottom of one of the stairwells to get the drum sound they wanted.
Below: A clipping from the *Foxtrot* era, 'the time,' Tony says, 'when we first started to become significant, in my opinion.'

The key track on this album was 'Supper's Ready', which had started off acoustically, like 'Stagnation' and 'Musical Box'. I'd written a descending chord sequence on the guitar, and, when we were playing in somewhere like Cleethorpes, I was in the changing room tuning the guitar and playing these chords. The room had a fantastic acoustic which made this particular chord sequence sound wonderful; Mike walked in and said, 'That sounds great, what's that?'

So he learnt the part and we played it together, and then we got the others in and played this sequence to them. I didn't know what we were going to do with it, but it was obviously something we could use as a starting point.

MIKE: The 'Apocalypse in 9/8' – the instrumental section from 'Supper's Ready' – was written at the Una Billings dance school, a rehearsal place just off Shepherds Bush. Peter wasn't there, so Phil, Tony and I started working on it; Steve didn't have much to do at that point. And it marked a start of what was later going to be the three-piece unit. And in a sense the piece was less written; the chords were set up and the mood was there. It was more like a group composition in that sense because the music was in place and Peter came in with the vocals afterwards.

TONY: We had this completely distinct song that Peter had written on piano called 'Willow Farm'. I took the left-hand part and played it on the Mellotron brass, and played the right-hand part on the organ, which created this rather ugly sound, and the first run-down had a very strange note in it that made you sit up.

September 30, 1972

Special review of the new Genesis album by Jerry Gilbert

"HAVE you got a copy of the new album yet?", Mike Rutherford inquired meekly as Genesis prepared to go on stage at the Marquee last week. Well I did have the album, and momentarily I found it impossible to reconcile his almost apologetic demeanour with what must surely become one of the major works of the year.

"Foxtrot" (Charisma CAS 1058) shows us the Genesis that we've seen all too often on stage and been longing for on record. This time they're . . . well they've almost achieved the perfect album on their first outing with producer David Hitchcock.

Vitality

There are occasions when the overall sound does lack the required vitality and other occasions where Genesis are trying just that little bit too hard, but these moments are sporadic

"It must surely become one of the major works of the year . . ."

unfortunate tenants, the property owner and his "winkler", closing with the immortal memo "With land in your hand you'll be happy on earth then invest in the church for your heaven", and offering other precious little gems like "It is my sad duty to inform you of a 4 ft. restriction on humanoid height". All good stuff.

Side one closes with "Can-Utility And The Coastiners", a strange allusion to King Canute which, although Genesis have worked it into their stage repertoire, I don't find the most exciting aspect of the album by any means.

Aside from a short Steve Hackett guitar introduction, side two is set aside to one composition called "Supper's Ready" which incorporates seven separate movements.

Peter on the flower costume: 'The flower was definitely from Bill And Ben and Little Weed. High culture, 'flobadob'. I can't remember who made all the costumes. Strat drew on some of his theatrical connections, as they used to call them, that whole Soho world of La Chasse and drinking parlours and Francis Bacon, a Soho that wasn't very visible but had influence in lots of areas.'

'Supper's Ready' was sounding quite pretty so I made a suggestion: 'Why don't we stop the song there, and just whang into 'Willow Farm' to see what it sounds like', because I always like contrast.

We all decided that sounded good and when it came to doing the vocals and lyric on it Pete, in the gap, said, 'A flower?', which was great, because it set up the contrast between what had been an ultra-romantic moment and what was about to come up, which was anything but. It's a key little moment.

The section of 'Supper's Ready' called 'Apocalypse in 9/8' was the best instrumental piece we'd created up to that point. Mike had a way of playing bass pedals and then putting guitar chord across it which just sounded great, and I said, 'If you can tie it down so you're playing an E on the bass, and then just play an F sharp and a B at the top, don't play any other notes. Then I can play any chord I like on top of that which will give me great freedom to write a solo on top of that'. Mike and Phil created a 9/8 riff, but I didn't want to be tied to the time signature so I just took it as a 4/4 thing and played right against their riff, starting off with cheeky little major tunes, almost a pastiche, and then slowly making it more and more sinister and unsettling, so you're not quite sure where it's going to go. And then I brought in the really big chords again, finally going back out of the minor key to an E major chord, which created this very serene, simple chord sequence, a strong, uplifting moment. It's like the angels have arrived, the heavens have opened. And it had taken about twenty minutes to reach this point: that was what was so great about it, and people often don't understand that. You have to have twenty minutes of build up, and then you get to that moment and wow, it really gives it to you. I like those moments which can send a shiver up the spine.

When I brought in this big sequence at the top of the solo, I'd assumed that there would be no lead vocal, so when Pete suddenly started singing over it – '666' – I thought, 'Oh shit, he's doing it again, he's singing on my best bit', but I have to say this time it only took me about ten seconds to think 'This sounds fantastic, it's so strong', even though that hadn't been my plan. That taught me another lesson, that however much you can climax a keyboard solo, if you have a vocal or even a guitar to finish it off, it takes it onto another level.

I think what I liked most about this song was that after writing it and sticking it all together we weren't too sure, because all the elements had been done very piecemeal and the first half of the song had been a bit traumatic, because that was when we'd changed the producer and engineer. We finally heard the whole piece back and thought, 'This is fantastic'. I remember playing it to Richard Macphail, who was hugely enthusiastic. He said, 'This is the best thing you've ever done'. We played it on stage and it went down really well with the crowd.

And even the album got to number 12 in the charts; of course the next week it went down to number 27 or something, but it was our first moment of scoring anything so we felt that perhaps we were underway, that we were heading somewhere different. *Foxtrot* was where we first started to become significant, in my opinion.

STEVE: When we finished 'Supper's Ready', I wasn't sure whether anyone would like such a great long piece of music. The word Elgar comes to mind for some reason, Elgar on acid perhaps. We weren't on acid, we weren't on drugs: we were on beer and wine and Earl Grey. I thought the game was up, no one was going to like it, the record company were going to sack us and we would disappear into a black hole. I was proved so wrong and I've never been so happy to be proved so wrong: it ended up becoming the band's anthem.

PETER: On the *Foxtrot* tour, I had a conversation with Paul Conroy, who was booking gigs for us: he was suggesting that we employ a person to walk around wearing a costume of the character Paul Whitehead had drawn for the album cover, the fox in the red dress, as an extension of the illustration. But then I thought, 'Right, I'll try putting that on, I'll see if I can get a fox's head made,' because I thought I should be the person dressing up rather than a stunt person. And my wife Jill had this red dress in her cupboard, which, believe it or not, I could get into. I decided to use it at a show in Dublin, at the National Stadium – an old boxing arena. I might have told the band my plan, but if so it would have been just beforehand. I certainly wasn't always upfront about everything because you'd end up having these endless debates and I'd think, 'Oh, fuck it, I can't be bothered'.

There was a silence when I walked out on the stage in this outfit. I think that very few people had seen a man in a dress at that point and certainly not one wearing a fox's head as well. There was a sense of shock and it was very exciting. And I thought, 'We're on to something'.

Peter on masks, costumes and radical haircuts: 'Nowadays there's very little shock value, but in those days when you arrived with make-up and a shaven head, it was other-worldly, scary and disturbing.'

Above: relaxation time – left, skinny dipping and right, Tony Banks and Richard Macphail with their new macrobiotic diet. Opposite: Peter sports his reverse Mohican hairstyle. Overleaf: Peter on stage in Jill's red dress and his fox's head. Following pages: Tony's wedding to Margaret, in Farnham, Surrey, July 1972. The wedding party, left to right: Peter, Steve, Jonathan Silver, Richard Macphail, Phil, Tony, Mike, Margaret, John Alexander (who had been pressed into service to give the original demo tape to Jonathan King), Ant, Little Paul and Guy. Inset: The tour bus transformed into a luxury limo for Tony and Margaret's honeymoon: they could only squeeze in one day in Dartmoor before he had to go back to work on *Foxtrot*.

PHIL: Pete had obviously decided by this point that he wasn't really open to the band discussion on this because he knew that it would get questioned or elbowed. I would never have elbowed it, but on the other hand I wasn't excited by it.

MIKE: Pete was very wise. If he'd asked us we'd have said no. Put to the panel, it would never have got through. I think the band scenario had always been a bit of hurdle for Pete because of the compromise situation, you've got to run things by certain people who've all got to agree about it enough. So we were playing the boxing stadium in Dublin, a rough venue, and he suddenly appeared in the gear. And it was like 'Bloody hell'. It was definitely different.

TONY: I don't know why Pete chose this particular gig, perhaps because it was in Ireland, and he thought he could probably could get away with it a bit more. It was a shock, this apparition coming towards me in a fox's head and a dress. I thought 'Christ!', but carried on playing, a true professional... and the audience loved it. Even more importantly a picture of him in this bloody fox's head was on the front page of *Melody Maker* the following week. Hey, this is interesting. Because we knew we had difficult music to get across, and with no TV, no national press, no singles, what do you do? You need something more than just music to attract a bigger audience. Suddenly this lifted us out of the general rank of people.

STEVE: Presentation is all important. Every band has got to have something. Either their playing has to be heroic or someone's got to be nominally a sex symbol, but I don't believe that a band can do it on just the music alone. A journalist needs something to get their teeth into and that didn't happen until Pete started dressing up in all manner of things. He became a focal point for the band, something to write about, because it's much harder to write about music – which after all is invisible – than PJ Proby splitting his drainpipes... I thought anything that got us in the papers was going to help us, otherwise we would be stuck in the situation when we were on the Charisma package tours and sometimes didn't get reviewed at all: as Mike Rutherford used to say, 'Genesis also ran'.

I'M GOING TO SOUND LIKE AN OLD GIT HERE
BUT IT'S A GOOD THING TO HAVE SOME MEASURE OF
THEATRICALITY. THAT'S STAGECRAFT.
YOU'VE GOT TO GRAB THE AUDIENCE'S ATTENTION.

STEVE HACKETT

THE NEW YORKERS' TALE, PART I: ED GOODGOLD

I first met Tony Stratton Smith when I was managing Sha Na Na in the late 1960s. I'd been writing trivia books and running trivia contests at Columbia University: Sha Na Na sang at some of the contests, when they were still known as the Kingsmen, and they contacted me at some point asking me to find them a manager. I said 'I'll be your manager', and lucked into the business.

I ran into Strat in England, at the Speakeasy. He was a great raconteur, remarkably entertaining and erudite. A friendship grew up between us, as well as a shared passion for Genesis. I'd seen the band's first New York appearance, and been impressed, but it wasn't until I saw them at the Hammersmith Odeon that I was blown away – both by their performance and by the relationship of the audience to them. Their music reminded me of Hector Berlioz, the 'Symphonie Fantastique', and they touched a spiritual nerve. I don't remember ever being at another concert where an audience showed such reverence. Reverence is not something you often see in rock'n'roll venues, but Genesis always had their believers. And I never walked out of one of their shows without a tremendously elevated spirit. The guys weren't aware of how they affected me, they were more matter-of-fact about what they were doing. But I think that's what was necessary for them to be who they were.

Strat asked me to help him organize the band's first US tour in 1973. It was one of the hardest things I ever did in the business. Nobody had heard about them and I had to cajole, lie, and squeeze out every favour I could to get them booked. And their equipment requirements meant that I couldn't put them on at venues like the Fillmore or the Boston Tea Party, they had to headline. So I ended up handcrafting the tour for them.

The guys were always pleasant to be with. My approach to management with Sha Na Na had been like being a sports coach: I used to throw a couch against the wall once in a while whenever they needed the energy, when they were in danger of getting slack. That didn't work with Genesis. When I did try that approach, Mike Rutherford ran out of the meeting; he couldn't take it. Mike was an interesting guy: his delivery reminded me of English actors of the '30s and '40s who I'd seen in movies.

Peter understood the spiritual component very well. I saw him as a rock priest, although as time went on in his career he moved into what I call the social gospel as opposed to the spiritual realm. But when Peter pulled off the priest thing, that was as good as a mass. In terms of the experience of the audience, namely me,

the only thing comparable to him in terms of getting me up was the Who when Keith Moon was alive – that ability to fill me with joy and lofty thoughts. To think that Peter did that relatively untutored. He created this magnificent persona, and his costumes were a very important element; the priest must have his vestments. Steve Hackett's guitar work was also transcendent, sweet, heavenly. I think he thought I was a little crazy, because I would use these spiritual terms to describe the rock phenomenon, but that's the way I feel, that's what moves me. Phil's drumming on a number like 'Supper's Ready', where his drums are basically melodic, was awesome, but I don't think he ever saw the group anyway near how I did... Occasionally they were not as realistic as I would have liked them to be, but I must say that whatever they said went. I never said, 'Oh what do you need this for?' Never. If they said they needed it, I would do the best I could to get it for them.

Towards the end of that tour, I was trying to organize a show in Chicago. I couldn't book them anywhere. The only thing I could find was an all-day festival at the Amphitheater, a huge indoor arena, on a bill headlined by Richie Havens; no one performing had anything in common with Genesis. I booked them and thought, 'Good luck, guys. Go and cast your bread upon the waters.' The group were introduced. Half the audience walked out of the arena to buy hot dogs, go to the bathroom, smoke in the hallways. I was sitting with the sound guy, thinking I'd really outsmarted myself this time, totally mea culpa-ing myself. And for some reason or other, the stage people had put a little too much magnesium powder in the flash pot. When the explosion went off, it was huge, the light blinded people, even the ones who were still out in the toilet stalls. All of a sudden everybody came back in, gave Genesis a huge standing ovation for being blinded and the band played three encores... Clearly this was the finger of the Lord in action.

Ed Goodgold was a pioneer of the trivia phenomenon: running quiz contests with fellow Columbia University student Dan Carlinsky in the mid-1960s. The pair wrote the first book on the subject, *Trivia*, in 1966, and later published *The Armchair Conductor: How To Lead A Symphony Orchestra In The Privacy Of Your Own Home.* Before and during his time with Genesis, Ed managed Sha Na Na, and he can be seen in the background during their segment in the movie *Woodstock*. He is now an administrator at NYU.

THE NEW YORKERS' TALE, PART II: NANCY LEWIS

Long before Genesis, I was working as a journalist in London, initially writing features for a weekly pop magazine, Fabulous. *Everybody in the music scene used to go to the same small circle of clubs and I'm sure I first met Strat at one of those clubs. Then I moved on to PR, and started working with him when he was managing a young group called the Koobas. Cut to a few years later. I had been going between London and New York working at various jobs – primarily for the Who – but finally came back to New York to handle the publicity for Buddah Records, a company run by Neil Bogart and Art Kass. Strat came over to do an American distribution deal – especially to launch Genesis – and of course he knew me. Neil and Art were very eager to set up the arrangement. And it worked beautifully.*

Because I'd worked for some of the English music papers, I'd been vaguely aware of Genesis, but nobody at Buddah had ever seen them, so I was flown over to London to see them play. And I was totally blown away. They were visually even more innovative and exciting than I'd thought. When I came back we set up a Christmas concert at the Philharmonic Hall with WNEW-FM – the band's American debut. I got in a taxi with Neil to go to the gig and he said, 'I've just realized you're the only person in Buddah who's actually seen this band. They'd better be good.' I laughed and promised him, 'They're going to be huge. Just remember this conversation when they sell out Madison Square Garden.' But both Neil and Charisma had left Buddah by the time that happened.

Neil was wonderful. Even if you came in with a crazy idea he'd give it consideration. Monty Python was a good example. Their albums were on Charisma and I told Neil, 'We've got to put these albums out.' He listened to them and said, 'Well, if they make you laugh and I don't have to pay an advance, we'll do it'. He was that outgoing front man; luckily Art Kass was much more practical. It was an ideal partnership. Strat, the intellectual Englishman, was totally different again. But he and Neil both had a childlike enthusiasm and energy for their projects. Neil really got into Genesis. I remember he would call everyone into his office and we had listening sessions while he played the Genesis album.

I went to a lot of the Genesis gigs – you always felt they were a group that needed looking after – and got to know them fairly well. They were delightful, but totally different from any other band I'd worked with. Peter was already married to Jill, and Tony was with Margaret; they appeared so settled. One of my favourite

nights on the road with them was, as I recall, in Cincinnati, Ohio. During the day, Jill had gone out walking and nearly been arrested. She was looking gorgeous in her stylishly unconventional English garb, and the police assumed she was a hooker – why else would a lone woman be walking around the streets of Cincinnati? Back at the Holiday Inn after the show that night, we broke out the Blue Nun – the decadent drink of choice – and played an energetic game of blind man's buff. In some madly extravagant gesture, Mike managed to break his finger. I remember saying, 'Only with Genesis...' It somehow seemed typical that their only injury would occur in this type of situation.

Because their music definitely fell into the 'progressive rock' category, Genesis were considered an intellectual band. Their fans tended to be very serious about the music – instead of trying to rip off band members' clothing, they struck me as wanting to discuss the meaning of lyrics. Mind you, being a very attractive band – in spite of Peter shaving various portions of his head – they also attracted their share of girls at the stage doors.

Charisma left Buddah to join Atlantic, but I stayed in touch with Strat and eventually went over to Atlantic too. By this time, Peter had left Genesis and, much to the amazement of many, Phil Collins had smoothly stepped into the role of lead singer. When the band were scheduled to play Madison Square Garden for the first time with Phil as singer, the folks at Atlantic thought it would be a great publicity move if Peter, who was in New York recording that week, came on stage for the encore. Peter and I were flying back to London the next day, so we negotiated with Atlantic that he would make the appearance if they would upgrade our tickets to Concorde. His appearance was a big hit, but during the flight, Peter went to the loo and was away for a long time. I was dozing, but I woke to hear a pounding noise: the lock had jammed – he couldn't get out! The crew came to the rescue, but this wasn't the way our glamorous, luxury flight was supposed to be. Not what I expected my lasting memory of Concorde to be!

After a career as a journalist in the US and UK, Nancy Lewis joined Neil Bogart's Buddah Records in New York. She later became Charisma's label manager in the US, and had a long involvement with Monty Python as their American manager. She is married to Simon Jones, the actor who created the role of Arthur Dent in the original radio and TV productions of *The Hitchhiker's Guide To The Galaxy*.

CHAPTER SEVEN

ON BROADWAY

MIKE: Just before Christmas in 1972 we had out first ever gigs in America: two dates, the first was a concert at Brandeis University near Boston, followed by a major show at the Philharmonic Hall in New York, a proper, pukka gig in a smart venue. People weren't used to travelling so much then, so at twenty-two years old it was pretty exciting going to America for the first time, living out what you'd seen on TV and in films, very intense, lovely memories. Within the first hour of our first day in the Gorham Hotel in New York, the phone went and it was reception: 'There's a man in the building with a gun, please keep your door locked until we tell you it's OK'.

PHIL: Being an avid reader of all the music papers, I knew Boston was the place that seemed to like all the English bands: the Nice, King Crimson, all these bands were big in Boston. So when we ended up going to the States, although the Philharmonic Hall was our first major performance there, I don't know if it was viewed as essential for us to have a warm-up gig or whether those were the only two shows we could get. I thought, 'Great, we're going to go to Boston. They love English music.' And when we turned up we were playing at lunchtime in a hall with windows, so it was daylight, and people were on rows of seats – it wasn't full – some studying, others eating packed lunches. I thought, 'This can't be Boston, not the same Boston, this isn't America.'

TONY: Richard had gone out to the States a little bit earlier for a recce and some preliminary work. I'm not sure what he was doing actually because everything was in complete chaos when we got there! When we reached Boston we discovered that because my organ had a cycle-controlled motor, and the American electricity supply was on a different cycle, the organ was sharp. We had to construct a power supply specially for it, but then there wasn't nearly enough power and as soon as I applied any volume the whole thing became distorted. We got on stage at Brandeis about four hours late, a complete nightmare, awful: this was meant to be our big moment, our first gig in America. At least it was only a warm-up show for the Philharmonic Hall, but that show was also absolutely terrible.

We were having real trouble with our gear: my organ was still problematic, and Mike's equipment had a buzz like you wouldn't believe. When we came off stage we were so pissed off: we were kicking and throwing things, muttering, 'That was shit' and then Strat came in: 'That was wonderful, my dears, it was beautiful, it was marvellous'. I said, 'It was absolute crap' and he said, 'No, no, it was good'.

MIKE: There had been a horrendous bass buzz all the way through. I got back in the lift that took us to the dressing room, feeling very grumpy, and I flung my Rickenbacker bass on the floor of the lift, thinking it was a complete disaster, we'd blown it. And actually they loved it. It was a good lesson that how you feel on stage and how you think you're playing can be so different to what's going on out in front. You can have what you think is a lousy show, but the crowd love it, and if they love it then maybe it is a great show. As Charlie Watts said, 'If it sounds crap on stage, you'll sound great out front'.

TONY: Gail Colson once told me, 'The thing about Genesis is that even if it's only seventy per cent on, it is still really good'. It was just that we knew it could have been so much better.

PHIL: I don't recall the Philharmonic Hall being a bad gig, frankly. I knew we had problems with the Mellotron, but I wasn't aware of that peripheral stuff. I thought, 'We're playing our music and these people love it.' I remember calling my dad and telling him, 'We've just been to America, it's been great. I'll see you at Christmas.' He said, 'Yes, I'll be at your mum's for Christmas' – they were sort of living separately because he had retired – and on Christmas Eve he died. So he never knew any of our success. I was just a struggling pub musician. I had come back from America and the band had been out gigging. It was all very strange, the best and worst of times. A monumental life change.

PETER: One of Strat's passionate projects was to get us to America. There were certain things on which he definitely took risks and swallowed costs and this was one of them. We didn't really know how we'd be received, but the warm-up college gig had been a very good idea:

Opposite: In central New York on the band's first visit to the United States in December 1972. Overleaf: Outside the Bitter End Café, Bleecker Street, New York in December 1972. The Bitter End was a coffee house in Greenwich Village and a focal point of the folk scene, where Peter, Paul and Mary first appeared, Arlo Guthrie recorded a live album, and comics like Woody Allen and Bill Cosby performed.

Above: Richard Macphail posing
in the US of A.

prog was esoteric enough in those days for students to be into it because it was not mainstream, so we found some aficionados right at the beginning of our American trip. The Philharmonic Hall was a bit touch and go, but in the end I think we felt we had just about delivered.

MIKE: We were a little disappointed when we returned the following year and realized that New York had forgotten us and the rest of the country had never heard of us.

TONY: We went back for a longer tour but there were only a few pockets of interest where we started building up a strong following, in cities like Cleveland, Philadelphia, Chicago and Detroit. David Bowie had introduced some Englishness into America through those cities and we followed on in the places where he'd been big.

PETER: Not many people would have believed that we were better supported in the hard-core blue collar areas than in the more gentrified areas you would expect. That was definitely true in America. You could touch people's hearts. It was a level of passion that we had only encountered in Italy. There was a spiritual connection that we sometimes were able to tap into. And when we did it was like hitting the mains cable when you're digging your vegetable plot.

MIKE: A friend of Strat's called Ed Goodgold, who managed Sha Na Na, started to get involved with us in America, but it felt quite uphill. We were so foreign to what was going on in America, an English rock band with hair down to here. Apart from New York and Chicago and the cities in the North East, the rest of the places were a bit like, 'What the fuck is that?' Yet for some people this English band seemed to represent something they could latch on to. As in England, we were popular in industrial towns, an escapism thing. So we did have a kind of cult following.

PHIL: Ed Goodgold had this remarkable knack of taking you aside and telling you that you were the most important member of the band. You ended up feeling ten feet tall... but slowly I came to realize that he had done the same to every member of the band! In the face of the struggle at the time, it made you feel it was all worth it. He was quite a good motivator.

PETER: Quite a lot of people, like Jann Wenner, the *Rolling Stone* founder, never really responded to the prog thing. We were once introduced disparagingly by Steve Miller on some TV show, and he said, 'Yeah, they're all talking about this "theatre rock" from London'. We didn't appeal to a lot of pure American music tastes. We weren't straight down-the-line rock'n'roll. We were a bunch of limey poofters and our music was full of classical references. So we attracted this quirky, eccentric following. Plenty of people today would not understand this, because they perceive the band as super-mainstream, and imagine punk as the alternative music which destroyed the behemoths of Floyd and Yes and Genesis. But at that time it was the other way round.

STEVE: I did enjoy America. I particularly enjoyed the first time we went to the West coast, when we were performing at The Roxy on Sunset Strip: two shows a night for three nights. I felt very at home on stage at the Roxy, which was almost like playing in someone's living room. It seated 500 people max and we were doing two shows a night, so we were playing to 1,000 people,

but I suspect it was the same people who came to all six shows: very relaxing, a residency where you could tweak the show each time. I felt that we were the best band around at that time.

Mind you, we were stuck for two weeks without a gig before then and it was costing a fortune to keep the band on the road, so financially we were a disaster. Luckily people had sufficient faith to keep bankrolling us. It was a very slow process of cracking America. It's like a number of different principalities; the people in New York don't feel the same as the ones in Los Angeles and just because you're a hit on the East coast doesn't mean it follows that they're going to like you on the West coast – and it took much longer to crack the South which had grown up on a diet of country music and didn't understand the brand of music that we were giving them.

MIKE: Shortly after we got back from the first trip to the States, we played at the Rainbow Theatre in London; by now our stage and light show was really starting to evolve. That particular show was a great example, probably the best example, of value for money in terms of production, because we had a great effect that cost virtually nothing. The guy who was managing us at the time, an old friend called Adrian Selby, was our age, very blusterous, but a doer. He always talked about dressing the stage to make it look a bit surreal, trying to create our own little world. He went out and bought a white gauze curtain for about a hundred quid, and rigged up some UV lights. He put the curtain up with all the amps and speakers behind it, and when he shone the UV lights onto the curtain, it suddenly looked like a solid curtain so all the gear behind it disappeared. It seemed so radical and especially when we were playing the *Foxtrot* material the effect was really, really strong, very special.

Opposite: Peter's Day-Glo eyes. Steve says, 'I suspect that the band were in two camps, the guys who were taking themselves very seriously, thinking like composers, and another guy who was giving Elvis a run for his money. I applauded the need for visual presentation.' Above: Drury Lane, January 1974. Overleaf: The Rainbow show, February 1973.

Above: Peter dangles at Drury Lane, January 1974. 'At the end of 'Supper's Ready', I had this 666 character in a big, heavy cloak with a fluorescent six-sided headpiece which would drop away to reveal a hammy but light lamé costume, a white out of black moment, the moment of ascent to heaven. It was supposed to be partly humorous but I think it ended up, in that great tradition of *Spinal Tap*, a little more humorous than I'd intended. In London you only needed one guy to operate the fly wire but in America there were about four to do the same job. This nearly ended up killing me because the person operating the wire was out of sight of the person giving the cue and they lifted me up before I was ready. I'd got a wire for the harness twisted around my neck in putting this mask on, which was serious because there was enough weight to hang me. The clock was ticking and I had to get this wire off my neck. I didn't really want to take the mask off because it would blow the visual moment but in the end I hid behind a piece of stage prop while I readjusted my hoisting wires and survived to live another day. But it was scary at the time.'

PETER: We knew our time was ripe. We had transcended Friars, the Angel at Godalming, the club circuit, The Rainbow was the prestigious venue at the time, so making that show special was important to everyone. I knew the band weren't into quite a lot of my costumes and masks, so I hid them out of sight until showtime, which was crazy because I couldn't really rehearse. But I didn't want a democratic discussion about how I was going to perform.

STEVE: When I joined Genesis it was in the days when you'd turn up and the house lights would throw strobes at you at the most inappropriate moments, or they put up an oil slide, making the whole thing look like a hippy love-in. I knew that we were never going to come across with this kind of hangover from the 1960s. We had to be able to control our environment. We had to be able to tell stories, we had to have the grand sweep of the orchestra.

TONY: We would start off with 'Watcher Of The Skies', with that atmospheric keyboard intro, and Peter would wander on with his bat wings glowing in the UV light and with the eyes shining through. I don't think the audience had ever seen anything like it. I'm a big fantasy fan and I liked the way we were able to create a fantasy on stage.

PETER: In the theatre world how you come in and how you go out are the two moments you have to think hardest about. The beginning of 'Watcher', with these rich, dreamy chords from Tony on the Mellotron, the lights and the UV make-up it was a moment that would give people the shivers.

STEVE: We developed this otherworldly look because of the UV and infra-red lighting: Peter used to put Day-Glo makeup round his eyes, so the first thing you saw was this unearthly black silhouette and then a pair of eyes staring at you plus the odd moment of dry ice, things straight out of a Victorian theatre by today's standards but nonetheless effective. I remember audiences saying afterwards when it worked, 'It seems like a fairy tale band compared to anything else'.

PHIL: It was all quite low-tech stuff. At the Theatre Royal Drury Lane Pete took off his cloak and went up in the air on the fly wire, but of course no one had taken into account the fact that when you're up there you're going to start slowly rotating. It looked kind of comical and it didn't sound that great, which also bothered me. I was never that interested in the visual side: later on when we would be sitting listening to the music at a lighting rehearsal using mannequins so we could see the lighting effects, I'd get bored really quickly. I suppose in the end my thing is that I'd love us to go out and just play the music without any of that to show how good the music is.

PETER: In many ways I was the aerial that was erected from the band box. It was my job to broadcast what the band was doing because that wasn't something they were really interested in doing or very good at then. Phil is a natural entertainer, but at that time he was a purist musician and didn't believe or buy into the visuals, which put a lot of responsibility on me. As well as transmitting our signals, I was also there to pick up the radio waves emanating from the audience.

STEVE: There was no doubt about who the star was. The rest of us were sitting like a pit orchestra, head down, concentrating furiously on our own little areas while Peter cavorted. I was growing enough face fungus to be able to hide behind it. It could have been anybody on guitar with a long-haired wig and a beard. In those days lots of us had beards, we wanted to look older. In my early twenties I wanted to look about forty. Perhaps we thought we'd be taken more seriously if we looked elderly.

IT WAS WEIRD AND SPOOKY AND DARK AND CURIOUSLY ASEXUAL COMPARED TO MOST SINGERS OUT THERE STRUTTING THEIR STUFF. PETE WAS STRUTTING A DIFFERENT KIND OF STUFF, PART SCIENCE FICTION, PART ALICE IN WONDERLAND... STEVE HACKETT

TONY: Richard Macphail decided to leave us at the end of another American tour shortly after the Rainbow gig. He had been an important friend, and it was a difficult moment when he went. I think the attitude to road crews had changed. They were becoming more professional and we were working with companies like Showco. Perhaps from his own life view, he thought it was time to move on, that he couldn't be doing this for ever.

MIKE: I think Richard felt that there would now be a more professional management around us, who might have slightly resented his link with the band; we had always been a bit funky in our organization: friends of friends, amateurs. There'd been a few cock-ups and things had to start getting more professional. One of our other tour managers hadn't kept any receipts for the first couple of tours and years later the tax man came to us saying, 'Our figures show you owe this'; our expenses were four times that, but we didn't have anything to show him. Richard wasn't the manager, he wasn't an accountant, and he probably started thinking more about what he was going to do with his life. I missed him because we used to bunk up together, share rooms. This was in my vegetarian days, and Richard was macrobiotic. We'd have a little primus stove in a Holiday Inn, and he'd knock up some late night food, we'd smoke a lot of dope and have fun. His energy and enthusiasm for all things was very infectious.

PHIL: I remember *Selling England By The Pound* being a very bright period of work. We wrote a lot of it in a little house in Chessington: a friend of ours knew somebody who had this rambling house and we moved in and took over the living room for a while.

Below. Steve emerges from behind his mask of glasses, moustache and beard. Overleaf: A portrait by Andre Csillag, taken a little later at the Savoy, London, on the presentation of Gold Discs for *Selling England By The Pound* and *The Lamb Lies Down On Broadway*, this was to be the last public off-stage appearance of Genesis with Peter.

PETER: I was very keen to try and focus our Englishness because American music at the time was the critics' darling and I thought it would be nice to respond with something of our own. Although we did have our American influences there were many English and European elements. The idea was to see how parts of an older Britain had been absorbed and taken on new life within a modern world; 'The Battle Of Epping Forest', for example, tried to graft an English gangland scene onto a slightly Hogarthian landscape.

STEVE: I still wasn't much of a writer and the more I worried about it the less the writing came easily to me. The worst thing about writer's block is worrying about it. By the time of *Selling England By The Pound*, though, my approach was just to come up with guitar riffs, not whole tunes but riffs, and see if we could find a way to use them, never mind whole façades of buildings, come up with a few good bricks, the odd window, the odd good bit of pointing. But my confidence was at a low ebb. I felt that the others were so much more accomplished than me in terms of writing. I always expected someone was going to put a line through it: 'Must try harder. Must come up with proper verse and chorus'. It was probably a product of the overbearing English school system: 'Knock them down and they'll get a very pleasant surprise by the time the exams come round'. But then chaps like me need encouragement. I need to be told that I'm better than I am. Flattery goes a long way with me.

Below and opposite: Cascais, Portugal, March 1975: soldiers form a barrier between the crowd and stage and the road crew watch the soundcheck.

TONY: For *Selling England* we were slightly dry of ideas. What we found was that we had about three or four pieces we were playing all the time because we didn't have that many things to do. One of those songs became 'The Battle Of Epping Forest', which probably ended up having too much in it, because we were adding new bits on a daily basis. And the other one we played every day was 'I Know What I Like'. Steve had played this riff a lot at sound checks and I would play some chords, and we would improvise: it was such a good riff. During one improvisation I started playing this line on the fuzz piano with the chords changing underneath it and we had our chorus. Peter sang along on top of it and he and Phil got together a melody line for the verses. We didn't over-develop the song, and I liked its simplicity, and thought that could have been quite a big hit, but the lyric was a little strange; it wasn't your average 'boy meets girl' lyric, but we weren't that interested in hits so we weren't worried one way or the other. That said, when we did release it as a single the following year, it did pretty well and there was a chance for us to be on *Top Of The Pops*. We turned it down. There were a few more quirky people appearing on *Top Of The Pops* at the time, like Fairport Convention. But it didn't suit us, and so we didn't appear, which I think was right. Pan's People danced to the track instead.

MIKE: Strat couldn't believe we wouldn't do it! That was in the days, though, where you were either a singles band or an album band and the singles charts were musically different. It was Picketywitch and Sweet. There was that sort of music and our kind of music and you couldn't be both.

PEOPLE ALWAYS SAID WE STARTED GOING FOR SINGLES IN THE 1980S. WE'D MADE SINGLES FOR YEARS. IT WAS JUST THEY WERE CRAP. Mike Rutherford

PHIL: With 'I Know What I Like', we had recorded the track, and Tony went home or out somewhere and the rest of us had this idea for a little motif on the outro. The Mellotron was there; Peter was playing it and he said, 'Let's record this'. And we had this fantastic moment when Tony came back to the studio. We were listening back to the track and Tony said, 'What's that, what's that?' and we said, 'That's this line we put on this afternoon', 'What is it?', 'It's a Mellotron', 'That's a keyboard, that's mine, that's my instrument'. It definitely caused a wave.

STEVE: Things would still deteriorate sometimes into a locker room punch-up over the most unlikely things. Suddenly it would go tilt and you suspected that there were issues from 1963 that hadn't yet been resolved: you swiped my wine gums back in biology, you always were a rotter. I think it was just the pressure and the fact that these guys had been together for a long time.

At the time my marriage wasn't going too well, so I found a refuge in music and I felt most at home when I was on stage with the band. And that level of joy of playing communicated itself in some way. There were moments in *Selling England By The Pound* that would have given the Mahavishnu Orchestra a run for their money: little bits of what I called guitar tapping, furious drums, great ensemble playing. And that's just the first number,

'Dancing With The Moonlit Knight', which starts off with Pete singing a cappella and runs through to a very floaty, drifty, pastoral exit from the song which we used to call 'Disney', the idea of a still, tranquil lake with each player slightly disturbing the surface: Pete using the reed from an oboe to make duck noises, over beautiful Mellotron chords from Tony and an arpeggiated twelve-string figure from Mike holding the whole thing together. True fusion. I always liked the term 'fusion', although nobody uses that term any more. I felt that it was more apropos than 'art rock' as we were described in America at the time or 'theatrical rock' or the ubiquitous 'prog rock' that we're stuck with now. I felt fusion did actually describe the idea of disparate styles combined in one.

TONY: In terms of my own contribution, the major track would be 'Firth Of Fifth'. I had a handful of ideas and had thought we might get two or three songs out of them, but Mike said, 'No, let's put them all on the same song', I suspect because he wanted to get them out of the way... I ran the three sections into each other, and on one run-through we were fooling around using Steve to play the flute melody, really loud in an expressive romantic style, so on the recording we used guitar and Mellotron for the repeat rather than with the flute and piano. It taught me how a melody can sound good being used in more than one way.

'The Cinema Show', again like 'The Musical Box' or 'Supper's Ready', had started off with an acoustic idea. But this time once we went off into the instrumental section at the end we didn't come back; it developed its own life. When we played that song to Tony Stratton Smith, who was obviously a big fan of ours, he didn't like it. He felt we were trying to move into the area of Emerson Lake & Palmer and that we were drifting away from what we did best. My feeling was that you can't stay doing the same thing forever and that particularly with 'Firth Of Fifth' and 'The Cinema Show' we were trying out things we hadn't done on the previous albums.

Opposite: The old man mask (top left) which Peter had used in performances of 'Musical Box' to replace the fox's head. The other images, from the *Lamb Lies Down* live show, prove how Peter had moved on again to the leaner, tougher approach he needed to portray Rael. Peter: 'In this post-MTV world it's very hard for people to imagine how strong being bombarded with different visual images in parallel with the music was for audiences at the time. Film had always been my passion and that was really the only place audiences had seen great images and music working extremely well together. We didn't get there always, but I think we got there more than most at the time.'

I have ambivalent feelings about *Selling England*. I like it a lot now, but at other times in my life I've been not so sure about the record, I thought maybe it was a bit too tricksy at times. And 'After The Ordeal' I think is a weak moment, pseudo-classical without any real spirit. That was probably my least favourite Genesis piece. In fact, I wanted it off. We were talking about what we should include on the album, something we had generally agreed about in the past. This time Peter and I both wanted 'After The Ordeal' off. But Peter also wanted to lose the second half of 'The Cinema Show' and I said, 'You can't put that off, it's great'. So we compromised by leaving it all on which meant that the album ran to about twenty-eight minutes a side, which was much too long and the technical restrictions of vinyl meant it sounded a little weak in comparison.

STEVE: I think Mike and Tony were disappointed with the album whereas I was very pleased with it. For me it was a more comfortable-sounding album and I liked being a guitarist in the band at that time. There were plenty of moments for a guitar to strut its stuff. Perhaps because it was a more riff-driven album, and less song-driven, more rock and less pop. It was still full of stories and character portraits: 'The Battle of Epping Forest', 'I Know What I Like', still very English.

TONY: We were helped a little by 'I Know What I Like' coming out as a single and giving us a higher profile. Overall our fans tended to stick with us. If they liked us they stayed with us, they didn't forget about us. What I liked, particularly at that stage, was that we were a very small number of people's favourite group. There was something quite exciting about that. We had a really fervent following. And that's why albums like *Selling England* did very well.

MIKE: Just before *Selling England* was released, our first live album had come out. *Genesis Live* is a good example of how record label bosses can make things work. That was Strat's: the recording had been for the 'King Biscuit Flower Hour' radio show in America, and he persuaded us to put it out, I forget why. There was probably a bit of a gap; we're a bit slow with albums. It kept the momentum going, and the album was a big success for us.

TONY: We didn't take *Genesis Live* seriously at all. We were asked to do this mix for the radio show in America and we obviously included 'Supper's Ready'. It came to the live album, and we couldn't put 'Supper's Ready' on because that would have taken up half the album, and it had already been half of the previous album. It was strange because it meant we were putting

This page: Tony Smith comes between Phil and Mike. Opposite: Mixing sessions for *The Lamb* at Island Studios, September 1974, with John Burns (top, far left) and at Glaspant in Wales.

out an album without including the best track. I don't know I've ever listened to *Genesis Live*. Not for years, anyhow. Live albums don't interest me all that much because they're just a representation of what you've done already; there's nothing new.

MIKE: On one tour we had done a show up in Glasgow, at Green's Playhouse, great gig: an old, old, theatre, really funky with a carpet that said, 'If it's good, it's Green's'. The audience there were tough. The first time we played there, we finished our first song and there was absolute silence. You could hear them thinking, 'Are they crap or are they great?' and it seemed about a minute while they made up their minds and then they went 'YEAH!!'. At one show there, a guy called Tony Smith – not Tony Stratton Smith – was the promoter, and our crew had managed to make the entire lighting rig live; whenever you touched something you'd get a shock. And the show had to be cancelled. We asked Tony Smith whether he would be interested in managing us and I imagine he thought, 'God, these guys need a bit of help'.

TONY: When we asked Tony Smith, 'Do you want to manage us?', he'd said, 'You're joking': he had a successful promotion company and here was this rather eccentric band who were completely un-together and losing money hand over fist. But some time later on, he was looking for a life change; perhaps he felt he had gone as far as he could in promoting, and the group was doing better. He came back to us and asked if we still wanted him to manage us, which we did. We really wanted someone who could look after the financial end for us and provide us with some kind of structure. Which were things we felt he would be good at. We didn't want anyone to tell us anything about the music. And he seemed like the man for the job. I think the band desperately needed someone like that to go on to the next level.

We said to Tony, 'If you manage us, it's got to be just us, and also we want to do it on a split basis. Any money we make, you make exactly the same as us. We all get the same amount, so if we do well, you do well, but you don't do well if we don't do well'. We were always a democratic band.

I think Tony Stratton Smith was cool about us having a manager. I think it took some pressure off him actually. What he felt about Tony Smith himself, I don't know, because Tony Smith took quite an aggressive approach towards Charisma, who needed a bit of shaking up. Technically we had been managed by one of the Charisma companies, Mother Management, but we knew that we couldn't really be managed by the record company. And although Strat had many, many qualities I don't think he was really right as a manager for us. He would always have split loyalties.

> **TONY SMITH FINALLY DECIDED TO STOP BEING A PROMOTER. IT WAS IN HIS BLOOD: HIS FATHER HAD BEEN A PROMOTER. AND THEN PETER LEFT THE BAND AND YOU COULD SEE TONY THINKING, 'OH MY GOD, WHAT HAVE I DONE?'** Mike Rutherford

Between recording sessions in Wales – and the mobile studio ready for action.

STEVE: Something changed in the mood of the band between *Selling England* and *The Lamb Lies Down*. It was no longer about fusion. I felt that Genesis by the time of *The Lamb* was almost like a vehicle travelling along a road and all the tyres have got uneven pressures. Everybody had their own agenda. Some of us were married, some of us had children, some of us were getting divorced. And we were still trying to get it together in the country so we were working at Headley Grange.

The place was falling apart. In fact, on the day that we left, I'd been washing at the sink, moved back three feet and as I did so the floor gave way and in front of me was a gaping hole where there had once been the ceiling of the room below. I don't know whether it had been gnawed away by rats. Robert Plant told me, 'I swear that place was haunted,' and indeed at night there were the most unearthly noises that kept me awake. I don't think anyone will tell you it was an easy period for the band.

PHIL: *The Lamb Lies Down* was at times a particularly miserable experience. We were staying in the house where Led Zeppelin had recorded 'When The Levee Breaks', fantastic. We arrived there to find that the previous band had left the place in an awful state. I don't think the owner ever knew how much we tidied up after them. There were rats everywhere. You'd be walking down the corridor and a rat would stop and look at you as if to say, 'What the fuck are you doing here?' and they would carry on walking, no scurrying, just sauntering.

TONY: The place was absolutely filthy. There was human excrement on the floor, absolutely disgusting. There was a big wisteria on the outside of the house and you could see the rats running up and down the wisteria and then going into holes in the wall.

MIKE: *Lamb* took a good six months to write. We had decided to do a double album from the outset, which gave us the space to improvise some of the longer, jamming pieces, an opening out, more freedom. But the length of the album did mean there had to be a lot of words; what became apparent was that there started to be a slight divide between the music and the lyrics, because on that album Pete wrote nearly all the lyrics, which was the right thing to do for the project. There were often times when he would be doing the words upstairs in the bedroom while we were downstairs working on the music. It was purely to do with time pressures.

And then he went off in the middle of that album. He got a call from William Friedkin, who had directed *The Exorcist*, and who'd read, on the back of *Genesis Live*, a piece of one of Pete's on-stage stories. Friedkin liked it, thought 'This is an interesting mind', rang him up and said, 'I'd like to talk to you about doing something'; whether he was thinking musically or more scriptwriting, I don't know. But I think Pete felt, 'I'd like to do this and I can't do this with Genesis'. So there was a tug-of-war going on within himself.

PETER: On the back of the *Genesis Live* record I had written a story which I used to tell in between songs, about this woman stripping in a tube carriage: she starts playing with herself and pulls her skin off and what you're left with is this column of light. William Friedkin saw this on the back of the album, called me up and said, 'I love the way you're thinking.' He was *the* hip and happening director because *The Exorcist* had just exploded, so he had carte blanche to do what he wanted. He thought he could revolutionize Hollywood and bring in a whole lot of people who had never been involved with film before. He was collecting together artists from Paris, Tangerine Dream, and he wanted me in there as an ideas person.

This was very exciting for me and something I wanted to pursue. I said to the band 'There's this great opportunity. I don't think it need take that long'. I think we were talking about six weeks. Of course later on everyone did do side projects, but at the time it was seen as a kind of betrayal because there was a work ethnic that you had to sacrifice your life in all sorts of ways and especially the family, in order to show you were part of the band, a military logic, really.

Above: Steve with wife Kim. Overleaf: The stage set for *The Lamb*. At the end of the *Lamb* tour, somewhere in France – Tony Banks is convinced it was the show in Besançon – one of the road crew, Geoff 'Bison' Banks, appeared naked on stage: a moment rooted in Genesis folklore. Bison tells the story: 'It was a spur of the moment thing, a chance to have a laugh. The tour had been all about this double concept album being played the same way every night, from top to bottom, so it all felt a bit strait-laced, not very rock'n'roll. In one part of the show Peter would get up on a platform behind the band, with three identical images of him on screen, and with a mannequin dressed in the same gear on the opposite side of the stage. When the strobe lighting went off, the idea was "Which is the real Peter Gabriel?" On the night in question, Geoff decided to put on the dummy's leather jacket – 'it looked like a waistcoat on me' – and jumped on stage wearing absolutely nothing else, much to the surprise of Phil Collins, whose drum riser was next to Bison, his eyes pretty much at groin level: Phil says it's an image he will never forget. 'It only lasted fifteen seconds max,' says Geoff, 'so I jumped back down and quickly changed into my T-shirt and jeans. We all had long hair then so I could merge with everybody else. "Who was that?" someone asked me. "I dunno." I was waiting to see if there was any flak – luckily there wasn't.'

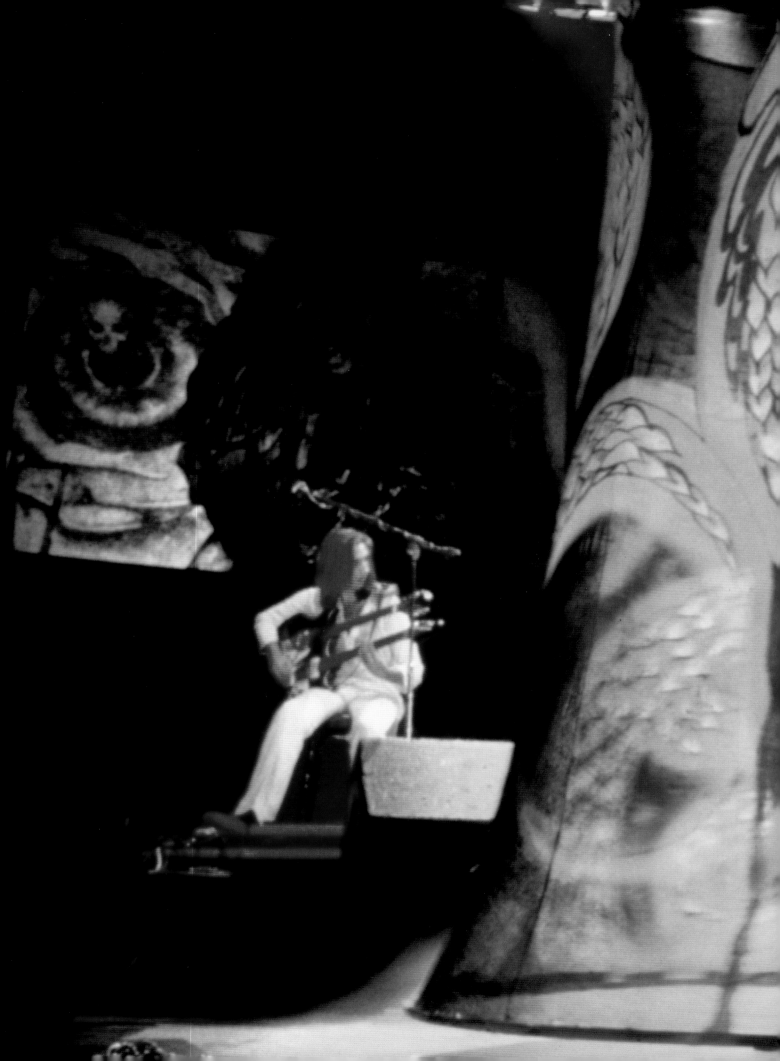

Jill was pregnant with our first child at the time, which was a huge thing for me. When Anna was born in July '74 there were all sorts of complications: Jill had taken an epidural and got an infection from the needle, Anna had the cord round her neck. We had been all set for a natural birth and then a sort of green-coloured thing came out and was taken away in silver foil like a chicken carcass. For the first two days the medical staff wouldn't let Jill go down to the premature unit because they thought Anna wasn't going to survive and they thought at that time it was kinder for her not to make the attachment.

It was a nightmare birth. Then when Anna made it through the first week and we were recording in Wales, the roads were terrible, it was like an eight-hour journey for me to drive to St Mary's, Paddington. And the band were really unsympathetic. They knew it was serious, but in my mind there was absolutely no question that on one side was life and death and on the other, an album, and I knew where they go in my priorities.

It was the combination of the Friedkin thing and Anna's birth and me deserting the band's recording session. We were still under financial pressure and I was making these absurdly long drives every other day to go and be with my family. I was torn... These external opportunities on the one hand and family life and crisis on the other were loosening the ground on which I stood.

Below: Peter, Jill and baby Anna, born July 1974.

Opposite: The Supperman. Peter says, 'I guess what I was interested in at that time was transformation, metamorphosis, journeys that would allow you to go through and explore different parts of your personality.

MIKE: Pete had always been inside the Genesis camp – one for all, all for one – and suddenly he was the one going outside the box saying 'Hang on, there's something out there I wouldn't mind looking at'. Anyway, Peter left for three days, but Strat rang him up and said, 'Are you sure about this, let's finish the album', and he came back. And in the meantime he'd spoken to Friedkin who also said, 'Wait, I don't want to break the band up, that's not the point'. So Pete came back and finished the album but I think those few days off had put the idea into his head – and our heads – about what might come next. So when he did leave we were slightly more prepared for it.

TONY: Peter and I were very close friends. But we always used to fight and argue a lot within the group, because we were both obstinate people and he moves at a snail's pace whereas I move at a fly's pace. I'm too fast, he's too slow. During the making of *The Lamb*, particularly when this issue came up with him and William Friedkin, I thought, 'Well, this project has got to be number one, otherwise it's not worth doing'. Now, in mitigation, he was the first of us to get the idea that there was more to life than being in a rock group. He'd moved on a bit, where we hadn't, and we weren't prepared to make quite the time for him that was necessary. The concept of him staying away for more than a day after his child was born was alien to us. And it just got more difficult. The magic had gone out of it.

ALTHOUGH THERE WAS A SENSE OF FRUSTRATION AND ANGER AND POISON BUILDING IN THE ROOM SOMETIMES, WE WERE EXCITED BY THE MUSIC. I STILL THINK IT'S ONE OF THE BEST THINGS THAT WE DID TOGETHER. BUT IT HAD NOT BEEN AN EASY OR SUNNY PROCESS. PETER GABRIEL

Above: A band portrait by Suzan Carson.

TONY: Of all my time in Genesis, my least favourite period was the writing of *The Lamb*. We pooled all the ideas we had. I had one fast piano introduction which Peter and I developed into a song, 'The Lamb Lies Down', the last song that Peter and I ever wrote together, just the two of us. And I think it showed our strengths: it had a good feel from what I gave it but much of the solidity came from what Pete wrote.

PETER: I'd still done a fair bit of writing on those songs and as always I had some semi-finished ideas to bring in, but a lot of the jamming which took place I was not participating in. I would go off and the others would carry on evolving the music through jamming; then I would come back and try to develop melodies on a piano in another room in the Grange.

I had taken on the bulk of the lyrics by choice. We had come up with a ton of music – we were talking about doing a double album – and I thought all this disparate stuff with no real purpose or glue would be much stronger if we could make it cohesive. The concept album was still a revered item in some quarters. I felt we needed a story and of course there was the odd argument about having to do it democratically, so I conceded on sharing some of the lyrics. But I felt I had to try and steer the story, and I think a lot of people still haven't got much clue what was going on in the story.

The Lamb Lies Down contained elements of *West Side Story* but it was also a kind of punk *Pilgrim's Progress*. A lot of my focus in Genesis had been on journeys into the psyche. I was reading a lot of Jung which was feeding that path. There was a film by Alejandro Jodorowsky called *El Topo* which was an influence – and in fact I asked Jodorowsky to write a screenplay with me later on. *The Lamb* was part psychedelia, part searching for spiritual enlightenment and part dealing with alienation, repression, rejection and trying to get a through-line to some transformative experience and hopefully some wisdom at the end of it. Nothing too heavy.

TONY: One of the bits I was most pleased about became 'In The Cage', something I'd seen as quite a rather dramatic piece in 3/4 but when Phil started playing the drums and he played against it, playing 2s instead of the 3s which made it much more driving and more exciting. Although it later became a bit of a classic Genesis song it was a slightly overlooked track on the album; in fact the album version isn't as good as what we did with it later.

I wasn't crazy about the overall story. It just didn't quite work for me as a totality, and I find the first two sides are much better than the third and fourth sides. I never think the fourth side really delivers, and if you are making a double album, you want the ending to be really strong. I felt that the album petered out. But I like a lot of it; some of my favourite bits are the instrumental moments which were done really as improvisations. There were two or three points where we had no music but Peter had written a storyline, and we had to create something on the spot. One was 'The Grand Parade Of Lifeless Packaging', which emerged from a couple of chords I'd started playing; the other was 'The Carpet Crawlers', where we had no starting point at all. Mike and I sat down and developed a chord sequence in a simple D, E minor, F sharp minor with a roll from the drums flowing through it, and Pete wrote a beautiful melody on top of that. It proved that you can slave for hours trying to get a song together and then, almost spontaneously, you develop one of the best tracks on the album.

And I particularly like the piece we called 'Fly On A Windshield', which starts as a very soft little thing and then this huge crash comes in from the drums with the guitar and the Mellotron. It's one of the strongest moments in Genesis, a physical 'pow' that really gives you that feeling of a fly hitting a windscreen.

PHIL: There were stand-out moments. The highlight of that album to me is 'The Waiting Room'. I remember when we first played the song, it was pissing with rain outside. We were doing this basic bad to good soundscaping and as Tony started to play some chords the sun came out, there was a rainbow and the rain stopped. It sounds very cosmic, but it actually did happen.

TONY: When we played *The Lamb* on stage there were quite a few pieces we never would have played live, had we not been trying to perform the whole album. Another problem I had was that at the time there was no real piano sound. None of the electric pianos had touch sensitivity. The RMI piano I was using was OK on a number like 'Lamb Lies Down' itself, but trying to play 'Anyway', which has a much stronger classical feel, sounded awful. That probably left a slightly bad taste in my mouth. And in all honestly, whatever anybody thinks, it never went down all that well on stage because people really wanted to hear 'Supper's Ready' and 'The Knife', and here we were playing them this piece they'd never heard before.

STEVE: On stage I wasn't sure what we were trying to be at that point. Robert Fripp came along to one of the shows and said, 'It seems obvious to me that the band are pulling in different directions.' Perhaps he was fuelling the flames there, because I know he wanted to work with Pete, but I had to agree with him. The band were doing one thing and the singer was doing another. But I have a tremendous amount of love for Pete and his far-reaching vision, so on another level I didn't mind. There were very few concessions to nostalgia with the *Lamb* tour. We simply weren't doing the old tunes, we had become a new band.

MIKE: We went to America and played the entire album live with only one or two old songs at the end. No one had heard it; the album hadn't come out. Which was quite brave. Because that tour was based round just one piece of work, it was rather limiting. But it was very, very strong visually, with all the slides and the projectors – and I think quite adventurous.

PETER: The Swingos Hotel in Cleveland was where I finally told the others I had to leave. The hotel was part of rock'n'roll culture and I realized, 'I'm part of this machinery and I don't feel this is where I should be or who I am.' I could feel the pressure mounting and I had to punch my way out through it.

It was crazy in every other way because we had accumulated quite big debts and were just beginning to pay stuff off and get our heads clear financially, and the music was going down really well. So all of the worldly stuff was going in the right direction, but for me internally it was more repressive and darker.

TONY: Pete finally announced that he was definitely going to go in this hotel in Cleveland, Ohio – a very unlikely place, a very strange hotel where every room was different but equally tacky. I had been given a room in this place which had orange walls. I've always hated orange, and couldn't bear to stay in it, so Tony Smith said, 'OK, I'll take the orange room. You can have my room', which was a sort of blue. Later on Tony called us to his room for a group meeting, and this was where he said that Pete had decided he was definitely going to leave – and there were these orange walls all around. Oh God, it was a nightmare.

Although I did spend a long time trying to persuade Pete not to leave, in a way it was absolutely the right thing to happen. He wanted to move into slightly different areas, and Pete was also getting too big for the group. He was being portrayed as if he was 'the man' and it really wasn't like that. It was a very difficult thing to accommodate. So it was actually a bit of a relief.

MIKE: As with Ant, I never thought to stand in Pete's way if he didn't want to be part of the band any more. But naturally I was sad about losing someone who had been a very close friend. You know you'll never be quite the same again, and although we are still good friends you never have that sharing thing in quite the same way: they've moved on into their own life.

STEVE: Nobody's departure from the band is without a certain amount of rancour, but it was as gentlemanly as it could be. Peter said he would honour the touring commitments of the band, and more and more shows were put in because nobody wanted to say goodbye to him. I think some of us hoped that at the end of it he would have enjoyed himself so much that he would come to his senses, realize how great we all were together and decide he wasn't going to leave, but by then he was obviously frustrated within the band format. The band had grown to the point perhaps where there were just too many ideas.

PHIL: I never felt any bad feeling, but the fact that we were touring with someone in the band who was going to leave was a very strange situation. I can't ever imagine saying I'm leaving and it being known and then going through those motions. I suppose we couldn't do much about it because we were committed to doing shows.

PETER: It was very difficult because the others didn't really understand why I would want to go when we were just about to achieve something we had worked so hard for. I think they felt I was sabotaging what was possibly their one big chance. I believe to this day that I had much more confidence in the band's ability to transcend my departure than they did themselves.

Opposite: And then there were four: rehearsals for *A Trick Of The Tail*, August 1975.
Overleaf: Thank you, and goodnight.

TONY: No one apart from the group, and the immediate circle of the group, knew that Pete was leaving and that this could well be our last tour ever. And the roadies always had to have some fun. There was this moment in the show where Pete would be on one side of the stage with a dummy on the other side and the strobe lights would flash on them so you couldn't tell which was which. And, of course, for one of the last shows one of the roadies got up there naked on the other side and took up the pose in place of the dummy... There were people watching this, my wife for instance, practically in tears because they thought that it might be all over for Genesis and we had a naked roadie on stage: was this how it was all going to end?

MIKE: The last gig was going to be in Toulouse and just before that final show, it was cancelled through lack of ticket sales. So the penultimate show in St Etienne suddenly became the last show, and an hour beforehand we learnt that this would be the last show with Peter, which was quite weird.

TONY: After the tour, I felt very determined to carry on. I was fed up because everyone was saying, 'Oh, Pete was Genesis' and I thought, 'It's not like that. Let's see what we can do, let's prove them wrong'. Mike was equally bloody-minded. 'We're not going to let it stop now. We've got to this stage and we can do it, we can write music which is just as good and we can carry on.' How we were going to accomplish it we had no real idea, but we felt we had an audience who were pretty enthusiastic and would stay with us. The main problem was we didn't have a singer of course.

MIKE: We assumed we would have to find a new singer, and started auditioning a few people, not that many and no one really well-known. And the funny thing was our singer was in-house all the time. He was staring us in the face.

MY INITIAL REACTION WAS THAT WE'D JUST CARRY ON AS A FOUR-PIECE WITHOUT ANY SINGING. Phil Collins

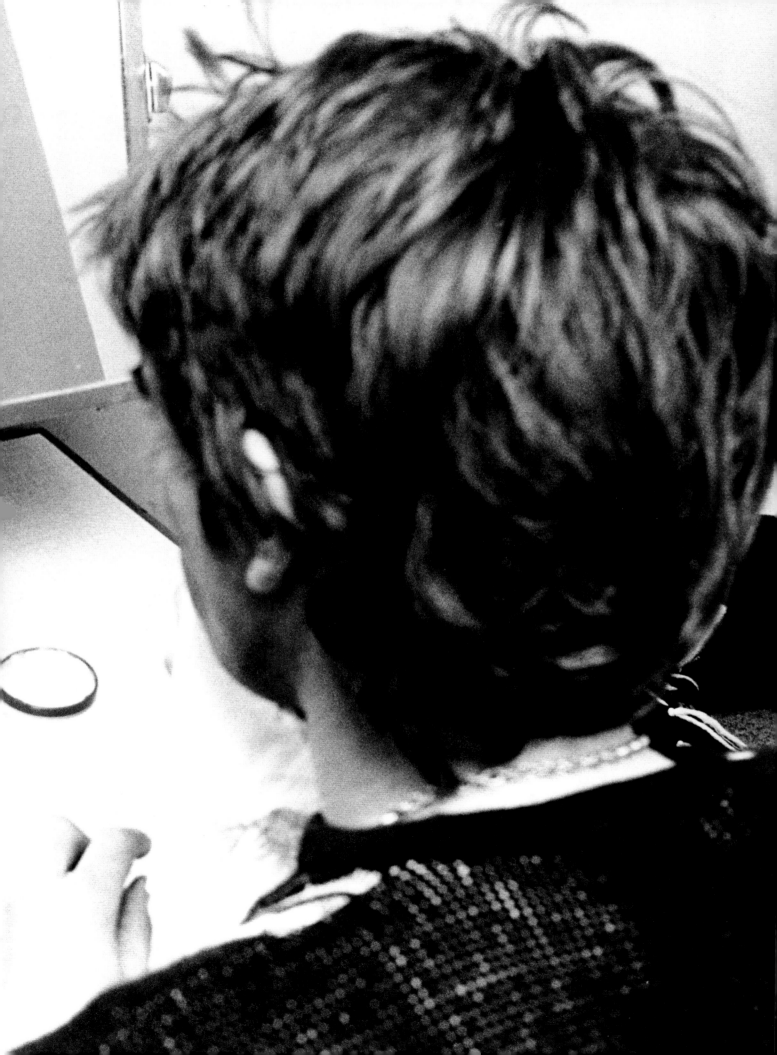

PETER'S TALE: PETER GABRIEL

After the final show at St Etienne, I sat around in the dressing room feeling very depressed, and also frustrated that I hadn't been able to tell the audience, 'This is my last gig,' because I needed to mark the transition somehow. And I was never able to – not if I was going to give the band a proper chance. Which meant I had to keep that internalized, and deal with a certain amount of criticism. I don't think there was a lot of support. People did accept my decision after a while, but I did have that Judas feeling that I'd betrayed the cause. However, I knew that I didn't have any other option.

Once I had made the decision to leave, and that I was going to get out of the music business altogether, that was my intention. I thought I might look at film again. I'd had the place in film school which I hadn't pursued because we had been concentrating on Genesis. The William Friedkin venture had fizzled out of its own accord. I think he had run into some problems, which was normal: often people start talking in a great revolutionary mode and then reality has a strange habit of setting in soon after.

My main objective, though, was to take a little time with my family at home. We had moved out to the West country shortly before – another change that had happened in that year of 1974 along with all the other issues. The geographical separation from the band made a difference, although the reason for heading out west was economic: we needed to look at somewhere like Bath, about 100 miles outside London, so that prices would be, at that time, low enough. I had come across one place in a small ad which had previously been an artist's house: a mill cottage in a beautiful little valley near Frome. It was a ruin, really, and when my wife saw the weeds growing up through the kitchen floor, what I saw as romanticism didn't quite appeal to her in the same way.

We continued looking around the area at other mill buildings and found a cottage in Woolley, just north of Bath. It was a village of fewer than 100 people. When the snow came the only vehicles able to get in and out were the farmer's tractor and my Range Rover, so we did the bread and milk deliveries and when one old lady sadly died it was a toss up between us who was going to carry the coffin and undertakers up and down the hill. This was the strongest sense of community that I'd ever had. I'd always liked the west country because deep down the people seemed open and friendly and more relaxed and there were hills and water, all of which I liked. It was very much a case of 'getting your head together in the country'.

After a while of twiddling my fingers, I tried writing some material with a friend called Martin Hall who was a poet. We wrote a few songs together, but it felt as if I'd gone the whole cycle back to stage one, where, in order to get anyone to cover your songs, you had to start performing them yourself.

In the meantime I was aware that Phil was going to take over the vocal duties for the band. It made a lot of sense to me. Phil was a good singer and is a natural performer. He'd had all that stage school training. In part it was true that he had been able to copy and absorb some of what he'd seen me do, but equally his voice had been a genuinely recognizable part of the Genesis sound.

I went to see the band on their first tour without me. It was a very strange experience, and I had mixed emotions. I hadn't been obliged to go; I was actually quite curious. I tried not to be precious about it, but I guess there were a few moments in the music and in the lyrics of the songs which had had some emotional significance to me and at times I felt that those moments of significance didn't connect or register with Phil.

Phil is a superbly talented natural musician. He can pick up almost any instrument and make it sound good and feel good, so there was never a question about the musicality. But perhaps some of the more obscure lyrical material which I had conceived quite naturally didn't mean anything to him. He was saying the words but not really feeling them. Although that was a slight negative for me, on the other hand the band were clearly firing on stage.

I think my reference points were more out of film and more noir and Phil's were from comedy, theatre and music hall. I had tried to add some humour into my performances, but he had a lighter touch. And as he grew in confidence and his writing style fed more into the band's character, they found another identity which produced the most popular period in Genesis's history, so he obviously found a way to connect with the audience.

That assuaged any guilt I might have felt, even though I had always been confident that they would carry on perfectly well without me, too. Clearly they were off and away after a period when things had been quite wobbly. I didn't know whether I had messed up other people's lives as well as, potentially, my own.

When I'd been the centre of the band everyone assumed that like Pete Townshend in the Who I'd been the main writer of everything, whereas I had been one of the main writers but not the writer. When I left and the band had more success without me, I suddenly felt that as people were re-evaluating the old work they were thinking, 'Oh, maybe Peter was just the guy who wore the masks', and that pissed me off!

When I started writing seriously again, I really tried to come up with songs that would be as different from the Genesis sound as possible. It was a scary thing to put an album together with other musicians, because I'd never been a trained musician. I had had some piano lessons, but I felt I couldn't score the musical ideas, so I was concerned about how I was going to express what I wanted and I needed people there who would understand me. I had no idea how to communicate with real session musicians, who seemed like strange, foreign people. So for the first demo sessions I involved musicians with whom I already had that shorthand – Mike, Phil, and Ant on keyboards: I used to like the way Ant had quite a simplistic approach to the piano but brought a lot of feeling and a lot of colour to it. He was very musical; I still think he was one of the most musical, if not *the* most musical member of Genesis.

For about ten years after I left the band I continued trying to do something else. I didn't want to be just doing more of the same. But there came a point when that was no longer important. I felt I'd found my own musical identity. By 2002, on a track like 'Signal To Noise' from the album Up, I was doing string arrangements which I might have not had the confidence to try in the earlier years of my solo career.

Today, however, I feel completely free to do anything that might have been considered old Genesis territory: on my last tour I was even thinking of including 'Supper's Ready'. I talked with the other guys about the dates for the Turn It On Again tour, but in the end it was building up to something bigger than I really wanted to do at that point in my life. I wasn't in principle against the idea of doing something for a short period. There is no forbidden territory now. Everything feels more open.

In February 1977 Peter Gabriel's first solo release after leaving Genesis was untitled, as were all of his first four albums. His third solo album in 1980 – featuring 'Games Without Frontiers' and 'Biko' – showed a burgeoning interest in world music, which led to the foundation of WOMAD (World Of Music, Arts and Dance). After the first WOMAD festival in 1982, Genesis reunited with Peter to raise much needed funds to guarantee WOMAD's existence. His 1986 album *So* marked a new commercial peak, and 'Sledgehammer' began a series of innovative, award-winning videos. As well as his solo work, Peter has had collaborations with Kate Bush, Laurie Anderson, Randy Newman and Joni Mitchell, composed film scores (*Birdy*, *The Last Temptation Of Christ* and *Long Walk Home*) and set up his Real World stable of companies. In 1989 he co-founded Witness.org, which gives digital video cameras and other tools of communication to human rights activists worldwide, and in 2000/2007 conceived and created the Elders.org with Richard Branson and Nelson Mandela. He also pioneered digital distribution of music with OD2 two years before iTunes was launched, and has continued his involvement with Filter.com and We7.com. As well as many awards for his contribution to music, Peter received the 'Man of Peace' Award in 2006, presented by the Nobel Peace Laureates.

THE MANAGER'S TALE, PART I: TONY SMITH

My father was a promoter: like most people he fell into it by accident. After the war he started organizing dances as fund-raisers for a local boxing club and developed from there to putting on shows for the Ted Heath Orchestra, Tommy Dorsey, Sarah Vaughan. He was the first person to ever book an Odeon Cinema for a live show. I have many memories of him going off in his dinner jacket and black tie, because that's what you wore if you were a promoter in the '50s. You had to do the announcing, be the MC, everything. He was quite a character, my father.

He moved into promoting bands and booking tours – trad jazz with Acker Bilk, Chris Barber and Kenny Ball, and the early rock stuff with Joe Brown, Cliff Richard and Tommy Steele. My father was desperate for me to have a proper job, so I trained as a mechanical engineer. But I helped him out in the holidays, selling programmes on one of the early rock and pop packages he put together with the Ronettes, Chuck Berry, Bo Diddley, the Four Seasons and the Rolling Stones. In 1964 he was doing some shows with the Beatles, but he also had Acker Bilk touring Ireland – my father was Irish and had connections there – and sent me off aged nineteen or so to manage the tour. He must have had a lot of faith in me, because the Acker Bilk Band were fantastic drinkers and it was certainly an eye-opener. And then I came back off the ferry at Holyhead and drove straight down to the Odeon in Worcester for the first of these Beatles shows. It was absolute chaos, one constant squall of screaming – extraordinary stuff and great to live through. I used to organize for ambulances to turn up or disguise the group as policemen to get them in and out of the theatres. That was my apprenticeship.

I tried engineering for a while, didn't like it, dropped out, and came back to London to get a job in a record store in Piccadilly, which I ended up managing. This was in '67, '68. All these great new bands were releasing albums, and I said to my father – who was now handling acts like Andy Williams – 'You ought to start doing some of this.' We began working together and soon we were promoting acts like the Who, the Stones, Led Zeppelin; I ended up doing about 300 shows a year. Towards the end of 1970 I was approached by Tony Stratton Smith, who had a bunch of bands on Charisma who were bubbling under. He wanted to do a nationwide tour and was prepared to subsidize it. We finally came up with the concept of presenting the three bands together for a ticket price of 30p. And that was the Six Bob Tour.

My initial reaction to Genesis was that the singer was quite extraordinary – a great voice and completely different on stage than off stage – and that they had a great drummer. It was only during the course of the tour that I realized how extraordinary Tony Banks's composing and chord progressions were.

But they were totally disorganized, totally. They were only just out of school and still acting like this was an after-school

activity. On the tour, I sat them down two or three times to tell them they really should get organized and either on that tour or the next, there was a great moment at Green's Playhouse in Glasgow when they were due to go on but there was electricity coursing through the equipment and we couldn't get anywhere near the stage. Finally we had to cancel and I was the one who had to get up on stage and tell the Glaswegian audience that the show wasn't going to happen, which didn't endear me to them very much. After that I definitely sat them down again to have a word. My memory tells me that they actually said at the time, 'Would you fancy managing us?' and I told them I was too busy, but that they should really get themselves sorted out. We went our own ways.

Amongst the tours I did was Monty Python Live, which we took to Canada. The Pythons didn't have a manager, just their individual acting agents. I found myself over in Canada with them, 3,000 miles away from their agents, and acting as their quasi-manager. It occurred to me that I rather liked the role. When I got back to the UK, I was driving back to London after a show in Cardiff, fell asleep at the wheel, ran into the back of a slow-moving truck on the M4 and ended up in hospital with forty-two stitches in my head and God knows what else. It gave me pause for thought...

During the next Genesis tour in 1973, Peter approached me and said, 'Look, we're still interested: would you fancy managing us now?' By this time I felt I had achieved as much as I could as a promoter in England at the time and based on the small amount of experience I had had with the Pythons, I said OK. There was a lot to learn and to sort out. When I took Genesis over they were £150,000 in debt, at 1973 prices. Their record deal needed drastic revision – without Tony Stratton Smith the band would not have been anywhere, but he was trying to be record company owner, manager and publisher all at the same time,

and that wasn't working. I didn't know much about the record business or the music publishing business or very much about foreign touring but I picked it up as I went along.

Shortly after I started working with the band, they had their first minor hit with 'I Know What I Like' off Selling England By The Pound. It was bubbling under at number 27 – a real breakthrough for the band. One of my first jobs as a manager was to tell Charisma that the band were adamant they weren't going to appear on Top Of The Pops, and the record company were going crazy because they needed them on the show that week to push the single up the charts. I agreed with Genesis that it was wrong for them because Top Of The Pops had such a pop image, which wasn't where the band were at. I had a huge fight with Tony Stratton Smith over this and I heard from several people that he said, 'I introduced this man to the band and now he's bloody stopping them being successful.' He was pretty upset about it, but he got over it.

A significant change in my relationship with the band came a couple of years later. Peter had left, but I was still managing his solo career, and 'Solsbury Hill' had been a huge hit. He was out on the road in America, as were Genesis who had also had a big hit with Trick Of The Tail. I was jumping from one to the other, couldn't ask for better: the records were hits, the tours going fantastically well. Towards the end of the Genesis tour the band asked if we could have a meeting. They sat down and said, 'We really don't think this is going to work. We don't think you can manage Peter and us. It's too much, and there may be a clash of interests.' I told them I'd think about it, and let it go for four or five days. Then I told them, 'I've come to the realization that if you make me make this decision and I decide to carry on with you, I will become your employee. I will no longer have an independent voice. So if you want to force this position I'm going to have to choose Peter.' I didn't hear another thing. However as both of them were becoming increasingly successful I needed to bring someone else in, and as Gail Colson was leaving Charisma I formed a new company, Gailforce, with her to manage Peter. Within the band, like all relationships that endure for thirty-five years, the dynamic does change. It's changed many times over the years.

There was always the potential for conflict within Genesis. If you're only putting out one record a year and everyone has their own writing, that is going to be the cause of tension. Financial issues, which are often a problem for a manager, have never arisen, only artistic ones. It came to a head on The Lamb. Peter had the concept for the story and wanted to write all the lyrics, so a whole area of the others' creativity was being cut off. Peter is not the fastest writer in the world and the band had virtually finished recording before the lyrics were available. He had just had his first baby, too, and was talking to William Friedkin about the movie possibilities. Suddenly where there had been closeness, there was a gap. It was very noticeable being around them all the time. The

mood was very fraught. During the course of all that Peter thought, 'Why am I putting up with all this pressure? The band aren't happy, and I'm being forced into making decisions and meeting deadlines which I don't want to do.'

He told me in Cleveland, early on in the Lamb tour. I'll remember it to my dying day. We were staying at Swingos Hotel, Cleveland and I had this godawful orange room – everything was orange, horrible. Peter came to the door and said, 'I need to talk to you, I've decided I'm going to leave the band.' There's never a good time for that sort of news. It was a total surprise to everyone despite the fact there had been those tensions. I think Peter was a little fearful, thinking, 'I'm opening a gate here and I don't know where I'm going', but at the same time excited, as anyone would be in that situation. What flashed through my mind first was, 'We've just launched the most ambitious record we've done to date, it's not the easiest of records to promote, and I've got 120 shows around the world that we really should be doing.' I realized that if there was going to be even the chance of a smooth transition, I had to convince him to stay on and finish the tour.

I believe we decided at the time that Peter and I should keep this to ourselves for a while. I felt that if the band got to know they wouldn't deal with it very well and it might reflect on the tour and on their performances, so my memory is that we actually kept it quiet for quite some weeks, though Tony Banks, I know, thinks it came out pretty quickly. I'm not convinced about that. It's not how I remember it. When it did come out we were in difficult circumstances. A lot of people hold The Lamb up as being a pinnacle in Genesis's career. The reality was that it was not a very successful record at the time. We'd come off the back of Selling England By The Pound, which had been fairly successful in their terms, to this very difficult double album that took quite a bit of digesting and which fans didn't really take to straightaway, although ultimately they loved it. We were out there touring this bloody double album, performing a wodge of new songs, which meant the reaction live wasn't that great because people weren't familiar with the album, certainly during the first part of the tour.

There was a lot of managerial smoothing of the waters over that period of time, but to give all of them their due they made the joint decision to finish the tour and give the record and the group a chance of success. I have to take my hat off to Peter that he was prepared to carry on – and with good grace. A lot of people wouldn't have bothered.

Tony Smith followed his father into the business of concert promotion and spent the late '60s and early '70s promoting tours and shows by acts including the Rolling Stones, the Who, Led Zeppelin and Monty Python. He worked with Tony Stratton Smith and Charisma to put on the Six Bob Tour of 1971, featuring Genesis with Van Der Graaf Generator and Lindisfarne, and took over as manager of Genesis, at their request, in 1973.

CHAPTER EIGHT

FOREIGN FIELDS

TONY: Since people knew we were looking for a new singer, we had been receiving tapes from all over the place. We used to see two or three people a day while we were actually writing *Trick Of The Tail*, and as we auditioned them, Phil would often sing the melody to teach it to them, and he actually sang a lot better than these guys. But, well, he was still the drummer – he wouldn't want to do anything else, would he? We had always thought Phil would sing a couple of the softer songs, like 'Mad Man Moon' and 'Ripples', because we knew he could handle them, but we never believed he could sing anything that had some body to it.

MIKE: Phil's voice was always very pure, like a choirboy's, and Pete's always had a bit of grit in it, so we couldn't imagine Phil taking over the whole range of songs because he didn't have that broken, husky sound.

PHIL: As time went on, I realized that we weren't going to find anybody. We eventually arrived at a position where we were down to only one or two possibles. We took one of these guys in to the Trident studios, having recorded the backing tracks without any consideration of whether or not he could sing them, and asked him to try 'Squonk'. The song was not in his key and doubtless he was nervous; for one reason or another it didn't work so we said, 'OK, call you tomorrow...'

TONY: I had missed this recording because I'd been ill. I came in the next day to listen to this poor chap trying to sing 'Squonk', which was pitched way higher than his range, which meant he had screamed his way through the song. The others said, 'Well, this is what we've got' and I said, 'You know, we're nowhere near, it's just not working at all'. So Phil offered to have a go. He sang 'Squonk', and did a pretty creditable job. His voice didn't sound bad – although it wasn't yet fantastic – but it sounded a hell of a lot better than the others we had on offer.

STEVE: When Phil stepped forward it seemed obvious because he'd sung 'For Absent Friends', the first song I'd ever written for the band, and also 'Star Of Sirius', which was going to be on my first solo outing. Plainly the guy had a strong voice; he'd been a star of stage, screen and musical. What must have been obvious to even the deaf was the fact that both he and Pete had such similar and sympathetic voices that when they were singing together it sounded like doubletracking, wonderful harmonies on tunes like 'The Chamber of 32 Doors' or 'I Know What I Like'.

PHIL: When Trevor Horn mixed a version of 'Carpet Crawlers' in the late 1990s, I had a bizarre feeling listening to it. I knew it was Pete singing when the track started but then it went to a verse and I couldn't tell whether it was me or Pete. I thought, 'That sounds like me but then I don't know – I don't remember us changing over at that particular point', although in fact I think it was me.

MY VOICE HAD ALWAYS BEEN THERE WITHIN THE GENESIS SONGS. PEOPLE HAD ALREADY HEARD MY VOICE SUBLIMINALLY. Phil Collins

TONY: Working on *Trick Of The Tail* was so refreshing. I loved making that record and taking it out on tour. I realized we didn't have to argue all the time. We could actually agree, and still produce music that was good. Everything had become so much easier and lighter. After the difficulties of *The Lamb* it was a breath of fresh air. That early period with Phil singing was one of the strongest periods we had: more musical – we seemed to be having millions of ideas – and closer to my own heart.

Previously there had been five of us all trying to write, all trying to get our stuff on the albums. Reducing that to four writers made a difference. You could get a bit more of your own material on, particularly if you shouted loudly like I did. At that point I'd got slightly fed up with the fact that people thought Peter had written everything, so we decided on this album to credit each song to whoever wrote it. And from that point of view one's ego was more satisfied.

Opposite: The announcement of the *Trick Of The Tail* tour of 1976 was made, no one can remember precisely why, in the London Underground.

Above: Phil takes the London Underground for the tour announcement.
Right: Dave Hentschel came on board as the producer of *A Trick of The Tail*. He had known the band since his days as an assistant engineer at the famed Trident Studios in London (on Dave's first day there in 1969 David Bowie was recording a *Space Oddity* session) and first worked with the band on *Nursery Cryme*. By 1975 he had picked up a Grammy for his work on Elton John's *Goodbye Yellow Brick Road*, and he stayed as co-producer with Genesis for five albums, through to *Duke*.

MIKE: It had been bothering us that the press that we got often talked about Peter, but made no mention of our music, so when Pete left we thought, 'God, if only the public knew some of their favourite songs were written not by him, but by us', because we always credited the music to 'Genesis', and it's natural for people to imagine that the singer is responsible for most of it. If only we'd written more credits, people would have known that 'Firth Of Fifth' was very much Tony's song, and that 'The Cinema Show' was by all of us.

In the early stages of writing the album, Steve wasn't there because he was working on his solo album. So the three of us – Tony, Phil and me – went into the studio and had a great first few days, including the beginnings of 'Squonk' and 'Dance On A Volcano'. Steve came back in, and it got better, but had those first few days not gone well, we might have thought we couldn't do it without Pete. It was a great start.

TONY: On the very first day we wrote what became a major part of 'Dance On A Volcano' and I thought, 'We're OK, we're underway'. This just sounded lovely and had a real Genesis feel to it.

I had a few ready-made pieces available, which I'd written thinking about a possible solo album, including a complete version of 'Mad Man Moon', and what became 'Robbery, Assault And Battery', which I'd written apart from the solo. 'A Trick Of The Tail' was something I'd written many years before, but with Peter's departure, I liked the idea of slipping in something lighter and more quirky.

'Entangled' was based on this really beautiful piece of song Steve had written, but it didn't have a chorus and needed somewhere to go. I happened to have this piece I'd written in 6/8, which was what the rest of the song was in, and so we stuck them together, getting the vocals to play what the piano part had been: it produced what is probably my favourite track on that album, ending with a great cathedral-type feeling. The Arp Pro Solo synthesizer I was using had a touch sensitive keyboard and if you pressed a key hard you got this vibrato, and could produce this marvellous high note that sounded like some wild cartoon soprano female.

PHIL: A lot of things were changing at that point. *Trick Of The Tail* was the first time we worked with Dave Hentschel as producer. I had been moonlighting at night at Trident Studios where Dave was a resident engineer – he'd worked on *Goodbye Yellow Brick Road*, and done some recording at Ringo's house – and we got on great, so I brought him in. Because I was the only one in the band who ever did anything else apart from Genesis. I was like the band's football scout, going out and seeing what everybody else was doing. I introduced Dave and he worked with us through to *Duke*.

TONY: For 'Squonk', Mike and I had been driving in a car somewhere in Germany and heard this song on the radio. Not being people who keep our ears to the ground, we said, 'This is fantastic; the drum sound is just so good', but we didn't know who it was. Afterwards we found out it was 'Kashmir' by Led Zeppelin, from the *Physical Graffiti* album. I'd never heard anything like this and I thought, 'I want our drums to be that big'. Mike and I played it to Phil and asked him to try the sound on 'Squonk'. We didn't quite get the sound we wanted but we did capture the slow tempo feel which produced a song that worked very well live, better live, in fact than on the record.

And 'Los Endos', which was a development of 'Squonk' and all the other pieces, was an idea which came more from Phil because he was very into jazz/rock, this idea of using all the melodies we had throughout the album and placing them into a slightly different feel to produce a song on its own.

PHIL: We had agreed with Pete that after he left no one would announce anything for as long as possible. And then suddenly the story had leaked. It was during rehearsals for *A Trick Of The Tail*. We bought a copy of that week's *Melody Maker* with Pete's picture on the front and the headline 'Gabriel Out Of Genesis?' That was it, we thought. 'They'll write us off now'. And a lot of people did, because for them Genesis without Pete was unthinkable. The positive side was that it gave everyone the chance to reassess us, and when we released the album, it was a surprise, because it was better than they thought it was going to be.

Below: The story of Peter's departure, a well-guarded secret, is finally broken by *Melody Maker* in August 1975.

MIKE: When the album came out it was a sudden turnaround. We'd been the underdogs: Gabriel leaves, it's all over. Then the album was released and people liked it and the reviews were good. Very good reviews, actually.

TONY: The reception for *The Lamb* had been mixed; I don't remember the fans being ecstatic about it at the time in the way that they had been about, say, *Foxtrot* or *Selling England*. So that gave *Trick Of The Tail* a chance, and I think people who had found Peter a bit difficult maybe preferred the album because it was a little bit less dense. And being able to replace Pete from within the group certainly eased the sense of a smooth transition. The next question was how we would go down on tour; I thought that live was where we were going to miss Pete most of all because he'd been such a strong focus.

MIKE: Even after finishing the album we didn't think Phil would want to leave the drum kit to sing on tour. And then one day he said, 'I might give it a try, and find a drummer – wouldn't that be easier?' It made sense. And because he was inhouse, so people knew him, and he had sung a bit on stage before, the audiences wanted to like him; they wanted it to work.

PHIL: Before we took *Trick Of The Tail* out on the road, we made another half-hearted attempt to find a singer. I'm not sure we even auditioned anybody, just wondered if there was someone we might have overlooked. So the conversation moved on to why didn't I sing on the road too. I must have been half-thinking about it anyway, and coming to the conclusion that if we were going to go out on the road with this great album we'd made, maybe I should be the one to sing it.

My real worry was actually what to say to the audience, because Peter had always had this offbeat charisma that gave the band a strange aura. I was much more friendly and approachable. So I spent more time on that journey, to London, Ontario for the opening show of the 1976 tour, worrying about what to say between songs than I did about what I was going to do once the songs started. We were very fortunate because we had an Ontario audience who were desperate for the band, their band, to survive and so they gave us every encouragement.

MIKE: In the first break between songs, I saw Phil go up front with a piece of paper in his hand, his hand shaking, so nervous. But it worked great. Of course, Phil had experience from his youth of being on stage; he was very comfortable there and the audience wanted to like him. He also introduced a calmer influence. Some of our songs were slightly distant, atmospheric, quite dark. Phil's more down-to-earth presence on stage counteracted the heavier parts of the set; he reduced the tension and helped people relax in between the songs.

This page: Genesis return to Central Park, this time with Bill Bruford (centre). Opposite: riding high in San Francisco.

STEVE: There was a feeling of confidence that on stage Phil would be able to deliver in a way that Pete found difficult. Pete tended to wreck equipment on stage. We didn't have cordless microphones in those days and when Pete was in his costumes he used to get caught up in the leads. There would be a certain level of collateral damage: objects used to go flying, gear used to blow up. There was probably too much ectoplasm emanating from the guy. Phil was much more consistent. You knew that he was going be able to run forward at the end of the drum break and hit his mark perfectly.

PHIL WAS AN EXCELLENT ALL-ROUNDER: A GOOD MASTER OF CEREMONIES, A GREAT DRUMMER, A GREAT SINGER. HOPE MY CHEQUE'S IN THE POST, PHIL. STEVE HACKETT

PHIL: Before the tour started, I knew I would have to find another drummer. I had played the drums and sung in my school band – it's not hard to do once you've mastered it – but visually it looks bloody awful because the audience can't see the drummer; they need to have a singer between them and the band. I'd been rehearsing with Brand X at Una Billings Dance Studio.

These pages: Phil's side project Brand X included (centre) keyboard player Robin Lumley. Phil says 'Brand X was originally more like an Average White Band funk thing, endless Tower of Power grooves, but then we became much more of a jazz-rock group. I was never going to leave Genesis for Brand X, but I was very much into the idea of playing some totally instrumental music.'

Bill Bruford was on percussion and I was playing drums; we were great friends. Bill asked me, 'Have you got anybody for the Genesis drum chair yet?', and when I said no, he said, 'Well, what about me?' I had never considered him; I thought he wouldn't have been interested. Bill had been there with Yes and King Crimson. When he was in Yes in their early days, the *Close To The Edge* era, they were one of my favourite bands, impeccable singers and players, what other bands like us looked up to; Crimson was another group we all admired. But he was really keen.

MIKE: Bill was very much Phil's choice. Phil had to feel completely comfortable about the person who will be coming in to play his parts live. Bill helped us too, because at the time Yes were popular in America, or had been, and he added a certain amount of kudos and credibility to that first tour.

TONY: Bill was someone Phil trusted, and he proved to be an asset for those live shows, because he had his own following: people in the crowd would be shouting out Bill's name. He also gave us the possibility of using two drummers live, which was something we hadn't thought of before, but which became an incredibly important part of the show; when he and Phil were playing together on 'The Cinema Show', that was one of the strongest moments on stage.

STEVE: Bill Bruford was a star in his own right. He helped the confidence on stage no end. I even shaved off my moustache. At last I was without facial hair.

MIKE: Bill's always at his best playing his own stuff. He's not a session guy. He is such an individual player he's not the best at playing other people's songs; he'd probably agree with this.

TONY: He is more of an analytical drummer. He has to think about things, he has to count things as well. I think he found some of the songs like 'Dance On A Volcano' not that easy: there was a fill in the middle which had to be played in 7, and you could see Bill's mouth counting it all out.

PHIL: Bill would never do the same thing twice, which I didn't really have a problem with, but on some of the songs, like 'Squonk', the drummer has to put a John Bonham hat on to get that Led Zep sound. Bill didn't want to put anybody's hat on. He wanted to play it like he wanted. He was trying to be a jazz musician. But there are a certain amount of essential cues, and with Bill it would be a different cue every night, so people wouldn't know what was coming where and there was always a danger that it would fall apart. At the same time I was on his side. I spent a lot of time on

the road with Bill, and I saw him get angry and frustrated a few times from all of the stuff that goes with being on the road and the feeling that the shows are derivative of something that you've already done. After a few months he had definitely had enough and eventually he left to form UK.

STEVE: By this time the band were very professional live. We were very good. Our timing had improved. Chris Welch at *Melody Maker* was giving us reviews saying, 'the band just played at Earls Court with a precision that would have done a symphony orchestra credit'. But for all the professional polish I had this nagging sense not so much of self-doubt but that I had to explore what I could do on my own. I felt I had to work with other people, I felt that the political games that one had to play within the group were perhaps something that I'd outgrown.

MIKE: The next album, *Wind And Wuthering*, was the first time we recorded abroad. It was purely for tax purposes. There was a weird loophole in those days; if you recorded an album abroad, you got a certain percentage of tax relief. So we looked for somewhere not too far away, and settled on the Relight studios at Hilvarenbeek in Holland; we did three weeks there and were able to lock ourselves away in the project. No phones, no interruptions, no family, it's a good thing to do for a short while.

Overleaf: A break in the *Trick Of The Tail* rehearsals, in the Acton garden of Phil's friend, the drummer and music shop owner Maurice Plaquet.

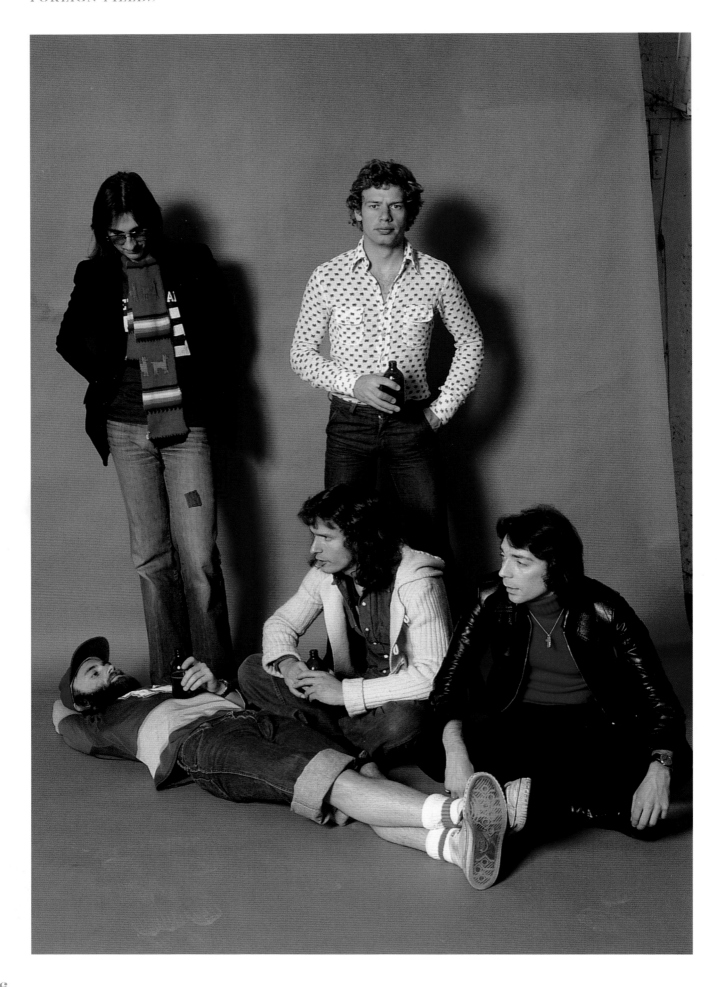

Opposite: Bill Bruford joins the 1976 tour. He says: 'If I were a better session musician, I'd have done what I was told.' Left: Tony with his RMI piano and ARP Pro Soloist synth, at the rehearsals for the *Wind And Wuthering* tour. Overleaf: A photo taken by Tony of the band's first Concorde flight, tucking into some caviar to celebrate.

PHIL: My eldest son Simon was born during that period. I was there at the hospital the day he was born, but I could only spend a couple of days before going back to work. It was one of those moments where you now think 'What the fuck did I do that for? What the hell was I thinking about?' You miss so much, because you don't think about it, and my attitude at the time was that this was what I did for a living. I made some terrible decisions. I don't think his mother and I would be still together now even if I hadn't made those decisions, but even so, I still get mad at myself.

TONY: *Wind And Wuthering* was about the confidence we had in playing as just the four of us. There are three tracks on that album which are amongst my favourite Genesis tracks: 'One For The Vine', 'Afterglow' and 'Blood On The Rooftops'.

I sat down and played 'One For The Vine' to the others on the piano with me singing 'la la la'. I always feel sorry for the guys when I do that. I don't know how exciting that was for them, really, but they liked it enough to take it into the studio, where we laid the whole thing down with piano, drums and a simple bass part and added everything else as overdubs. That was fun for me because it's got loads and loads of keyboard overdubs, a whole orchestration of synthesizers and Mellotrons. It was an elaborate piece that took a long time to write and a lot of honing to get right. It was a total contrast to 'Afterglow', which I wrote pretty much in the time it takes to play it, and consequently has a spirit about it that comes from being less contrived.

'Blood On The Rooftops' was one of the best pieces of composition Steve ever did with us. He had written a great introduction and a beautiful verse, but again it was just a wonderful piece of music with no chorus. Phil had a simple chorus that sounded good, with the line 'blood on the rooftops' but no other words, so Steve wrote the lyric based around that. I love that song. It's a beautiful song and because I had nothing to do with the writing of it, I can be a little more detached; it still moves me when I hear it now.

MIKE: *Wind And Wuthering* was one of Tony's favourite albums, but it's not mine. I found it something of an anti-climax after the excitement and the challenges of *Trick Of The Tail*, Phil's first singing album, I couldn't get that same kind of buzz.

> ## I CALL WIND AND WUTHERING THE 'FEMININE' ALBUM. IT'S THE FEMININE SIDE OF GENESIS, A LITTLE LESS BOLLOCKS IN IT.
> ### MIKE RUTHERFORD

PHIL: *Wind And Wuthering* marked the beginning of the end for Steve – especially his angst about how much material he had on it.

STEVE: My first solo album, *Voyage Of An Acolyte*, had come out just before *Trick Of The Tail* was released. It had been officially sanctioned by the management, I think because when I took to Tony Smith the idea of doing a solo album, it seemed like I'd thought it through very thoroughly. I had it organized: I had a team in place, I had the studio and the schedule in mind, I'd worked out a budget. What I was trying to do was to make something more romantic than the direction that Genesis had moved towards, to create something that was much more instrumental. It was a great period for me. I wasn't sure if I'd come up with nothing more than

a collection of outtakes, but in fact I'd written a lot of solid material. I recorded the thing in a month; it would take me at least that long to do one song these days.

We recorded at Aviation House in Kingsway, near Holborn, a place Fleetwood Mac had used for a lot of their recording work and which was either completely or partly owned by Ian Gillan, and some of the other Deep Purple chaps. There was a noise restriction: you couldn't record until after six o'clock in the evening when people were no longer aviating, so these were all night-time sessions – which helped give a feeling of working after hours.

On the very first night in the studio, the first thing we recorded was a piece with my brother John playing flute, I was using a Mellotron and I'd borrowed Mike Rutherford's twelve-string guitar; we came away with this semi-acoustic piece that sounded absolutely beautiful. I was starting to fall in love with the nylon guitar, the beginnings of a gradual transition from twelve-string to nylon guitar and a shift towards a more classical direction.

Above and opposite: Rehearsals at Little Chalfont Farm, November 1976, for the *Wind And Wuthering tour*. Chester Thompson's first time playing with the band. Chester, who took over from Bill Bruford, remembers that 'from the moment I sat down with Phil, we both, as drummers will do, started doodling around. I don't think I've ever locked with someone as quickly.'

MIKE: I think we all felt Steve that was going solo a bit too early. A band starts off and for a while you have to concentrate on that exclusively, nothing else, until you've built it up to a certain level. And we hadn't reached that stage yet. We were at a point in Genesis's career where we needed to put a lot of energy into it. Maybe Steve had seen Pete's solo success and felt he could achieve the same. But if we'd all done solo albums at that point then we wouldn't have got anything done. Just after Steve left, the time felt more appropriate. But Steve will say, and I'm sure in some ways he is right, that there were more songs of mine and Tony's on *Wind And Wuthering* than his. But I always like to think that there was more of a group feeling for the songs.

STEVE: In many ways it's very frightening taking on a solo album, because you realize that you're going to have to carry the can for its success or failure. When you're in a band, there's a shared responsibility for everything, from accountancy to who's going to make the tea. It's different when you're the captain of your own ship. When you're doing a solo album you're running your own show. People are looking to you for all the answers. Once you've successfully negotiated that, going back into a band is like returning to the crew. You realize you've outgrown the need for permission. And I also made the grave error of having a hit with the thing. I suspect from then on I became much less containable within the group.

Even if I am running a band, I always want to get the best out of people. I sense if anybody is not completely happy with something, if they want to do another take. I'll do whatever it takes to get the best out of someone. I wear them down with niceness rather than beat them over the head for not having played it properly in the first place. I can be a very enthusiastic character, for all my reserve and Englishness. If someone plays something I think is really great, I tell them. Then they're no longer a competitor; I'm just proud to work with them.

For instance, in the early days of Tony possessing a Mellotron, something that I had pushed for, when he played the opening strains of 'Fountain Of Salmacis', it sounded so beautiful, I said, 'We've got to use that'. I like to think that when anyone comes up with a good idea I would immediately enthuse about it because I was always interested in the whole being as strong as possible rather than trying to superimpose my idea simply because it was mine. And probably usually quite happy to sidestep and let someone else take over. I suspect it didn't go down at all well within the group on the few occasions when I said, 'No, I insist, my idea has to go on the album', because when you're operating outside your regular character it's much harder for other people to understand what's happening: 'Hang on a minute, isn't this the guy who always agrees with us?'

I think we all changed character over a period of time. Obviously everyone became more forceful, and unless you have a number of solo projects running in parallel I don't think you can have a band working like that. I feel everyone should have been encouraged to do some solo work earlier on and, if we had, perhaps that five-man team might still be treading the boards this very day.

TONY: I had always felt that Steve would not be around for ever, that we would be part of his career rather than his final resting-place, but on the other hand I had no idea how long we were going to last for. Steve had finished his solo record just before *Trick Of The Tail* and had not been around for the earliest writing sessions on the album, which was quite significant. But then on tracks like 'Los Endos' he and I had been swapping licks and I loved that. It was great to have someone who could come up with ideas and play in harmony and unison.

STEVE: After my solo album, I spent two years acting the part of the well-adjusted rock guitarist, but I wasn't. I felt that I was biding my time and I was looking forward to doing another solo album at some point. It was made clear to me that that was not an option whilst I remained as a band member, and from my point of view things were becoming claustrophobic once again. You can't keep a good Hackett down.

There had been many times when people talked me into staying with the band. Sometimes it was the others in the band, sometimes my father, who spoke very good sense. At one particular juncture, just before the tour of *The Lamb*, I injured my hand. I'd been to see the Alex Harvey band at the Palladium – a brilliant band live – and gone on to the aftershow party. I was getting a bit out of it and I heard someone at the gathering saying, 'Of course the band would be nothing without Alex'. And it had made me think of someone saying the same thing about Genesis: 'the band would be nothing without Pete'. And I must admit I tensed; I had a wine glass in my hand which broke, and I severed a tendon and a nerve. I was rushed off to the hospital, got stitched up, had an operation later to reconnect everything and just before we were about to go off on tour, with my hand in this weakened state, I felt it was madness. I remember my father talked me into carrying on. He said, 'You're not going to get all the answers to everything you need to know at this point but it's a good time to go with the flow, a time to coast'. He used the word 'coast' as I recall. And I did. But there comes a point when you can coast no more.

TONY: Perhaps Steve was a little distant, because he'd released his solo record and it had done OK. And we weren't quite sure whether he was going to hang about. I was actually a little pissed off that he'd done his solo album at that point, because we needed all the material we could possibly have, and we could certainly have used the song he ended up doing with Randy Crawford. I'd been thinking about doing my own solo album at the same time because I had quite a few pieces like 'Mad Man Moon' which I thought would be fun to do, but had made the decision that if we were going to carry on with the group we would need to pool everything. And then when it came to *Wind And Wuthering*, I felt that of all the albums that we had worked on together, there was more of Steve's contribution than on any other, particularly on 'Eleventh Earl Of Mar' and 'Blood On The Rooftops'. So I had been thinking, 'OK, he's been a bit apart from us, but maybe he's finally in there now; that's great'.

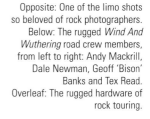

Opposite: One of the limo shots so beloved of rock photographers. Below: The rugged *Wind And Wuthering* road crew members, from left to right: Andy Mackrill, Dale Newman, Geoff 'Bison' Banks and Tex Read. Overleaf: The rugged hardware of rock touring.

NESIS
UITARS
GENESIS
STEVE HACKET
GUITARS
GENES
PHIL CO
DRUM

These pages: Touring can be so tiring – Bunking up (above) and lying down from sheer exhaustion (opposite). Following pages: Tour images from Berlin and Paris, 1977.

MIKE: We were mixing the *Seconds Out* live album. Phil passed Steve in Ladbroke Grove and Steve acted a little oddly. He said, 'Hi Phil' and then never came in, obviously because he got to the studio and thought 'No, I can't do it', went back home and we never saw him again for a while. I think by day three we realized he wasn't coming in. Ideally all of us should have sat down and had a chat and said, 'Look, what's going on? If you want to leave, you want to move on, that's absolutely fine', rather than him not appearing and calling us up to tell us.

PHIL: Steve was living near Ladbroke Grove at that point, and I was driving in from West London on my way to Trident Studios. Just opposite the Hilton on Holland Park Avenue, I saw Steve walking along or waiting for a taxi. I stopped, wound down the window and said, 'Get in.' He said no, that was OK, he'd speak to me or call me later. I thought, 'Fine, maybe he has something to do before he goes to the studio.' I got to Trident, parked, went in and told the others I had just seen Steve. Mike and Tony said, 'Oh, you haven't heard, he didn't tell you? He's left.' I know that Steve has his own take and his own feelings about what happened that day and I realize now I may have underestimated him a little.

STEVE: I think we'd just mixed 'I Know What I Like' and I was thinking, 'I can't face listening to this song any more. I've heard this song a thousand times; we're going over old ground here'. Plus I'd got what I felt were all these very strong ideas that I wasn't able to get on *Wind And Wuthering*. I had this song called 'Hoping Love Will Last' that I wanted Randy Crawford to sing, and no one had heard of Randy Crawford in the UK at that point. It was a song that only a girl could sing. I thought it was a great song, but I felt that the band couldn't do it. There was another piece called 'Please Don't Touch' that became the title track on my second solo album, but which was something that Genesis had rehearsed and I thought was enormously strong and why the hell didn't we use that? I said to myself, 'They're going to take forever, maybe another ten years if I'm in this band, and I can't hang on to ideas for that long'.

So I phoned Mike and said, 'I think I should leave', and he didn't try and talk me out of it. He knew I wasn't happy by then. 'Fine Steve, if that's what you want to do'. And then I bumped into Phil in the street either the same day or the following day. He asked, 'Aren't you going to the studio?' and I said, 'No, I'm not, I'm... Speak to Mike, he'll explain'. I just couldn't bring myself to say the words, couldn't face talking to Phil about it. And I know that he feels slighted by the fact that I wasn't able to, but I thought that if I did speak to him, he might just talk me out of it and convince me to stay. If he and I had had a conversation and I'd gone through the reasons why I felt the need to leave, perhaps I would have gained an ally. Instead of which my mind was made up, I wanted to leave. It was very much Hello, I Must Be Going! And it's not that I didn't love Phil and not that I didn't respect him – and maybe for all the wrong reasons he'll have felt snubbed for the past thirty years – but the fact is I felt I couldn't say anything within a band concept any more.

MY WIFE AND MY FATHER ARE BOTH PAINTERS AND I'VE SAID TO THEM, 'CAN YOU IMAGINE WHAT IT'S LIKE IF YOU'VE GOT FOUR OR FIVE ARTISTS WITH PAINTBRUSHES WORKING ON ONE CANVAS AND YOU CAN'T AGREE ABOUT THE FOREGROUND, THE BACKGROUND, EVEN THE SUBJECT MATTER?'
STEVE HACKETT

TUNING

No Wallys,

Borin

TONY: When Steve announced he was leaving, I was surprised, and disappointed, given the way I felt about his contribution to *Wind And Wuthering*. He had seemed to be asserting himself. Steve was really good for us and had brought certain new elements to the group but there were equally some aspects of what he liked to do that we weren't so keen on and so never got explored, which frustrated him. And, particularly at that stage, I was very much getting my way all the time, which he found a little disconcerting. I think he said as much in various articles afterwards, that I was controlling it too much – and he's probably right. I think he always thought that for some reason I had it in for him, but I really didn't. It's just my way. I always appear to be like that. I actually used to champion him; I remember a few times championing him against Peter, who wasn't quite so sure.

The other thing was that we had started off as five people all trying to write and produce and get our bits on records once a year, and even after we went down to four there wasn't enough room for all of us.

STEVE: I suppose my main disappointment with the band was not that the occasional good idea was passed over in favour of something which was politically expedient, but the fact that we hadn't grown to incorporate other players, other than the ones we needed for live work. I would have liked us to have been able to use an orchestra occasionally, or to have admitted when we were out of our depth and needed somebody to play flute to the standard that my brother plays, for instance. Or get in a fantastic cellist, which is something that I got to explore in my solo years. On reflection, with Genesis, there was this contracting team, the Ten Little Indians effect, getting smaller and smaller every year.

MIKE: When Ant and Peter had left, those were major moments which raised significant questions: are we done now, should the band stop, has the band run its course, was it time to move on to something else? This time, when Steve went, we didn't think that. I'm not trying to say anything brutal about Steve at all; it's simply to do with the time he chose to go. Plus a lot of the guitar parts on the album were not lead guitar at all, more like rhythm parts.

It passed rather smoothly in a way. I don't mean that in an unfair way; it's just that suddenly Steve wasn't there and we mixed the live album and we had to find a way forwards. I'm not really a lead guitarist, and although we thought I could have a go at doing what Steve did a bit, of course I couldn't because he has a very strong and distinctive sound. It took me a while to find a style of playing lead.

TONY: I think we felt we had got past Pete's departure, which was a far more significant thing in terms of public perception. After Steve announced he was leaving there was never a moment when we thought we wouldn't carry on. We did often think, 'Do we get another guitarist?', but the answer to that was no. Mike had obviously played the majority of the rhythm guitar over the years, and he felt he could adapt himself to handling a bit of lead. I felt we could easily carry on after Steve left. I didn't think it was going to be a problem; we could work it out. It would just be different.

And we liked the idea of trying to keep it just to the three of us. We were good friends, we worked well together, we had written the main part of 'Dance On A Volcano' on our own, the three of us. Of course, when we came to record again, I did miss not having a guitarist of the quality of Steve, his ability to play lead lines fluently. And Steve was perhaps a bit more left field than Mike and Phil which would make some edgier things happen.

But there was a sort of clarity about how we could work together that I really liked: fewer personalities to cope with, fewer arguments, far fewer. The three of us writing together was the ideal in a way. We had had five writers, which was tempestuous, and then four, which was easier but still created a sense of two senior and two junior members. With the three of us it felt liberating.

Opposite: At the end of 1977, Steve Hackett headed off in a new direction.
Overleaf: Phil was used to the spotlight from his stage-school days. He claims the cross on the tambourine meant 'Hit here'!

I'M A GREAT BELIEVER THAT CHANGE,
VERY OFTEN NOT LOOKED FOR,
BRINGS SOMETHING NEW AND DYNAMIC,
WHICH IS ALWAYS GOOD. Mike Rutherford

STEVE'S TALE: STEVE HACKETT

It is a strange fact that bands manage to create music which is so cohesive that there appears to be some kind of presiding consciousness which has dreamt it all up. But it is easier when you are inside a band to subscribe to someone else's magic.

I have spent many long hours chatting with Ian McDonald, who spearheaded the original King Crimson, about what we thought were the strengths of our respective teams. He was describing a bunch of gigs that Crimson did at the Marquee. This band was the hottest band on the block. Bowie was a fan. Hendrix went to the shows. Donovan jammed with them. Name drop, name drop. I tried to see them as often as I could, absolutely loved what they did: a band that combined jazz, classical, pop, rock, humour, you name it. In many ways they were a prototype for what we, Genesis, were trying to do. I'd ask Ian, 'What was it like playing those gigs?' 'Oh,' he'd complain, 'it was so hot, that summer of 1969, so hot.' So I'd say 'Well, what about the way the sax worked with the guitar?' and he'd come back with, 'Yeah, wasn't that a terrible sound with the sax miked up through a Marshall cabinet?' We're talking about the difference between heaven and hell, because seeing it as a member of the audience you are not concerned about the details of whether the drummer's ears are being bombarded by the speaker cabinets because the other guys are refusing to point them in a different direction, but you'll get that story from Ginger Baker when he's talking about Cream: this poor sod being deafened by these two bastards either side of him.

When you're out front in the audience you're not suffering under the lash, are you? You're seeing this wonderful ship and its wonderful crew wending its way on a seamless journey. But when you are part of it, it's a bugger: some guys in the band will be smoking in the van, others are non-smokers and why should they have to put up with me and my poisons and my filthy habits? There are so many minor issues and external pressures.

After Genesis it wasn't until I was on stage doing my own shows – and going down well – that my confidence was entirely restored, because I was very scared and suddenly there was no one to blame but myself. It's been a very long journey to the complete restoration of my confidence and the vindication of my own ideas over the past thirty years or so since I left Genesis.

I gave a press interview after I left which raised a hackle or two. It's a very long time ago now, and let me tell you diplomatically... One wishes one could take back words. I suspect that all of us have given our equivalent of that type of interview and when I hear or read Peter saying, 'I'm tired of working with those bastards,' I laugh at it. But I wish I'd

played the diplomat and not so much the young blade trying to cut a dash at the expense of his whole regiment. It's never worth being rancorous in print because it lasts a very long time although the spoken moment is fleeting.

Most journalists are looking for an exposé; it's far more interesting to feature somebody sounding off, firing off a few ill-chosen words or a few broadsides at the mother ship. And for some reason those sort of things tend to happen in America because of the amount of ground that you've got to cover and the sheer number of interviews you have to do. It's a bit like the process that every aspiring president undergoes: you're on tour, you're talking to as many people as possible and you're barely human by the end of every excursion because on an average day of meeting the American press or talking to them by phone, you are doing twenty or thirty interviews. In the end you crack. Much as I love America, it can break you down and leave you a babbling wreck.

It's far far better to place your frustrations into your forthcoming work rather than having a go at people you've worked with. I like to think the others laughed it off and I like to think that I've apologized to them since for anything that I may have said. I think there's still a lot of respect towards each other. I get that feeling.

My career since Genesis has pursued its own organic furrow. I tend to have a big hit once every ten years. The rest of it is a gigantic experiment, but it doesn't matter to me whether it succeeds or fails, I'm more interested in creating unlikely constructions. I suspect that Genesis operated in the same way.

I'm very happy with the idea that you should approach the song with a different ethos each time. It is a very good thing. It means that if I produce a song like 'Camino Royale' which I think is perhaps my greatest tune, from an album called Highly Strung, I know that one day I'll record a version of it that is extended with an orchestra. In fact we named my record company, Camino, after that song, a track which uses both the idea of lead chords and Latin rhythms, where Latin grooves meets the blues, and as far as I'm concerned, it's like a jam session in heaven that's performed and refined into some finished version where all the instruments have their say, and all the forms converge. You can't put your finger on it. You can't say it's jazz, you can't say it's classical, you can't say it's Latin. It's all of those things and yet it's none of them. I like the idea of fusion, the idea that all these things that shouldn't co-exist can.

Music is this potential time machine, a vehicle that can convey you to all manner of times and places. We did a certain amount of that with Genesis: yes, here we go, now we're off to Greece and the world of the myths. Music is a limitless thing and I find it amazing that Genesis has pretty much tried to cover the whole of music, from Phil working with Eric Clapton, doing a blues session with BB King or playing with one of my personal heroes, Paul Butterfield, to Tony's classical album Seven.

Fusion does not have to lead to confusion. It should be possible to make the join seamless between all these various forms and they should be able to speak to each other and be relevant to each other. The Dorian scale in blues becomes relevant to convoluted chord changes that appeared in baroque times and you've got an aspect of almost gospel in there that needs to be addressed as well. Collision is a term that I believe scientists are using to describe multiverses. Well perhaps that same thing can exist in music. I gather the multiverse theory collides again with the idea of the big bang, that it may have been a number of big bangs, any number of universes impinging one upon another. I'm digressing and yet somehow it's the nub of all of this. Digression seems to be the name of the game for me rather than containment, if there is such a thing.

Steve Hackett's first solo album, *Voyage Of The Acolyte*, was released in 1975 while he was still part of Genesis; his first release after leaving was 1978's *Please Don't Touch*, featuring vocal contributions from Richie Havens and Randy Crawford. Exploration has been a keynote of his subsequent career, whether the straighter pop sensibilities of *Cured* in 1981 or the influences of Brazilian music on *Till We Have Faces* three years later; he co-founded supergroup GTR with ex-Yes guitarist Steve Howe. He has successfully ignored the constraints of genre pigeon-holing, recording Vivaldi's Guitar Concerto with the London Chamber Orchestra and releasing *Sketches Of Satie* with his brother John, a regular collaborator, on flute. In 1996 Steve put together a diverse team of musicians, including Chester Thompson and Bill Bruford, to create *Genesis Revisited*, a series of re-interpretations of classic Genesis tracks.

THE DRUMMERS' TALE, PART IV: BILL BRUFORD

There was a time, I think, when Phil Collins used to set up my drums. I recall one gig at Barnstaple Town Hall when I was in Yes and Phil was with his group Flaming Youth. He wasn't getting much work at that time and quite liked what I was doing with Yes so he would come along and do the odd drum roadie job. He was younger than me and probably saw Yes as a famous group at the time. Even after he joined Genesis I wasn't terribly aware of him until we fast forward to 1976, when he was running Brand X, and asked me to come and play percussion to his drums.

I think everybody in Yes and King Crimson thought that Genesis would never make it because they sounded like a combination of the two groups. We thought they might be too late – we'd been there and done it. We saw them along the lines of 'Genesis are quite fun, but they've got a guitarist who sits down like Robert Fripp and a drummer who plays a bit like Bill: the Americans have already had that...' How wrong can you be? We were an arrogant lot, and I was pretty insufferable around that time, cocky as hell. So I think when I re-established contact with Phil in the Brand X set-up I was the senior guy, and when I joined Genesis they probably thought they had a bit of a rock star on their hands.

I was rehearsing with Brand X and Phil was moaning away about Peter Gabriel leaving. Evidently, they had been trying out various singers and he was exasperated by wading through the auditions. He said something like, 'They're all bloody useless. I can sing better than they can,' as people do. And I think I suggested to him, 'Why don't you sing and I'll play the drums for a while, so you can get yourself comfortable.' Phil once told me that if a drummer goes up front to sing, his nightmare is that the rhythm will fall apart behind him. He knew our styles were similar and probably thought, 'Bill's reliable and if he could hold the drum chair down then I could sing.' The fact that he wanted to sing was not a huge surprise. Everybody knew he sang back-up vocals for Genesis and could do them while drumming. I'd also heard him do wonderful feats of musicianship in Brand X, singing melody lines entirely independent of the rhythm he was playing.

Phil's a considerable natural talent. He's one of these guys who can figure out the sticking pattern of a double paradiddle if he ever needs to use one, but even when he's figured out how to do it, he's unlikely to know what it's called. He is also an amazing mimic. He could do a brilliant impression of a sea lion – if you closed your eyes, you'd swear that there was a sea lion in the room. He very quickly absorbs new mannerisms in voices, in sounds, in drumming, a bit like blotting paper. It's a very useful ability. And when he

began to sing with Genesis, we all thought he sounded just like Peter Gabriel, which was not at all a bad thing for smoothing the transition period.

When the idea of playing with Genesis came up I was in quite a tricky place. I'd left Yes for King Crimson, which had instantly fallen apart. I'd been off and played with bands like Gong, National Health and several other scratchy bands of the day, so the offer of a tour with Genesis didn't sound bad to me. First of all I'd make some money – as I recall I was getting £500 a week, which was a huge sum of money, an absolute fortune then; secondly the tour was going to the right kind of big stadiums in Northeast America. It sounded about right as a career move.

The band were immediately very friendly, funny and very accommodating: the mechanics of daily life were very well taken care of. We went to America first for ten days of rehearsal in Dallas. It seemed incredibly extravagant. I'd barely spent ten minutes rehearsing at such a high level of production. I like to wing it a bit on stage, but Genesis were very, very precise. I'm much more accustomed to making it up as I'm going along, but they wanted the right notes in the right place, everything to be tickety-boo. There was no music, nothing written down; I'd learnt the tunes from the albums, and if it felt a little different from what Phil would have done, people would look at me and say, 'Hey, Bill, could you make it sound a bit more like the record?' I'm probably not as good at mimicking Phil as Phil is at mimicking others, and my style doubtless stuck out a bit, but nevertheless they knew that the beat wasn't going to fall apart and that the stage performances were going to function OK because I was a reliable, if independent, character. Maybe a bit of a loose cannon!

It is quite possible that I caused irritation, because my nature is to play a piece differently every night even though there are only so many ways you can play 'Supper's Ready' on a drum kit without the song unravelling. I probably annoyed the heck out of Tony and the others: 'Why doesn't Bill just stick to the parts?' They must have gritted their teeth and bit their tongues, because they were always extremely nice about it. If I were a better session musician I'd have done what I was told, especially as providing exactly what was required was really the basis on which I had been hired. However, not being much of the session type, I didn't do terribly well at just delivering the parts. In fact, what finally drove me out of rock'n'roll was the repetition. That's what had separated me from Yes. Why I had found King Crimson so attractive was because they were way more open: 'Surprise us, go ahead, let's improvise, terrific.' And having gone from that atmosphere back into Genesis who were the most regulated of the lot, I think I behaved rather badly – and I have been apologizing to them ever since.

The overall touring environment was great. We swam a lot, because the tour fell over the summer, and in those days it was great because you could relax. The chances were that there were no interviews to do because the band were handling all the press, and once I'd arrived from the airport at midday, I generally had the rest of the afternoon to myself. The group were very pleasant. They didn't waste money, but they didn't stint either. Tony Smith was a wonderful manager: I can remember sitting down at my kit on the first night of the first tour, a deafening roar coming from the audience, picking up my sticks and looking down and there was something on the snare drum, a small note from Tony with words to the effect of 'Great, Bill, glad you could come, here's your return ticket'. And there was my return air ticket, because I'd probably already been making a fuss about it.

The mood in Genesis was such a contrast to the chaos of Yes, where nobody could agree what day of the week it was and any time anyone said, 'Shall we make a record?', everybody would start arguing. It was hopeless. How we in Yes ever got anything done, I still don't know. Within Genesis the musical, staging and logistical decisions seemed to be made quite efficiently and rather quietly between, presumably, Tony and Mike with Phil. Steve I remember was unhappy about something for much of this period and left very shortly afterwards.

Phil and I were soul mates, drummers together, we liked that side of things. I think he liked the drumming more than the singing, to tell you the truth. In fact, I think he may even still prefer the drumming to the singing. We had a terrific, powerful double drum thing together in 'The Cinema Show', and I also enjoyed 'Squonk' and 'Dance On A Volcano', and much of 'Supper's Ready'. Like the other drummers in progressive rock I tended to like the gritty bits where all the action was happening with the drums. I never much cared for the twinkly bits where it all goes fey; I still don't.

1976 was my Genesis year, and it wasn't even a full year – only March to late summer. At the end of the tour I had a feeling that I ought to get back to work. In a very patronizing way, I felt this had all been good fun, a bit like a reunion tour, but I should now concentrate on what I hoped would be my first record, which did subsequently happen. All along I am sure the group had assumed I'd get off at the next bus stop. It was a short moment in a longish career. But I realize that I came away with a valuable lesson – although I hadn't really absorbed it at the time – that the musician exists to serve the music rather than the music existing to serve the musician. It is a much better way round, but it took me a while to understand that. I'm eternally grateful to Genesis for being so nice to me while I sniped gently from the sidelines. If anybody was at fault, it was me. Honestly, I'd be much better now. Do you want to have another go, lads?

Bill Bruford became a professional drummer in 1968, and spent the next six years touring with Yes and King Crimson. After a period working and appearing with Gong, UK and National Health, as well as his 1976 tours with Genesis, Bill was ready to release his own albums under the group name Bruford. Following a reconstitution of King Crimson between 1980 and 1984, he founded Earthworks, an electro-acoustic jazz group with pianist Django Bates and saxophonist Iain Bellamy. Alongside Earthworks' continued development, Bill has toured extensively, established a successful series of drum clinics and set up his own record labels, Summerfold and Winterfold records.

CHAPTER NINE

THREE POINT TURN

MIKE: After Steve left I wasn't gagging to be the band's lead guitarist. But if we had started to bring in someone brand-new at that point, given the chemistry of the band, it would have been a major deal. We had to weigh that against the chances of me finding my feet, bolstered by the fact that much of our material did not rely on a traditional lead guitar role.

TONY: Mike's playing was a little thin on *And Then There Were Three*, I think. There was one guitar solo, on the song 'Burning Rope', which I had written the line for. If Steve had been playing the solo, I would probably have hoped to have gone further and expanded it, but Mike just played the notes – and it still sounds all right. He obviously needed to gain confidence to feel comfortable in the role, and by the time we got to, say, *Abacab*, his guitar playing had really improved and he was able to contribute fully as a lead guitarist in addition to everything else that he did.

MIKE: We did miss Steve's input, of course, but at the very start of writing *Trick Of The Tail*, when Steve had been off on his solo album and missed the first few days, Tony, Phil and I had written as a trio, so we'd been through that moment before in a way. Nevertheless the album did suffer. I managed to scrape through the lead part, just. And when I hear it back it sounds slightly dodgy because I lacked – and consequently the album lacked – Steve's ability and his lovely way of playing, which I didn't possess. Of all our albums *And Then There Were Three* was the weakest, without a doubt.

TONY: I always felt that *And Then There Were Three* was a slightly strange album. Phil was somewhat distracted during this period, because of his divorce, and in all honesty he hadn't contributed very much as a writer right up to and including this album. Which left Mike and me as the main writers: Mike provided 'Deep In The Motherlode', 'Say it's Alright Joe' and 'Snowbound', and I brought in 'Undertow', 'Many Too Many', 'Burning Rope' and 'The Lady Lies'.

The most exciting moment for me in the studio was when Mike played a big flanged guitar riff and I started playing a few chords along to it; suddenly the combination sounded fantastic, this very simple little thing, which became 'Follow You Follow Me'. And having worked it up, we decided, 'Let's keep this really simple'. Mike went off and wrote a very simple love song lyric on top of it, trying not to move away from the flavour of the piece, because it was a song that made you feel warm. It was a happy song – which is something that we're not really very good at – and it needed a love lyric where everything went right. It was a whole new experience.

We were lucky that we had the hit single with that song, because it gave out the positive impression that we had survived all the changes we'd been through in the two or three years before. We had dropped down to a three-piece, which might have been a drawback; punk music was coming in and was supposed to be doing away with groups like us. But at exactly that moment we had our first hit single and so the first of our albums that sold in any quantity. It was a very strange juxtaposition, Having been an underground group, we were suddenly being played on the radio, which was a novel experience for us. And for many of our friends and relatives, it was the first time we had ever appeared in their personal consciousness. If Genesis had never released 'Follow You Follow Me', if we'd split up before it came out, most people would never have heard of the group.

Although we had slightly missed an additional guitarist on *And Then There Were Three*, for the live band we had been able to introduce a guitarist of the quality of Daryl Stuermer, who was so versatile he gave us another strength. We were at our strongest live, because we not only had Daryl, we also had Chester Thompson on drums.

MIKE: Phil had first introduced us to Chester for the *Wind And Wuthering* tour in 1977, when he took over the drum seat from Bill Bruford. There are other drummers I know who might be able to copy Phil better, but that was not what we were looking for. We wanted someone to bring their own style of playing.

Opposite: Rural retreat on the common by Phil's house, the Old Croft at Shalford. Phil is the clear winner in that year's Tony Smith lookalike contest. Tony Banks has always believed his T-shirt says 'Genesis' in Japanese. Overleaf, clockwise from left: Tony's kit including (bottom of the left-hand rack of keyboards) the long-serving Mellotron; the Relight studio in Hilvarenbeek in Holland, where both *Wind And Wuthering* and *And Then There Were Three* were recorded; and outside the studios at Shepperton, where the 'Follow You Follow Me' video was shot, February 1978.

Above: Chester Thompson soundchecking for the Knebworth Festival in June 1978. Chester remembers that when he first joined the touring band, it took him a couple of weeks to tune his ear into the different British accents. 'It would be the strangest feeling to sit in a room when you're supposedly speaking the same language and not understand anything of what was going on'.

Phil always had a great overview, knowing what Chester could add, but always within the bounds of what was right for any particular song. Chester comes from a very musical background and from an area of drumming where he works in many different musical genres. I'm sure that at some point he must have wondered, 'What am I doing here?', but also he enjoyed the challenge, because for him playing our kind of music was quite foreign.

PHIL: I'd seen Chester perform with Weather Report, but that wasn't what convinced me. Although there were certain versions of Weather Report I really liked, I wasn't particularly in love with the version Chester was part of. What convinced me was that a friend of mine played me Frank Zappa's album *Roxy And Elsewhere (Live)*, which featured Chester and Ralph Humphrey on drums. I had always liked Zappa, and would check out whatever he was doing, and this live album was fantastic. There was one song called 'More Trouble Every Day', which had a particular drum fill where these two drummers played a great move together. And I thought, 'I want to do that with that guy'.

I had never met Chester, but I managed to track him down, called him up and said, 'Listen, I play in Genesis, I don't know if you know us. Do you want to join us?' And Chester said, 'Sure'. He flew over to England to rehearse with us. And that was the first time he met everybody. Bizarre to think that there was no audition process. Mike and Tony just trusted me.

TONY: When Phil had originally suggested Chester my immediate reaction was, 'God, I wouldn't have thought somebody who has played with Zappa and Weather Report would want to do this'. But when he arrived he was very up for it, and I noticed he really liked some of our more elaborate musical moments like 'One For The Vine'. That was significant to me, because a piece like that is not to everybody's taste. It is very structured music and requires every beat to be in the right place. But Chester was happy to do that even though he is a naturally jazzy drummer.

PHIL: Sometimes Chester would be trying to interpret things I had played on the albums, which I had based on things that he might have played. I'd say, 'But I'm just trying to play like you guys, like an R&B player.' So sometimes the musical influences would go round and round in circles. What Chester and I found, when we later worked with the Earth Wind & Fire guys, was that musicians from the R&B world did not quite get this English style of music initially, because it was not part of their musical culture, and it offered something else, whether that was being quaint or English or unAmerican. That is the way I think the music of Genesis should be described, not that it is stiff or lacks swing, because I was trying my damnedest to make it swing!

TONY: Although Chester came from a slightly different area of music, he was very able to adapt to what we were doing, and he added to our very English kind of music a hint of something which I really liked. A song like 'The Cinema Show' really developed and came alive with the double drumming between Chester and Phil – which we had first tried out with Bill Bruford.

SECONDS OUT WAS A MUCH BETTER LIVE ALBUM THAN GENESIS LIVE. WE HAD TAKEN IT SERIOUSLY AS A LIVE ALBUM. BUT ALSO WE WERE NOW MUCH BETTER LIVE PERFORMERS. Tony Banks

MIKE: With Chester in place, when the tour for *And Then There Were Three* came up, we needed to add a guitarist to the live line-up. There was no question in my mind, and I think Tony and Phil would agree, that American session musicians at the time were way ahead of their English counterparts. They had the chops, as they say; even a few guys playing in a Holiday Inn bar band would have fantastic licks. America had a much stronger array of top players; there was no comparison with England, and had there been guys of the same calibre we would have looked in the UK. England is all about the feel – the Sex Pistols came from England and I don't think they would have worked if they had come from the States – while Americans have that technique.

I flew over to New York to find a guitarist. There was a deadline because we were due to go out on tour a couple of months later. The first person we had got hold of was Alphonso Johnson, who had played with Weather Report and Billy Cobham. Part of our thinking at the time was to decide whether we should bring in a bass player or a guitarist, or maybe somebody who could handle both so he and I could interchange. Alphonso was a lovely guy, but definitely a bass player who could play a bit of guitar, rather than the other way around – and it seemed that really what we needed was a guitarist who could play some bass.

TONY: Alphonso Johnson's strengths were that he had already worked with Chester in Weather Report, and as a bass player he might be able to free Mike up to play more guitar. But Alphonso himself didn't feel he was a good enough guitarist to take on the role, and in fact was the person who recommended Daryl Stuermer.

MIKE: I had seen a few guys, including Elliot Randall, a great session musician with Steely Dan amongst others. What was wrong with Elliot was not his ability, because he's a great player, but I gave him four or five songs to listen to, and when we played 'Squonk' as a kind of audition piece Elliot said, 'How do you want it? Do you want it country, or what?' His skills were fantastic, but he couldn't quite see that within the context of Genesis there was only one possible way to play it. Daryl Stuermer came in and saw that straight away. It was a very easy choice. He totally understood our music.

Overleaf: Daryl and Mike continue the distinguished Genesis tradition of perfecting the art of twelve-string tuning, backstage in Ohio on the *And Then There Were Three* tour, 1978.

TONY: Mike brought back some tapes for us to listen to and Daryl stood out. He'd been working with Jean-Luc Ponty, and with Chester being from the jazz-rock world, we thought that it was more than likely that they would gel. We were intrigued to learn that there were musicians in that world of American session players who seemed to like the kind of music we were making, who actually liked the fact that it was very unAmerican, which was curious.

Daryl, it was immediately obvious, could play anything and he could adapt to what we were doing: he was a very lucky find and another great asset alongside Chester. He could play by ear and pick up everything extremely quickly. When we were running the rehearsal sessions for the tour, Daryl knew the stuff better than we did. We kept asking him, 'Hey, how does that bit go?', so we knew that if something went wrong on stage, it was never going to be Daryl's fault.

DARYL HAS ASTONISHING TECHNICAL ABILITY. SOMETIMES IT'S IMPORTANT TO SLOW HIM DOWN BECAUSE HE PLAYS SO INCREDIBLY FAST – ALTHOUGH THAT WAS GREAT FOR OUR ENERGY LEVELS ON THE LIVE SHOWS. Mike Rutherford

TONY: Having a guitarist of probably even greater technical ability and fluency than Steve meant we could do things we'd never have tried before. We decided to include 'In The Cage' as a separate song, taking it out of context of *The Lamb*. It might have seemed an unusual choice, but when we brought Daryl in, he added excitement because he could play very fast and extremely in time.

We did consider the possibility of using both Daryl and Chester on the studio albums but when we actually reached the recording stage on the next album, we thought, 'No, we're here and there's a vibe going, we'll stick with it', even though at times we were a little restricted by that.

Above: Daryl and (right) Mike. Daryl says of Mike that he has always been easy to work with. 'If he could tell I wasn't sure what I was supposed to do he would say, "Oh, you can just do this" and that's the way it's always been. Nothing has changed. It's just got even easier over the years.'

PHIL: The first tour with Chester, back in 1977, included three American tours, two European tours and a Japanese tour – that was really what broke my first marriage up: the absence from the family. There was a point when my wife had gone back to Vancouver, where her family had moved to, and our two children were with her. I remember going to the Crown in Chiddingfold to have a meeting with Tony and Mike and Tony Smith and saying, 'Listen, I've got to go to Canada. I've got to bring my wife and kids back', because obviously I was missing the kids terribly and I thought there was a chance that the marriage could survive.

'And if we can do everything out in Vancouver' – which was totally unrealistic – 'if we could do everything there, then I'm in the band, otherwise I'm off'. They said, 'Well, we've been writing a lot of stuff. Why don't you go and sort yourself out and we'll do our solo albums'. And that's how their solo albums got going.

TONY: Phil was having trouble with his marriage; he wanted to try and salvage it. So rather than push him into a corner by saying, 'Right, that's it', we decided to put everything to do with Genesis on hold for a few months. Mike and I had wanted to do solo albums for a long time. And that proved to be a great experience for us.

MIKE: It's another example of how this band works. We've never had a master plan that we have to stick to. When Phil said, 'Listen, I may have to move to North America, I've got to go to Vancouver', we told him, 'Well, go and see'. I thoroughly agreed with his choice: I always think that family has to come first. So if that's where he was going to be living we would find a way to carry on. It was only a question of geography. And while he headed off to Canada we concentrated on our solo albums.

TONY: I used the opportunity of a solo album to go a little bit further than I had within the band. I allowed myself a bit of space. I'd come across a lovely little 1950s science fiction story called 'Flowers For Algernon', by a writer called Daniel Keyes, that I wanted to base the thing on. I wrote all the lyrics and was quite a long way down the line when I learnt that, amazingly, a stage musical version of 'Flowers For Algernon' was being put on in England. I had no idea whether this musical was going to be the new *Jesus Christ, Superstar* or not, but the advice I got from everybody was that I should consider changing tack.

Below: Tony playing guitar in his home studio, August 1979.

So I decided I could create a new story by using a lot of the same lyrics I'd already written – I'd worked hard on them, and didn't want to waste them – and changing two or three key plotlines. I regret doing that. I think the album would have been good as I initially conceived it, because the original short story was great. And especially as the musical – which I went to see; it wasn't bad, Michael Crawford was the lead – only lasted for about nine days.

Dave Hentschel had found us Polar Studios in Stockholm, the recording studio set up by ABBA. I went out there, and Dave got mumps, so for the first couple of weeks on the album I was there with just the tape op, Dave Bascombe, who later went on to become a successful engineer/producer. We laid down all the basic tracks ourselves, with me playing all the instruments apart from drums, including guitar and bass; and I brought in a singer called Kim Beacon, because I wasn't going to do the singing myself. For the drums I asked Chester Thompson to come and play; I thought it would be nice to have a familiar face. And I think the result had a very strong atmosphere. In terms of production values it's not that brilliant, but as a unified piece it's one of the best things I've ever done. I'm still very proud of it. It was released while we were writing *Duke*. The first week it came in at number twenty-two and I thought, 'Hey, this is it, I'm off'. The next week it was number twenty-three and then after that it sank without trace.

I had thought that it would be bought by the same people who had liked tracks like 'Afterglow' from the *Wind And Wuthering* period, pieces I'd written which had been quite highly rated. But there were no singles on the album and then Mike's solo album came out about a week later and did better than mine, which was a bit frustrating – although nothing like a year later when Phil brought out his...

MIKE: In those days, if you were a successful English band, there was still a reasonable market for a solo album, which might be quite average but still perform OK and reach the top twenty. That wasn't why we did it, but it did mean there was a chance to try out things in a different area.

I had read a book called *Smallcreep's Day*, written by Peter Currell Brown, a guy who worked on a production line in a factory. I can hardly remember the story now, but it talked about the way that real life can be like a conveyor belt moving through the factory's machines. I decided not to sing myself, and in the end found a singer called Noel McCalla, lovely voice, huge range. I also booked ABBA's Polar Studios in Stockholm and went out with Simon Phillips on drums, Morris Pert – and Ant on keyboards. As a leader I think I slightly missed the sharing we experienced in Genesis, but because I had to make all the decisions it certainly sharpened up my instincts.

Above: Mike backstage at the Knebworth festival 1978.
Overleaf: The Genesis family outside the Hotel la Trémoille in Paris – left to right: Mike, Angie Rutherford holding Kate, nanny Karen who later married Genesis sound man Craig Schertz. Andy Collins with Joely, Phil with Simon on his shoulders, Margaret Banks holding Ben, Tony, Daryl and Michaela Stuermer, Chester.

Above: Phil with his son Simon in Vancouver, 1979.
Right: Phil writing on the road.
Opposite: Drawing on his repertoire of theatrical faces for 'The Lady Lies'.

PHIL: I came back from Canada after a couple of months – domestically things had not changed – by which time Tony and Mike were well into their own albums, so I started to look at my studio equipment. The first time we'd been to Japan, although it was very disorientating and at home my life was falling apart, something had happened that musically was really significant for me. We were offered the first Roland drum machines off the production line. They were brand new; they'd hardly reached outside Japan. Initially I had said I didn't want one, because I thought the sound was robotic and tinny. I didn't think I needed one. But by the end of the year, with my wife and the two kids gone, and the two dogs gone, my home just outside Guildford was in a bit of a state. I was there with all this recording equipment and playing with anyone who asked me. I'd always played with everybody, but especially at this stage I was throwing myself into anything and everything that came along. Brand X was still around and I met Eric Clapton, who was a neighbour, John Martyn, Phillip Bailey. I worked with Peter on his third album. It was a very busy, but very productive, period, and some great music came out of it, but it was wall-to-wall work. And I decided that maybe the drum machine wasn't a bad idea if I was to start writing.

That's when I started writing my own songs. And I really loved it. I didn't see it as making a record. I was learning how to play the piano. I only had eight tracks on the recorder, so I used the stereo Prophet synth, a stereo electric piano, the Roland drum machine, added a guide vocal and the song was almost there. I was just writing little doodles: if I saw the meters moving I was quite happy. And that's why on *Face Value* in particular there are odd bar lengths, and if you had the separate tracks up, you could hear the phone ringing or the fridge motor clicking on and off, because it was all very low tech. It wasn't cathartic but it was obviously therapeutic.

> BECAUSE I WAS NOT VERY ARTICULATE OR I FELT THAT I WASN'T VERY ARTICULATE, I WAS WRITING THESE SONGS AS MESSAGES IN SOME RESPECTS. THE SONG-WRITING WAS LIKE KEEPING A DIARY.
> PHIL COLLINS

MIKE: We hadn't had much communication with Phil during this period, although Tony Smith was obviously in touch with him. We hadn't set a timescale. It was up to Phil to say when he felt ready to start working with us again.

PHIL: I was ambling, meandering through these little sketches I was writing. Mike and Tony finished their albums and we decided to get back to do a group album, so everybody moved into my house because I was living on my own. Brand X had been living there on and off, we'd done some recording there, and things had gone off the rails a bit, drinking too much...

The studio was in the master bedroom, which basically had nothing in it apart from my piano, the keyboards and the demo equipment. There was a secondary bedroom which I also took everything out of and put the Genesis equipment in.

MIKE: We wrote *Duke* at Phil's house. Prior to that, *And Then There Were Three* had been very much some of my songs with some of Tony's songs, whereas Genesis had started off as a collective. We had gone full circle after Peter left and ended up with songs written by the individuals, and I think the previous album had suffered precisely because there were fewer group songs. Having been out there doing solo work, I felt, probably subconsciously, it would be good to get back to what we used to do, which was writing together. And with *Duke* we turned that corner.

PHIL: Because Mike and Tony had completed their albums, and I was doing what I didn't even know was going to be my first solo record, there was a scarcity of good material, which we

Previous pages: Images from the *And Then There Were Three* tour, 1978.
Below: The new Genesis line-up, including touring members Daryl Stuermer and Chester Thompson.

used as an excuse to start writing together again, and we wrote some great group compositions like 'Turn It On Again' and 'Duchess'. I have very fond memories of those rehearsal days at that house, the Old Croft in Shalford.

Tony and Mike each had a couple of pieces left over from their albums, and asked me, 'What have you been doing?' I played them the material I'd been working on and they chose two of the songs, 'Misunderstanding' and 'Please Don't Ask', which was the most personal song I've probably ever written.

TONY: During the time we'd been away Phil had started to write material on his own, which is something he'd never really done before, and he played us some of these pieces for possible use on the Genesis album; we made a selection of the ones we heard including 'Misunderstanding' and 'Please Don't Ask' which we liked a lot.

PHIL: Tony Banks claims to this day that I didn't play them 'In The Air Tonight', because he reckons that they'd have chosen it if they'd heard it, but I know I played them everything. I didn't want to hold anything back because I didn't know I was going to make a record at that point.

TONY: Phil didn't play us 'In the Air Tonight', because if he had and we'd rejected it I'd be very pissed off. I don't think he'd written it at that point, that's why.

MIKE: No one can remember whether we heard 'In The Air Tonight'. I'd like to think that if I had heard it, I would have remembered.

TONY: Mike and I were slightly more devoid of ideas. So we started writing in the rehearsal room, improvising and developing ideas. I had one little four-bar idea and didn't know where it would go or what we could do with it but working with the group, it became an extended instrumental piece leading into 'Behind The Lines'. I found that exciting because it hadn't existed before we got into the rehearsal room. The same happened with 'Duchess', which was a little drum machine sound I was trying to imitate on the keyboard: that turned into what is probably one of my favourite Genesis songs. I love the way the song comes out of nothing and goes back to nothing, a very simple approach to the career of a female rock star, called Duchess obviously. In the first verse she's up and coming, in the second verse she's made it and by the third verse she's on the way downhill again. A very simple little tale, with simple emotions.

Mike had one riff left over from *Smallcreep's Day* which was fantastic, so good I wondered why he hadn't used it on his album... We stuck his riff and one of my leftovers together, thinking originally it might form a link within a longer song, joining 'Behind The Lines' and 'Duchess' with 'Duke's Travels' and 'Duke's End'. We put in this bridging section, 'Turn It On Again', but when we heard it back we thought, 'This is much too good to be just a link' so we doubled it up, span out the chorus at the end and wrote a song on top of it. What really transformed that song was the drumming. Both Mike's riff and my piece were slower and heavier, but Phil's drumming made it brisker and more rocky, and the lyric, which Mike wrote, was easy for people to relate to. Phil had also developed as a singer. On *Trick Of The Tail* and *Wind And Wuthering*, and even on *And Then There Were Three*, there were times where it sounded as if he was not totally convinced himself, although on stage he was getting stronger and stronger. But his singing really started to happen with *Duke*. With all the demos that had been recorded at his house on top of everything he'd been through, he had developed a way of singing that sounded great on tracks like 'Behind The Lines' and 'Duchess', real singer's songs.

Duke is my favourite Genesis album. It was a good time all round in our career. It was far and away our most successful album, our first number one album in the UK, even a bit of a hit in the States, where 'Misunderstanding' did well as a single. It was a good moment. When I hear it now there is still something about the opening of 'Behind The Lines'. It is so optimistic.

Overleaf: Cast and crew members, including: back row, fourth from right, the late Craig Schertz; front row, from left: Tex Read, Alan Owen, Dale Newman, ML and Andy Mackrill; at the very front, tour manager Dik Frazer.

DUKE BROUGHT THE BAND BACK TOGETHER AGAIN AFTER WE HAD ALL BEEN OFF ON OUR DIFFERENT TANGENTS. Mike Rutherford

TONY: We had never had a particularly positive reaction from journalists. The only moment I ever remembered getting reasonable press was when Peter left in '76, as did Peter. And we actually got quite good reviews then. One or two people, journalists like Barbara Charone and Hugh Fielder on *Sounds* were big fans and wrote good things about us. But by the time we got to around1980 we were considered public enemy number one. Because we had survived. We were supposed to have been killed off by punk, and yet we were bigger than ever. And at that point our press just became terrible. What happened was that the writers on newspapers like *NME* – who I have to say, unfortunately, were pretty good writers – decided that they were really going to get their teeth into people like us, and they did. Fortunately it had no effect on our popularity. But they did write pretty badly about us and to this day it's never really recovered. And now that the journalists from that period are distributed throughout the mainstream newspapers, they still hate us. That's in the UK. It's not been the same in other countries, where our press has always been an awful lot better. The lack of critical acclaim was depressing, especially as Peter was getting very good critical acclaim. Much as I thought Peter deserved it – don't get me wrong – it was still irritating.

I stopped reading reviews in about 1978, particularly when my first solo album, *A Curious Feeling*, came out. There had been a review in one of the papers, which Phil had read. I asked him what it was like. He said, 'How shall I put this, par for the course. I wouldn't read it if I were you'. So I never read anything after that.

PHIL: While I was rehearsing with Brand X during those difficult days, Tony Smith had come down to ask me if I was OK, because I was a bit depressed about the marriage break-up, and he asked me what I'd been doing. I told him I'd been recording some of my own songs, but it was not on my horizon to do a vocal solo album. If I was thinking of a solo album it would have been a jazz-rock thing. Tony said, 'I'd love to hear some of the songs', so I took him to my Mini which was parked outside and I played him some of them on the cassette player – and he was really positive about them.

Later I had a meeting with Ahmet Ertegun from Atlantic Records who was in England at that time. I liked Ahmet and he liked me – he always called me the son he never had. So I had been nominated as the person to go and play *Duke* to him at his house in Kensington. We wanted to see what he thought because I guess after *And Then There Were Three* and 'Follow You Follow Me' the record company was keen for us not to lose the plot. I took a cassette of my demos with me and Ahmet, like Tony Smith, asked me if I'd been OK; I felt like an invalid. 'Yeah, I've been writing'. He said he'd like to hear some of the tracks, and his reaction to my demos was incredible. He said, 'I'd do anything you want me to do to make this record happen. You have to make this an album'. And because it was Ahmet saying this, I suddenly saw things from a different point of view.

I played the demos to Hugh Padgham, who co-produced *Face Value* with me, saying, 'I can't face playing this stuff again, it has spirit, it has an atmosphere', and Hugh said, 'We can probably use the demos'. We copied them onto 16 track at the Townhouse studios and started adding stuff on top of them. A guy called John Kolodner, who was with Atlantic in the UK and went on to become a bigwig at Geffen, told me, 'Give me a wish list of who you'd like to be on this record with you', so I wrote down everybody I liked, from Eric Clapton and David Crosby to Stephen Bishop and Earth Wind & Fire, and John made most of that happen. Ahmet came down to the final mix in the cutting room in New York, because he'd been so involved in every process, and supportive every step. We were playing back 'In The Air Tonight'. The drums don't come in until the end but Ahmet didn't know that at this point, because on the demo the drums hadn't come in at all; it was only drum machine all the way.

And he was saying, 'Where's the down beat, where's the backbeat?' I said, 'The drums come in in a minute.' 'Yeah, you know that, I know that but kids don't know that; you've got to put the drums on earlier.'

So we added some drums to the mix and put it out as a single. It was a surprise. The single came in at number thirty-six, I did *Top Of The Pops* with Dave Lee Travis, and in one of the down moments he said, 'This record is going to be top three.' I didn't believe him, because it had been made so haphazardly, but the next week, there it was at number three. And then Mark Chapman shot John Lennon and that was that.

Below: The threesome at work in a hotel room, Scotland, 1980. Overleaf: The live line-up of Tony, Daryl, Chester, Phil and Mike, photographed in 1980 by Jill Furmanovsky.

THE GUITARIST'S TALE: DARYL STUERMER

In Milwaukee I had a band called Sweetbottom with my brother. One day we all went to Chicago, which is only ninety miles away, to see Frank Zappa's band, and dropped in to Frank's Drum Shop so our drummer could pick up some drum sticks. There was another guy standing at the counter buying some sticks. Our drummer Mike asked him if he was going to the Zappa concert that night, and the guy looked over and said, 'Well, I'm in the band.' It was Chester Thompson.

The next time Zappa was in Milwaukee we invited the band down to Sardino's, the nightclub where Sweetbottom played five nights a week. Chester, the keyboard player George Duke and some of the others came over and sat in with us. As soon as Chester started playing I could feel the hair on my arms rise. I had played with some very good musicians but Chester was on this next level. The groove he set down was better than any groove from any drummer I had played with. Right away I felt some kind of synergy with him.

After a couple of songs I said, 'Maybe I should sit down so some other guys can come in'. But George Duke said, 'No, you stay right there', which was flattering because I was a big fan of his. Some time later he was responsible for getting me an audition in LA with Jean-Luc Ponty, the jazz violinist, who was looking for a guitarist. I got the gig and had to go back to Milwaukee and tell my and band that I was off to join the

Ponty group. I had been on the road with Jean-Luc for about two years or so when I ran into Chester again at the O'Hare Airport in Chicago. 'Oh, Chester, what are you doing?' He says, 'I'm out here with The Wiz,' 'Really?' 'But I'm going to be playing with the group Genesis,' and I thought, 'What?'

First of all, I didn't know that much about Genesis. I had seen Peter Gabriel in a music show on TV being interviewed alongside Mike Love from the Beach Boys, Charles Lloyd, the jazz saxophone player, and John McLaughlin. There he was with his hair shaved down the middle, and then they showed this film clip of Genesis performing 'Willow Farm' with Peter Gabriel prancing around wearing a flower. Now I was a jazz fusion guitar player. I thought this wasn't serious enough for me, it was theatre. So when Chester told me he was joining Genesis I'm thinking 'Chester Thompson with flower buds on his head?' I was just surprised. And I said to myself, 'It must be for the money'.

A little while later I was talking to Jean-Luc Ponty at his house about this and he said, 'Oh no, this Genesis band is good. You should listen to them.' He put on 'Squonk' and said, 'I'd like to use this drummer on our next album.' I was thinking to myself 'Wow, this does sound good, this band sounds great.' Jean-Luc gave me a cassette with Trick Of The Tail on one side and Wind And Wuthering on the other, or nearly all of them, because Genesis always made records that were a little bit too long to squeeze onto a 45-minute cassette. I was amazed by the group because prior to becoming a jazz fusion musician, I had been a big fan of Procol Harum, Yes and King Crimson, and the sounds and the orchestration of Genesis was what blew me away, and now I could see why Chester might find it challenging and intriguing to work with them.

Time went on and during a break when Jean-Luc was off the road, his tour manager phoned and said they'd had a call from the Genesis management, that they were looking for a guitarist and they wanted to know if they could have my number. What that told me was that either Jean-Luc wasn't planning on doing anything for a while or else I'd been sacked...

I was invited to fly to New York, and arrived having learnt the songs they'd sent me, and thinking I was going to audition with the band. I was supposed to get to the SIR studios at ten in the morning but I gave the cab driver the wrong directions, which made me five or ten minutes late, but to me that's too late. I'm pretty much an on-time person and I was thinking, 'I can't believe this, I'm going to blow this audition.' I reached the studio and there was just Mike with a monitor system, a cassette player and a pedal board on the floor.

Mike says, 'We'll just put the cassette through the monitors and you play along.' I start playing and get through about half of the first song. Mike stops it and says, 'OK, we'll fast forward to the next one,' and he does the same thing. Mike and I are getting along very well right away even though I find him a little hard to understand – I still do – because he has this fast-talking mumble. We get to the last song and he says, and I can quote this verbatim, 'Well, anyway, I think you're the one.' 'What? I'm the one, I didn't really do that much.'

Mike said he'd ring me at the hotel at five o'clock, because he had three or four other players to audition. And I was thinking in my head, 'But what if one of them turns out really great too?' I went back to my room, rang my wife right away and said, 'I think I have the gig, but I'm not sure if I really want it,' because I had been so used to playing in a virtuoso kind of role in a jazz fusion outfit, and I didn't know whether the role in Genesis would be quite secondary. My wife told me, 'What are you doing? You're not in a band right now. Just take the gig.' Mike rang back about six, and said, 'We're going to start rehearsals in a few weeks…' It surprised me that they were that close to starting rehearsals and they still didn't have a guitar player, but Mike told me later he knew he would find somebody in America. He gave me a song list of twenty-six songs and after Christmas I sat in my room and learned five songs a day, learned the whole lot and thought I'd get to the rehearsal and these guys were going to come in and hit it. I turned up at the first rehearsal and we didn't play one song, not even a note that first day because they were getting the gear together…

One thing I wasn't used to was tea breaks. I couldn't believe how these guys would often walk away from their instruments and I'd be wondering where they were going. 'Tea break.' There was a long table of food in the room, and I was watching what was going on there, observing, because I didn't know what kind of guys they were, whether they were uptight, upper-class British guys. I looked over at the table where Mike, Tony and Phil were talking and I'll never forget this because it made me very comfortable. Mike was standing there running a fork through his beard, Phil was biting his nails and Tony Banks was leaning with his hand casually lying on a loaf of bread. I thought, 'These guys are not uptight. I don't have to worry about this at all.'

With the Jean-Luc Ponty band, the biggest venue we played was maybe 3,500 seats, and most of the time it was around 1,000 or so. The first show I played with Genesis was somewhere in Pennsylvania, and as soon as we came out I couldn't believe the sound of the audience. My skin just rose. Before the first show of a tour everybody's a little tense. But as soon as that audience started my nerves went away. I thought, 'They are with us no matter what.' That's what makes the difference. When I play jazz gigs I'm not sure the audience is going to be with me. I have to prove myself every time. Genesis does have to prove itself, but the audience is predisposed to love the band as long as we're as good as they think we are.

On that first tour we were in Germany and I found myself sitting across from Tony after we had ordered enough beer to be getting drunk and I realized he didn't dislike me. There's always a thing between a keyboard player and a guitar player. Either they get along or they don't and I get along with anybody musically, but I initially found Tony much more reserved than anybody in this band. Mike and I had hit it off at the audition, Phil is very easy and I knew Chester already. But Tony I wasn't sure about, I couldn't tell whether he resented me being there or not. I really couldn't tell. I would walk up to him during those first rehearsals and maybe have to ask him, 'Now, what chord was that you were playing?' And he would give me a look and say 'Well, it's like that.' I think his mind was usually on something else, but also maybe he was just as uncomfortable with me as I was with him. I don't even know to this day that he ever thought that way, but it was the way I perceived it and I thought maybe I haven't proven myself to him yet. The truth was that I had never sat down and talked with him. And all it took was getting drunk together.

Tony sets up an incredible atmosphere with his arrangements and his writing, especially his ballads. There are certain things that Tony plays, where if an even more proficient keyboard player played the same notes, it would sound corny to me. But when Tony Banks plays it sounds fine: it sounds like Tony Banks and no one else can imitate that. The same is true of Mike when he plays the guitar. I might possibly have more finesse than Mike as a player, but it doesn't matter. It matters what he's playing and how he executes that playing and if I play the same part, I might almost play it a little too clean. I've been to watch a couple of the Genesis tribute bands and every time I see them I think they're all playing the right notes but even though the tribute bands love the music of Genesis, I don't feel the passion there. You can't replicate that.

Daryl Stuermer formed his first band, Sweetbottom, with his brother Duane in his hometown of Milwaukee. After successfully auditioning for Jean-Luc Ponty, he toured with the French jazz violinist for four years, during which time he also became the touring bassist/guitarist for Genesis, a role he held until 1992 (rejoining for the 2007 Turn It Up Again tour). Like Chester Thompson he has worked on Phil Collins's solo tours, and has also recorded with Phil, Mike Rutherford, Tony Banks, Joan Armatrading and George Duke. Daryl has released half a dozen solo albums since *Steppin' Out* in 1987, and appeared in a reformed Sweetbottom in 2002.

CHAPTER TEN

THE FARM

MIKE: When Phil's solo album, *Face Value*, was released it ought to have been a weird time for us. We were in the studio writing *Abacab*. 'In The Air Tonight' came out and charted in its first week. I think if had we been in a period when we weren't busy, it might have been harder to deal with. But because we were in the studio working with a new producer, Hugh Padgham, trying to develop a more pared-down, tougher sound, it didn't affect us. All three of us were in there together working side by side, concentrating on Genesis. From then on the different careers ran side by side. We were one of the few bands who managed to co-ordinate our solo releases to alternate with the band's albums in a constructive rather than destructive way.

TONY: As we began to write the material for *Abacab*, it seemed we might be in danger of repeating ourselves. It seemed a good time for us to change things around, to make our writing and recording process more streamlined and straightforward. So we got rid of the big choruses and the tambourines and the keyboard solos and aimed to hone everything down, something we also tried to reflect in the album's abstract cover design.

We underlined this change of direction with *Abacab* by bringing in a new producer. We had had a good relationship with Dave Hentschel, but to make any significant kind of change in what we were doing we really needed to change producers too. Although Phil had already been working with Hugh Padgham, one of the main reasons we chose Hugh was on the strength of his work on Peter's third solo album, *Number Three* – or whatever it was called, because Peter never gave them names, did he? – the one with 'Intruder', 'Biko' and 'Games Without Frontiers' on it. Phil had played on the album and been very impressed with Hugh's engineering. While we were writing *Duke*, Phil brought along a tape of the drum loop which was being used on 'Intruder', just the drums with no cymbals. and with the compression techniques that had been applied by Hugh, they had created an incredible drum sound. As Pete said at the time, 'With a beat like that you don't really need to do anything else. That on its own is the hit'. We had already been talking about how much we liked the John Bonham drum sound on Led Zeppelin's 'Kashmir', and this was even more John Bonham than John Bonham.

PHIL: The album represented a pivotal scaling down of the Genesis monolith. One reason we wanted to reinvent ourselves was as a response to punk, although we were convinced that we were different from all the bands punk hated. I once saw an interview with John Cleese in which he said that after they'd done the accountant sketch for *Monty Python*, which was critical of being an accountant and how boring it was, he realized he was due to have a meeting with his accountant the following day and he thought, 'Fuck'. He went to see the accountant and asked him if he'd enjoyed the show. 'Yes, fantastic'. Cleese said, 'You weren't offended, then?' – 'Oh no, because I'm a *chartered* accountant'.

WE FELT THE HAND OF PUNK WAS SHAKING THE TREE. WE DIDN'T LIKE MOST OF THE BANDS THEY DIDN'T LIKE EITHER, SO WE WERE ALL FOR IT, BUT UNFORTUNATELY THE PUNK PERIOD SAW US AS ONE OF THE THINGS THEY WERE TRYING TO SHAKE OUT OF THE TREE. PHIL COLLINS

PHIL: We had realized that we sometimes had tensed up when we were recording what had originally sounded great when we had written it on our own in our own environment. Tony is not a natural performer. he's a great musician, but he's not a natural performer. Mike's the same. So if you put them both into a studio under a certain amount of time pressure, they tense up. So it was inevitable that we would want to find our own place where we could stop and start whenever we wanted without worrying about the clock.

Opposite: At Fisher Lane Farm. Overleaf: Rehearsing at the Farm. The Fisher Lane Farm was found for the band by Dale Newman, who first met the band in 1975. Dale says, 'I had been a guitarist and songwriter in the States and following the death of my brother had spent time in a hermitage there and taken on a day job delivering flowers, while working on an idea for a musical. Craig Schertz, a friend of mine from home in Fort Wayne, Indiana, had gone to Dallas and found work with Showco, who handled Genesis's sound and lights'; Craig ended up touring with Genesis handling their sound. At the end of 1974, Dale got a call: 'Genesis needed a guitar roadie for a couple of weeks. Genesis and Yes were two bands I would have done anything for, and I was intrigued by Mike's position in the band, which I found indefinable, a little different.' Dale was a twelve-string guitarist and in the days before electronic tuners, had the ability to tune Mike's twelve-string by ear; the two hit it off, and Dale took on a role as guitar roadie. Two or three years into his work with the band, Dale mentioned that he fancied doing something more, but not on the road. 'Sometime later Mike remembered that, and knowing I was interested in recording and studio work, told me the band were thinking of buying their own equipment to record their next album. He asked me to help them look for property for their own studio, which had to be near their homes. I said, "Yeah!"' Dale spent the summer of 1979 driving round the south of England looking for a barn where the band could rehearse and record, located Fisher Lane Farm, near Chiddingfold in Surrey, and stayed on to run the studio. Dale says it is easy to see why Genesis succeeded: 'They have a work ethic like no other band on the planet.'

MIKE: We bought this place called Fisher Lane Farm in Surrey as a base to work out of. We weren't planning to build a big studio. We just felt that we ought to have our own place, somewhere we could write, a writing room. We weren't even sure we were going to record there. It was our place to work. The first stage was to take an old cowshed on the farm which had previously been converted into a garage, and soundproof it. But it became obvious quite quickly that we needed a studio as well.

PHIL: We bought the Farm with the idea that the crew would live there, which would give this beautiful farmhouse a reason for being. We converted the six-car garage into the studio, and imagined the roadies would live in the house. But of course the roadies all had girlfriends and wives. As you get farther away from dropping the stone in the pond, all the ripples become less and less related to each other and even though we have a relationship because we're in the same band, and all the roadies have got a relationship because they've been with us, there is absolutely zero relationship between all their girlfriends and that idea soon fell out of bed straightway. So and so didn't get on with so and so, so and so had to move out and in the end we had an empty house, or maybe one couple left.

MIKE: The original control room was not top of the range. It was something that would do for now. We asked some sound specialists to come in and design the main playing area, but they were about six weeks late, and by the time they finally turned up we'd already been playing for the previous month, so we told them, 'No, bugger off, take the stuff back'.

TONY: When we started working on *Abacab* the studio hadn't been built, so we were up in the farmhouse itself for the writing, trying to keep everything concise. I was trying to avoid reiterating some of the things I'd done in the past. It was an interesting exercise, and I think pretty successful too, particularly the track 'Abacab' itself and 'Keep It Dark', another favourite track of mine, both of which are very succinct tracks with a definite identity.

I had one little moment on *Abacab* where I could afford to revert to my old ways. On 'Me And Sarah Jane' I poured all my flowery, beautiful stuff into one song, and for the rest of the album kept thinking, 'Really keep it simple'. 'Me And Sarah Jane' was probably the last time within Genesis that I wrote a song which goes through loads of chord changes. You could call it a piano study, where I started with a two-note riff which I slowly altered to create an effect; the first two or three minutes of the song are just that one idea, followed by a middle section that is very, very romantic and an ending that has a certain finality about it that I like. Our later producer Nick Davis calls these my 'terminal songs', where everything's over, it's bye, bye, people walking down the beach and the world's about to end.

PHIL: Leiden in Holland was the first place we played *Abacab* live, and they booed us. They genuinely disliked the new approach. In particular they hated 'Whodunnit?', which we originally called 'Weird Synth' as a working title, and was basically a punk pisstake.

TONY: 'Whodunnit?' is a notorious track. I had a Prophet Five synthesizer which I really used to abuse. If you played certain notes and then changed the tones while you held the notes down the keyboard would produce some very strange sounds which I loved. I think I was the only one who did like these sounds, and the others probably thought, 'Oh god, Tony, any way to shut him up, let's record it'. We put the track down; Phil added some filthy drums, Mike the bass, and Phil went off to write a silly lyric for it. I've always loved this track and virtually everyone else, it seems

Above: Producer Hugh Padgham at the tape machine.
Opposite: Fisher Lane Farm in September 1981.
Overleaf: Relaxing on the grass at the Farm. Mike says that living and working in the countryside in England helps maintain a sense of balance. 'I have a theory that American artists go home after tour to find that their fellow Americans believe all the fame thing, but in Britain we never pander to that. We could go down the pub and everybody would ignore us, even at the height of our fame.'

to me, hates it. There's something about it that appeals to me, the fact that it managed to provoke such strong emotion in people. It was unlike anything I had ever done or ever did, a hypnotic piece, a brave track to include.

When we played the album to Atlantic in the States, we had a couple of extra tracks to chose between, one of which was a more straightforward, pretty Genesis song called 'You Might Recall', and there was some debate about whether we should include that track or 'Whodunnit?'. I remember that Ahmet Ertegun said, 'No, I'm afraid you've got to put that track on'. He called 'Whodunnit?' 'that track' and everyone knew exactly which track he meant. It gave the album a very definite character and became a focus whenever we played it on stage. The crowd would boo and I found the whole thing very funny. The band wore silly hats, I'd put on a little snorkel and play a Prophet Five keyboard specially tuned just for that one song. It was supposed to be a joke, but I think it also has a certain charm that I like a lot.

ABACAB OFTEN PROVOKED A STRANGE RESPONSE, BUT IT WAS AN ABSOLUTELY NECESSARY ALBUM IN OUR CAREER. WE HAD TO CHANGE, WE COULDN'T CARRY ON AS WE WERE. IT MARKED A WATERSHED. Tony Banks

TONY: Although *Abacab* is not one of my favourite albums I think it did produce some good results. Above all we gave ourselves a healthy kick up the arse. Although we appeared to become more commercially successful and popular, that was a side effect of the fact that we were writing so spontaneously. Often I'd play something which I would normally have gone on to develop into a really long piece, but Mike or Phil would stop me and say, 'No, that's great. Just leave it like it is'. It helped me focus more on the good bits.

PHIL: After *Duke* we wrote more as a unit. On *Abacab* I think we brought in one song each and after that there were no individual songs, because we all had solo album careers. This gave Genesis a genuine reason to carry on, because the band's music was something we couldn't do individually and therefore anything we created as Genesis was nothing like what we did on our own records.

Right: Phil's kit at the Farm. Below: outside the barn where the Vari-Lites were first demonstrated. The technical installation of the Farm studio was undertaken by Geoff Callingham. At the end of 1979, Geoff got involved with Genesis when they were about to go on tour with a Prophet Five keyboard, a piece of equipment notoriously prone to breakdown, and they needed his expertise. He became the band's electronics engineer, 'their Mr Fixit', as he calls it – building kit and sorting out a vast range of problems on the road and in the studio. When the Fisher Lane Farm premises were acquired in early November 1980, Geoff and the team started work to make the building ready for recording in March 1981. 'It was quite tight,' Geoff says with a certain level of understatement, 'to convert an old cowshed into a studio in four months. In fact, when the band started recording the concrete was still wet.' The band had been writing *Abacab* up in the main farmhouse, but as recording sessions began Geoff was still completing the wiring, and after the band had finished recording during the day, he would dive back in and work through the night to carry out the final jobs. He is proud of the fact that the band were able to record within their own environment and without any pressure, so they could get exactly the sound they wanted. 'Everything was tailor-made for them: for example, there was a quite innovative foldback system that allowed them to create and modify their own individual headphone mixes in the studio. The studio really was custom-built for the way the three of them worked.'

MIKE: Phil's album had taken off in a huge way. He was off doing TV shows all round the world. And I'm sure I must have thought that if things were going that well, it was probably only a matter of time before Phil would think, 'It's time to move on'.

TONY: Phil didn't really talk much about his solo success, but he seemed very happy to stay with the group. I think Ahmet Ertegun at Atlantic Records had said to him, even before *Face Value* came out, 'You should stay with the group whatever happens'. I'm sure that had an effect on him. And he enjoyed being part of Genesis. If you can manage to sustain two careers in tandem for fifteen years and be successful in both, why not?

PHIL: It's a cliché, isn't it: any member of a band gets some hint of solo success and they're off. It never occurred to me to leave. Here we were, we had recorded *Duke*, which I was really proud of, and I thought that for the first time with Dave Hentschel at the ABBA studios we had captured some of our live energy on tracks like 'Duchess'. It had also been the first record that I felt had a bit of me on it, because on *And Then There Were Three* I only wrote a few bits and on *Duke* I had two complete songs. By *Abacab* I felt much more involved in the writing and the production was sounding even better so I had no reason to think about leaving. Genesis and my solo work were not in competition. Both sides of my career were quite happily running in

parallel – to the point where when I did finally leave, I was sitting at Tony Smith's kitchen table with Tony Smith, Tony Banks and they said, 'It's not a surprise. We're surprised you stayed so long. Why didn't you go earlier?' But for me it was never really an issue. I had the best of both worlds.

I also had the time and space to do a lot of different work. I was no longer married; I was going through the process of a divorce. Before long I met Jill, who became my second wife, but we became a couple based on the fact that this was my life. I've always tried to see my oldest two children as much as possible but that was made more difficult by the fact that my first wife Andy had chosen to live as far away from me as possible, in Vancouver, where her mother and siblings were, which made having every other weekend with the kids impossible. As a result I had twenty-four hours available every day.

I was being asked to do fantastic things. I'd met Eric Clapton and we'd become good friends – someone had suggested to him why don't you use Phil Collins on your next record, not knowing that he knew me – and my life changed a bit. Robert Plant called up one day. These were life-changing phone calls for me, when I felt that if I didn't say yes I wouldn't be asked again. So I tended to work all the time. But Jill knew what she was getting into.

TONY: *Face Value* did take a moment or two to recover from. If Phil could produce that on his own and be more successful as a solo artist than he was with us, it felt a bit strange. You are always aware of the commercial aspects. With Phil's success, it didn't worry me quite so much because Phil was the singer. It was the same with Pete: they both have an instantly recognizable voice and as long as they released something good – and they both did very good things – they were going to do well.

And perhaps because Phil's solo success happened when we were about thirty years old, I was able to accept it in a way I could never have done at twenty-one. When finally Mike as well started having massive success, I decided, 'I'll just be the one the completist record collectors have to really search for'.

MIKE: I only ever saw Mike + the Mechanics as a very low key thing. The amount of success Genesis has had, plus Phil's solo career, Peter's, and the Mechanics' has been unreal. There was a time when we all had a single in the American charts, Steve too with GTR; it was ridiculous. The Mechanics was a real pleasure for me; the music came out without me really thinking about it. I'm very proud of what we did. We had a great era. Who'd have thought it.

What I also gained from the Mechanics was the opportunity to write with other people like BA Robertson, Paul Carrack and Chris Neil, which taught me a different way of approaching things. And whereas Phil, on his solo projects, was in charge, I was trying to make it more collaborative. I realized that Phil, Tony and myself were on the same playing field all the time; our lives have been similar, we had the same mentality. Other people have different agendas, which I had never experienced, and different kinds of ego, and I got a shock with all sorts of people. In Genesis there was no such thing, and being away from it made me appreciate that.

TONY: Phil becoming a household name did have one unfortunate downside, which was that in the public's eyes we were back to being a singer with a group, the very same perception we had experienced with Peter, which was frustrating.

PHIL: We've always been very British. It's the playing of the game, not the winning, you know. Tony Banks is a classic at that: 'It did very well, but that doesn't necessarily mean it's the best'. Tony is very cynical about any kind of success, so there is never any danger of getting above yourself, because immediately the band will knock you down a peg or two. From my point of view I felt that it was more luck and fluke than something I had earned – something that had hit at the right time. Genesis was a band and this success would obviously add something to the band's credibility. It certainly brought us to a different and a larger audience in various parts of the world.

Left: Tony with his wife Margaret.

TONY: Success was a very slow process for Genesis. We had our first hit single in 1978, which was when we started to break even, because we had built up a lot of debt before that. Even when the commercial success happened, it was gradual. I don't think that success affected anything we did, or what we wrote. It didn't affect the way I approached anything. I had bought a house in 1978 which stretched me quite a bit because we weren't very well off then, and at the point I bought the house, Phil had these family problems and might have been heading off to Vancouver, which made me a little nervous. But I decided to stick with it, and I'm still in the same house.

As a five-piece on stage, we had always gone for quite extravagant effects. There were a couple of things that always pissed us off. One was the fact that we had all these lights overhead and they could only be one colour. The other was we didn't like being obliged to use the in-house follow-spot operators, particularly in America where you were locked into the union guys. They would wobble all over the place and the effect was awful. We really wanted to operate the follow spots ourselves. One way we thought we could do this was to have the spots onstage and shine them off mirrors set above the stage. It didn't really replace the follow spot but it was an addition to it. And the bonus was that the mirrors could move so you could effectively move the light around.

It was clear that if you could get a light that could change to become any colour and also could move, you would have a very powerful tool. People had been trying to achieve this, the lighting companies had thought of the same thing, obviously, but we thought we'd put money into it. We talked to the guys at Showco, the sound and lighting company we were using in the States, who were thinking along the same lines. And the Vari-Lite was born.

MIKE: We were shown the Vari-Lite for the first time in the old barn at the Farm. Our original brief had been for a one-off special effect for the tour. We had always had a thing about a neon club light, which was like a wheel with a gel going round, and we asked Rusty Brutsché at Showco to find us a light that could do that. He showed up one day with these prototypes. I think one of them blew up and another kept going round in circles, but we could immediately see the potential of a light that was able to change colour.

The way I remember it is that we had tried talking about our ideas to the regular lighting companies, but because they were in the business they were all blinkered. Their response would be, 'Ooh no, that can't be done because of this and you wouldn't be able to make that work, no.' Rusty Brutsché and Showco could think outside that particular box. To me it's no coincidence that it was what was primarily a sound company who got the idea working.

On the first couple of tours it was a disaster: the lights kept blowing up, but it was still exciting – a genuinely new look, which is really rare to find in this day and age. This was lighting that moved, literally a revolution.

TONY: We took the Vari-Lites out on the road as prototypes and we had as many technicians as we had lights, it seemed to me. By the end of each show, you were lucky if ten of them were still working, so they were constantly being dismantled and re-built, but as the tours progressed they became more and more reliable. They went much further than we had originally imagined: they were computer-controlled so you could move the lights to anywhere you wanted and change them in an instant from one setting to another setting – and the movement between the settings could itself be very attractive. So you could have an incredible effect where you could move the lights in unison and have them all red one moment and then suddenly all the same lights would be green. You could also get great beauty out of these lights by putting a bit of smoke through them, which created a dreamy and lovely effect which worked really well on a song like 'Afterglow'.

Sometimes we'd incorporate an effect that was absolutely stunning, but use it only once in the course of a show. We'd get comments like, 'You've got all these bloody lights and you're not using them', but if you could hold the effect back until three quarters of the way through the

Previous pages and opposite: Phil and Chester grab some valuable relaxation and headspace on tour. Overleaf: Bringing the live shows to light.

show and suddenly something happened that no one had ever seen before, that was visually very powerful. I used to say to people, 'Look, even if you don't like the music, get some ear plugs and come and watch the lights'.

Phil was a good stage performer, but Mike and I probably weren't very good at doing anything on stage. I certainly wasn't. And the bigger the venue you're playing, the less important the guys on stage are. We used to sit dummies on the stage for the lighting rehearsals, which in my case was pretty much as mobile as me.

PHIL: I tend to take a percentage of the glory about the lights, but without really earning it. There was a day in Dallas, rehearsing as the five-piece band, where the mannequins were on stage and I was watching them go through the tapes with the lights and someone was saying, 'Well, there are 100 lights up there, but we've got twenty-five reds, twenty-five yellows, twenty-five blues, twenty-five greens, why can't you have something that is like a fog spot lamp, a gel changer, so you have a hundred lights that are all one colour…' I remember that conversation and thinking, 'Yeah, that's a great idea.' And really if I was truthful that was the last I heard about it until they went into development and came up with the Vari-Lite.

Because I'm more of a player than an imagineer I was much more interested in what was happening on stage than what it looked like. I became more interested when I became a singer but it still wasn't really something I felt very comfortable with. So whenever someone says to me now, 'Genesis, you discovered the Vari-Lite!', I say, 'Yeah!'

THE VARI-LITES GAVE US A FANTASTICALLY DIFFERENT LOOK ON STAGE. WE WERE THE GUINEA PIGS, SO WE PAID FULL PRICE FOR IT, BUT IT BECAME A REALLY IMPORTANT PART OF THE STAGE PRESENTATION. MIKE RUTHERFORD

TONY: Towards the end of 1982 Peter needed some financial help because WOMAD had gone a little pear-shaped. People had been asking us to organise some sort of get-together for years and years and this seemed a very good reason to do it at the same time as helping Peter pay off this particular debt. We did need a reason, because it wasn't something we were itching to do.

PETER: In typical Gabriel style I had had big dreams. My general philosophy is go for what you want and accept what you get, but with WOMAD we ended up in a financial disaster. The first festival, in 1982, was a magnificent event, with Echo and the Bunnymen, the Burundis, Jon Hassell. We put it on during schooltime so there were a lot of schools working on projects about world music; it was very exciting, fresh, passionate. But the people just didn't come. There was a rail strike that weekend and even though we thought we had enough names to pull in an audience we were hopelessly under each day, and suddenly realized the financial consequences.

Below: left to right – Chester on the *Three Sides Live* tour; Phil, Mike and Tony at the *Abacab* stage rehearsals; Daryl with Geoff 'Bison' Banks; Tony on the *Three Sides Live* tour.

Geoff Banks started working with Genesis in 1974: 'A friend of mine from Cumbria was in London working with a band who had a regular gig on the pub scene, and I thought I'd come down too. So like Dick Whittington I headed south and found work on the circuit, including a stint with Hot Chocolate. Someone gave me the phone number of a band looking for help, and one night, after a couple of gigs where I'd had to drive hundreds of miles and only got £20, I phoned the number. Genesis were offering three times what I was normally getting. Initially I was employed to look after Tony's keyboards, and because we are both called Banks, it was always assumed, particularly in the States for some reason, that I was his brother. However much I would point out that we were like chalk and cheese, me from the north of England, him from the south, and the fact that we look completely different, no one would ever be persuaded. 'Man,' they'd say, 'having to work for your brother...'

The debts were more than I could ever hope to sort out personally. I had some horrible phone calls and death threats from people who I owed money to. It was a very oppressive nightmare. Tony Smith offered to speak to the band to see if they could help and they were extremely gracious. I do think it helped that I had been a little generous at the time of my leaving and they were certainly extremely generous on this occasion. The money from that reunion concert was enough to pay off the debts and allow us to keep WOMAD going.

PHIL: It had come up that Peter had put this event on and it had been a financial disaster. He was on the verge of going under, and we offered, and he agreed, that maybe we could do something to help, which ended up being the Six Of The Best concert. Whether or not he felt he needed our help to get himself out of trouble, it made sense to us, and it certainly was not a condescending gesture.

We gathered at the Odeon Hammersmith one afternoon to run through some of the tunes. We were very under-rehearsed because we only spent a couple of afternoons working at it, but I guess it must have fallen back into place quite easily, otherwise we would have been in trouble. I was quite happy playing the drums behind Peter. I certainly didn't have my ego dented. I always relish the chance of going back to the drums.

TONY: It was a weird day out. It was extremely wet, and for some reason I was wearing a red tracksuit with the words 'Kamikaze' written on it. I really don't know why. It summed up the day...

PETER: It was pissing down with rain. I wanted to be brought on in a coffin, in a typically humble gesture. We had only done about four days' rehearsal, and I was frustrated because it was very sloppy. I was certainly not sharp enough. You can memorize stuff and work on your own until you're blue in the face but actually you need to be sitting in with the band and doing some warm-up gigs. So it was frustrating and yet it felt a warm occasion, there was a nice feeling up on stage. A lot of the fans seemed to enjoy it even though it was very loose. It was a bit like going to school when you haven't been there for thirty years; in this case it was only six years, but it still felt like a lifetime.

PHIL: I don't have too many memories of the show at Milton Keynes apart from the fact that it was pissing with rain, as it always did, and that John Martyn and Talk Talk were on the bill. And Peter came on in his coffin, still able to spring a couple of surprises even at that stage. As it seems that he always felt that anything he brought to the band would be the subject of democratic decision-making and that sometimes the things he wanted to do would not get through the sieve.

If he had told us he was thinking of coming on in a coffin we would probably have said, 'Is that really the best thing?' But he did it and it was funny.

TONY: The whole event was strange: Phil was playing drums for some of the numbers that Chester had been playing drums on during the live shows, which changed the nature of the performances. And Pete was trying to play bongos on 'Turn It On Again', not realizing that there was an extra beat every fourth bar or so. When you just listen to the song you wouldn't think it contains anything odd, but when you start trying to play it you think, 'Where have I gone wrong?' I could see Pete throwing his hands up in the air in frustration or confusion.

It felt like a bit of a dream. I was very glad when it was over, because I hadn't particularly enjoyed playing that stuff at the time. I always tended to be into what we were doing either at the time or whatever the next thing was. I was pretty glad to have left some of those old songs behind. But the audience reaction was very good, and I believe that show did go some way to sorting out Peter's financial problem; now WOMAD is a monster thing.

MIKE: We were on tour at the time so we had to squeeze the rehearsals in between dates. And on the day itself it was raining, it pissed down. These things are always so surreal, they go by so fast and before you know it the event is over. Your mind is so taxed with trying to get the parts right, you miss what's going on. I regret it now but I was keen not to record the show. I thought it would be a bit rough and ready and that it was better to be there and in the moment.

Overleaf: Rehearsals in September 1982 and the performance at the Milton Keynes Bowl for the 'Six Of The Best' reunion and WOMAD fundraiser, 2nd October 1982. Peter gets his flower costume out of mothballs. Top right and bottom right: at Hammersmith Odeon, September 1982.

Previous pages: Phil works up a sweat on the *Three Sides Live* tour, August 1982
Above: Michael Winner with Tony, who wrote the music for the Winner movie *The Wicked Lady*. 'It was a good experience and I got on well with Michael Winner. He was very enthusiastic about everything I wrote.'
Opposite: 'I'm sorry but press do say no news is good news', a line from 'Paperlate'.
Overleaf: Tony Smith, Daryl, Jill Collins and Phil in Venice.
Following pages: I only have eyes for you – Mike and Daryl.

TONY: I had a phase working on film scores. The first soundtrack I had been involved in was for *The Shout*, in the late '70s, which Mike and I were asked to do together. I had written a long introduction to 'Undertow' on *And Then There Were Three*, but the others were keen not to use any introductions, and it had been dropped. I took a small part from the middle of that intro and expanded that, and cut down the major part, and because it was a scary film, I added some spooky chords.

Both Mike and I were closely involved with the making of this film in terms of crafting the music with the action, but on the day they added the credits we weren't there for some reason. Eventually we saw the film and the credits started rolling just as the music was going through its big climax. Suddenly there was a huge wind noise which really ruined the musical moment. By the end of the film Mike was so upset that he got hold of the producer and had him up against the wall shouting 'you've ruined it, you've ruined it'. I'm normally the one who starts throwing things about. That marked the end really of my filmwriting career at that point. I think that if Mike hadn't had that guy against the wall, I might have been involved – even if Mike wouldn't have been – in the next film made by that guy.

I continued telling everyone who would listen that I wanted to write film music. Phil Carson, who was Atlantic Records' representative in the UK, heard that Michael Winner was looking for a composer for a new film called *The Wicked Lady*. He wanted someone cheap but interesting, and so I was suggested. I had one piano theme I'd written but wasn't planning to use on my next solo album: I played this to Michael Winner, who thought it was great, and I got hired.

It gave me the opportunity to work with an orchestra, which I'd never done before; an arranger called Christopher Palmer came in to take what I played on the piano and orchestrate it to sound beautiful. I was working on another solo album, *The Fugitive*, at the same time and in a way I almost resented doing this *Wicked Lady* music simultaneously because it represented such a lot of work. But when I heard this main theme I'd written played back by a full orchestra, it sounded fantastic. Unfortunately the film itself, although it had a fantastic cast – Faye Dunaway and Alan Bates, Denholm Elliot, Prunella Scales – never worked. It's only narrowly famous for the fact that Marina Sirtis, who appeared in *Star Trek: The Second Generation*, had a topless whip fight with Faye Dunaway, and that has always guaranteed it a certain level of cult status…

On *The Fugitive*, I did the singing. I knew I could sing it, because I'd made demos for a couple of tracks on the *Abacab* album, 'Keep It Dark' and 'Me and Sarah Jane', to show Phil how they could be done. It was pretty nervewracking stuff but occasionally my voice sounds all right. It's as good as Bob Geldof's. It's better than Bob Geldof's actually. I ended up sounding a little bit like a cross between Al Stewart and Neil Tennant from the Pet Shop Boys – quite appealing but a little fey for the music I was writing, so I tried to put a bit more balls into it. Although I'm not the greatest singer in the world, the songs stand up and I think a lot of the fanbase liked it because it was me singing, which was unusual. I learnt an awful lot about writing music and perhaps my writing after that did get melodically simpler.

SINGING MY OWN SONGS TAUGHT ME WHAT I HAD BEEN PUTTING PETE AND PHIL THROUGH OVER THE YEARS, MAKING THEM SING MY MELODIES, TELLING THEM, 'YEAH YOU CAN DO IT, HIT THAT NOTE', AND GIVING THEM WEIRD LYRICS LIKE BREAD-BIN. TONY BANKS

THE PRODUCERS' TALE, PART I: HUGH PADGHAM

In 1978, after a couple of jobs learning the craft of a recording engineer, I had the chance to work for Virgin Records, who had decided to build a studio in London and run it along the same lines as their studios at the Manor near Oxford, in other words as a residential studio in London. They found this property with a bunch of flats in it where the bands could stay, called it the Townhouse and the place took off almost immediately. It was an incredibly cool and trendy place to be.

I joined as one of the staff engineers and very soon met up with Steve Lillywhite who was the same age as me, but

already an independent producer. We worked together with several groups, the most well-known of which was XTC, and through the success we had with XTC, Steve was asked to produce Peter Gabriel's album, oscillating between the Townhouse and Peter's house in Bath using Virgin's Manor Mobile. Phil Collins was the drummer on some of the tracks – Jerry Marotta, Peter's regular drummer, was also playing on the album. We had discovered this particular big drum sound which obviously impressed Phil quite a lot at the time. Coming into the late 1970s many studios were very, very soundproofed, with a dead sound, and we wanted to have more live areas. At the Townhouse there was one big room where the walls were lined with Cotswold stone that had been dug out of the garden at the Manor Studios.

Peter's idea was not to use any cymbals on the album, which was a recording engineer's dream come true. Cymbals can be horrible things that swish and splash their sound around everywhere and cover up everything else. We experimented with sounds endlessly. One of the girls in the studio brought her new-born baby in one day and we stuck the baby in the middle of the studio and miked it up while the mother came into the control room. After a minute or two the baby started crying and we later took the baby's sound and slowed the tape down: it sounded like a man crying, so horrendous. After my previous life, doing sessions against the clock all the time, recording jingles for soap powder in a morning, when everything had to be done in double quick time, being able to spend days doing one thing was fantastic fun.

A few months after we'd finished Peter's record, I was rung up by Tony Smith, who asked me if I was interested in working with Phil because he was going to do a solo album. 'Bloody hell, yes.' I had an MGB at the time and drove down on a lovely day to meet Phil at his house in Shalford just outside Guildford. He was on his own in the house because his wife had left. We played Frisbee in the garden, listened to his demos and made a game plan from there. We both had very much the same kind of production ethic: to keep things really simple. We used the bones from his demos which we took from his 8-track machine and copied onto 24-track and we carried on working on those, which of course endeared me to Phil a lot because he loved the demos he had done.

Peter and Phil work in very different ways. Peter nowadays works very, very slowly, which would probably frustrate Phil, who has always been a workaholic and he would be the first person to tell you that. If we were meant to start at ten o'clock, if you weren't there, it was like, 'Well, where are you?' When mobile phones first came out, it was really bad to have one because Phil could ring you on it. Supper break would be at 7.30 on the dot and the minute he put his knife and fork down he'd be back in the studio and expect you to be there as well. Sometimes I had to end up saying to Phil, 'Look, come on, I need to have an hour's brain break here.' On the other hand, Peter can be almost too laid back. Years later when I worked with him on 'Shaking The Tree', he'd have so many things going on that we might manage five minutes in what was meant to be a day's recording. They could both drive you crazy in different ways.

Duke was the first Genesis album Phil had written any songs for, and 'Misunderstanding' marked his evolution from being the drummer and the singer of the band's music to a writer in his own right. Genesis had always been lyrically somewhat esoteric or fey, a little bit nutty – and as a teenager I had loved those lyrics where you had no idea what they meant – but when Phil started writing lyrics they were coming straight from the centre of his heart. Your old-school Genesis fan will say that the era I came in on – and I hope they would not necessarily blame me – destroyed Genesis, because when I started working with the band their songs became shorter, more understandable and subsequently more commercial and a lot of people thought that that commerciality was selling out. But certainly up until I started working with them, they were still on the bones of their arse financially speaking. Duke had started to make some sort of sales inroads but they were not yet a wealthy band by any means.

My aim with Genesis was to move them to a better place sonically because their previous recordings – to my ears – had been very wishy-washy. I wanted to make Phil's drums sound louder, like drums, rather than like somebody tapping away rather quietly in the background. That meant being very, very careful and particular about the equipment we used and how I recorded the drums so they came across sharp and clear. If you listen to Duke and then Abacab, I would like to think that you can really tell somebody new was twiddling the knobs.

We built the studio at the Farm coming up to record that album. It was exciting but hairy because we were spending a large amount of money and I had a lot of responsibility to get the studio together. Even though I had been on staff when the Townhouse had started, and knew a reasonable amount about building studios, it was not at any deep level. It sounds easy to say, 'Let's make a studio'. At the time it was a big deal, quite nervewracking, and I'd be up extremely early in the morning trying to sort stuff out before the band came in. I can't recall the details, but I can remember being scared shitless if it was going to work or not. Two or three years later, in 1984 and '85, we re-built

the studio: the control room was purpose-built from the ground up, and that was totally the dog's bollocks, seriously as good as if not better than any London studio at the time.

I actually liked the long tracks. of which we didn't really do that many, and to be honest if anything I would almost have liked to have done more tracks with the original Genesis feel than the poppier songs, but that was what they wanted to do at the time. I was only ever – and I feel quite strongly about this – a co-producer with the band, not an autocratic producer stamping my sound on each album. My job was to make what they created sound good or sound like a record. In both Genesis and Phil's case there was absolutely no record company input at all, which was brilliant, because record companies know nothing about making music as far as I'm concerned. And whenever they do try and get involved it's usually a disaster. All we used to do was say to them at the end of the day was 'Here's the record'.

Sonically, I was very, very proud of Invisible Touch when we did it, and it was very successful as well which was great. But looking back, what I really don't like is that we thought we were being cool experimenting and fiddling around with electronic drums and trying to use a set-up combining electronic drums with real drums so Phil could play it all together. The electronic drums sound absolutely unlistenable to me now, even though the songs are great. No one else would ever probably pick up on it or necessarily care as much as me but if somebody ever let me do it, I would re-do those albums and replace the electronic drums with real drums.

It annoys me that I can't boast about my involvement with Phil and Genesis any more. It's really upsetting because together they helped launch my career. But the climate changed and their credibility curve amongst large sectors of the music business tumbled. I'm really looking forward to the day that Genesis become a flavour of the month again.

Establishing himself as a tape op and engineer in the 1970s, Hugh Padgham was a staff engineer/producer at London's Townhouse studios in the latter part of the decade, working with XTC, Peter Gabriel and Phil Collins. The 'gated' drum sound Hugh created for Phil's 'In The Air Tonight' single created one of the most influential templates for 1980s drum sounds. He co-produced Genesis from *Abacab* to *Invisible Touch*, and has won four Grammy Awards, including two in 1985/86 for his work with Phil on *No Jacket Required* and one in 1990/91 for 'Another Day In Paradise'. He has also produced a long list of artists, including the Police (*Synchronicity* and *Ghost In The Machine*), Sting (an engineering Grammy for *Ten Summoner's Tales*), David Bowie, the Bee Gees, Elton John and McFly.

THE IMAGINEER'S TALE: RUSTY BRUTSCHÉ

I started working with Genesis in the Peter Gabriel days, when they began touring the States. The thing about Genesis was that their shows were always memorable and cutting-edge, theatrically oriented and daring in what they wanted to do. Very innovative and extremely creative people.

At the time I was one of the co-founders of a company called Showco. We had started out as a sound system company in the late '60s: by the mid '70s we added lighting to the repertoire and started dabbling in all kinds of things: building stages, trucking, crew buses. There wasn't anyone else around supplying those services. The rock touring industry was still in its infancy.

By the middle of the decade we were handling Genesis's sound and lighting and much of their staging, and had a good relationship with the band. Tony Smith was a tremendous manager, so astute at what he did and always honest and straightforward. The rock'n'roll industry in those days was pretty wild and woolly, still evolving, and there were plenty of people in the industry who were pretty crazy. Tony was always very businesslike and very stable.

Genesis came up with a lot of concepts to do with their lighting. They were the ones who knew what they wanted and we helped them to execute the ideas. One innovation in 1977 was to use large frames with Mylar stretched over them which

created a reflective surface, and to mount these mirrors up in the rig over the stage. Tony had contracted a Belgian company to build the mirrors and motorized gimbals and we provided the trusses and other lighting equipment for the tour. We shone follow spots into the mirrors and by using motorized gimbals could tilt them this way and that to direct the beams around the stage.

Then we turned our minds to the question of colour. The lighting standard of the day was the par can, which was essentially a car headlight about eight inches in diameter stuck inside a steel can. Rock'n'roll tours used the par can because it was lightweight, cheap and simple – and you could put a gel in front of it to create a colour. But if you wanted a red wash, you had to have fifty red ones and if you wanted to go to a blue wash you'd add fifty more blue ones. It didn't take us long to fill the stage with par cans. We'd have two or three thousand of them and by the time we got through there was no space left over the stage to do anything else. So we realized we needed some way for the light to change colour.

We tried various ideas including squeezing liquid dyes between plates to vary the thickness of the dye and the colour saturation, all this crazy stuff. But in 1980 we had a very creative engineer named Jim Bornhorst working on audio equipment and I asked him to have another look at this. In the workshop we had a follow spot that used a new metal halide bulb, the Marc 350, which General Electric had developed for a 16mm film projector. It was an arc light, where there's no filament but a gap between two electrodes – a modern version of the kind of technology used in WWII searchlights. The breakthrough with this new bulb was that it was very small, self contained with an integral reflector and extremely efficient, so a little 350-watt bulb could put out the same light as a 1000-watt par can. But when we put a piece of gel in front of the bulb, it just evaporated because all the energy was focused down into a tiny area.

Now Jim Bornhorst was a photographer and familiar with photography equipment, particularly photographic enlargers which used equipment called dichroic filters, a technology that was different from gels. When you put white light through a red gel, for example, all of the light other than red is absorbed in the gel. So the gel heats up and melts eventually. Dichroic filters work in a different way by reflecting light away. So a filter that reflects away all light other than red light actually dissipates the heat, and so it can take a lot of energy. Jim found a bunch of these filters in a scientific hobbyist catalogue and started playing with them in front of the metal halide bulb. He found that the dichroic filters would handle the heat from the Marc 350 bulb and they also had a very interesting property, which was that as you tilted them the colour would shift because it changed the frequency of the light it was passing.

Jim and his team constructed a light using four different colour filters each operated by a motor so they could pivot in the beam and thereby colour tune virtually the entire colour spectrum. That was already a breakthrough. And then one day we were having lunch at Solly's barbeque place in Dallas – it was run by a Lebanese guy called Salih but nobody could pronounce his name in Texas. The group consisted of myself, Jim Bornhorst, one of my partners, Jack Maxson, and two other Showco employees, Tom Walsh and Tom Littrell.

We were sitting there talking, all excited about this colour-changing light, and Maxson, just out of the blue, popped up and said, 'Well, if we can make the light change colour, we could make it move.' We all stopped talking, because we'd never put that together, and said, 'Damn, of course we've got to make it move.' All of a sudden this whole idea of an automated light came into being right there at lunch.

I contacted Tony Smith to talk about the Abacab *tour coming up in the summer of 1981. They were working on the album at the time. I mentioned the new light and Tony said he'd like to see it. We built the prototype in twelve weeks flat. Jim and I put together a team including Brooks Taylor, a software engineer, John Covington, an electrical engineer with expertise in power supplies and motors, and Tom Walsh, a digital electronics engineer who built a hand-made one-channel controller for the prototype light that could store sixteen cues. I called Tony Smith to tell him we had the prototype ready, and Jim and I wrapped it up in towels, put it in a regular suitcase, brought it over on the plane and drove out to the Farm, where Genesis had built their recording studios and were recording* Abacab.

It was mid-December, really, really cold. We had to rig the prototype up in an unheated barn. There was no way to attach the light to the beams because they were centuries-old oak that was hard as steel. We were freezing our butts off out there but we finally strapped it or roped it onto this beam. When we first turned the light on it wouldn't work because the temperature was so low everything was sluggish, but as it heated up it began to work properly. We asked Tony and the band to come out, demonstrated it, and went back in the house where Tony and I struck a deal on the spot, sitting beside the fireplace. I told him how much money I needed – around half a million dollars for fifty units, which was a lot of money back then – and he said, 'If we do this, we want to invest.' We agreed to set up a partnership. I said we'd have to create something outside of Showco, and would need a name for the product, so Tony said, 'Why don't we call it Vari-Lite' – and that's what it's been called ever since. We only had six months before the tour. We built fifty lights and a controller from scratch in six months and we worked insanely hard, at least fifteen to twenty hours a day, seven days a week. But we got it all together.

We hadn't really envisioned what was to become the defining feature of the product. The colour changing was very important – the dichroic filters produced very rich, saturated colours and we had worked out how to make the lights change colour instantly – but the thing that was really impressive was when you programmed a cue and all of these white, sharp-edged beams moved together in a synchronized movement. The moving, kinetic beam effects with the instant colour changes had never been seen before.

The first gig was in Barcelona, 27th September 1981, in a bullring with a lot of dust in the air from the dirt floor, an environment that was good for reflecting light. When the lights came on it was absolutely astounding, and from there word about these lights went around the industry like a rocket. We started building more and more gear and renting it out; we couldn't keep up with the demand. Out on the road we were constantly solving mechanical, electrical and computer problems. We had built the very first computer from scratch and the only way that we could load the software was via paper punch tape, which had to be fed into the console, and we were always having to glue it back together.

Genesis were the pioneers of automated lighting and their tours became testing grounds for the technology, and on each tour we would add and improve and develop. But the tour that was the most exciting for me, because automated lighting was still so fresh, was the 1983 tour. We had constructed 180 units, more than three times the number we had built for the first tour. Nobody had ever seen anything like that before. There were two particular moments within the show that stood out. One was what we called a 'panic' cue, which caused all the lights to randomly move and change colour. And the other one was when every single one of the 180 lights would turn and focus on Phil playing drums. Now that was awesome.

The sound systems that Rusty Brutsché and his college friend Jack Calmes created for their Texas-based blues band in the late 1960s sounded so good, they decided to set up the Showco company with engineer Jack Maxson in 1970 and concentrate on building systems for local shows. Three Dog Night were impressed when they passed through town and asked them to create a touring version, which led to tours with Led Zeppelin, James Taylor and Genesis. In 1980-81 the company created what Genesis manager Tony Smith dubbed the Vari-Lite, which quickly set new industry standards. The new Vari-Lite company continued to develop the system for music shows and later moved into TV and theatre, winning a primetime Emmy in 1991 for Outstanding Achievement in Engineering. Rusty is currently Vice Chairman and Chief Technology Officer of the umbrella company PRG.

CHAPTER ELEVEN

THE WORLD AND ELSEWHERE

TONY: By the time of the album *Genesis*, in 1983, we were a bit dry of ideas. I don't know why; we didn't seem to have quite as many ideas as on other occasions. That's why there are no spare songs from that period and perhaps on a couple of the tracks it felt at times as though we were stretching the material as far as we could.

However, we knew that we had this one really strong piece that Mike had got from a drum machine which he'd put it through an echo machine and then through his speakers. It produced a wonderful slappy sound and once we heard it we knew, 'That's a good song, we don't really need any more.' I added a dark, atmospheric drone down at the bottom of it and a spooky sound on one of the synthesizers. I had this way of pulsing the keyboard in time with the drum machine, and when we put all those ingredients together and Phil bluesed some vocals on top of that, it sounded really strong: and the result was 'Mama'. Phil's laugh on the track was great, something which came from a record he'd been listening to. 'Mama' was one of those songs that obviously had to build. It was a question what to build to. My idea was to have very minimalist chords throughout the song and then at a certain point bring in these massive major chords – I thought that would do the trick. It was an unusual single, but still a big hit for us.

Another section that emerged in the studio was what became the instrumental part of 'Home By The Sea'. Phil had a drum riff which he repeated with Mike and I playing on top of it. We recorded two or three reel-to-reels of improvisation, around sixty minutes of music in total. We listened back to it and clocked the parts we liked, learnt what it was we'd played and then repieced it back together. It was another new way of working, and something we couldn't have done without the comfort of our own studio.

I also have a lot of affection for 'Silver Rainbow', which is something of a forgotten track from the second side – it was originally called 'Adam Ant' because of the drum part. The other hit off the album was 'That's All', which was quite a distinct track in our collection, almost Beatle-ish.... There's no track on *Genesis* that I find weak.

PHIL: This was a period of continual rise. There was a point at that time, and we're talking about '84, '85, '86, where everything I did on my own was working out, whether it was with Phillip Bailey or 'Against All Odds' or *No Jacket Required*: four or five top five singles, a couple of number ones in the US and God knows where else around the world, and with Genesis we were building up to *Invisible Touch* which was a number one Genesis album with a number one single.

THE MID-1980S WAS THE BIGGEST WE EVER GOT. I WAS WAITING FOR SOMETHING TO GO WRONG. PHIL COLLINS

MIKE: Once you put hit singles out you attract a new hardcore fan base. The downside was that this coincided with the rise of MTV, so suddenly a hit single created a profile so big it dwarfed the rest of the tracks on an album. We were doing songs like 'Home By The Sea' which was eleven minutes long, yet the public perception of us was based on the tracks that got played on the radio and MTV.

TONY: I would like to have been part of Live Aid. Definitely. I felt at the time it would have been great to have done. But it fell during a period of Phil's solo work, and we were never asked. I did suggest to Mike that we could go up there and join in on one of Phil's songs or something. I know Steve Hackett was also quite keen. He rang me up and said, 'I think we should get together as the old lot and do it.' But nothing ever came of it. It was one of those events that became Phil's thing and not ours. I didn't even see it on TV. I felt all the time that we should be there. I just didn't want to watch it.

The only drawback with Live Aid was that it was the point at which pop music became the establishment, a defining moment, when suddenly it developed a conscience, and paradoxically something died at the same time.

Opposite: Chester, Mike, Phil, Tony and Daryl prepare for take-off on the *Mama* tour, Philadelphia, November 1983. Overleaf: Phil and Genesis manager Tony Smith on the plane from Philadelphia. Doug Morris, a music industry heavyweight, who joined Atlantic Records as President in 1980 – and is currently Chairman and CEO of the Universal Music Group – has fond memories of working with both Genesis ('the band was pure class') and with Tony Smith: 'Tony is a particularly intelligent fellow, one of the finest managers I've ever worked with. A good guy, but tough. We would have screaming arguments on the phone. Genesis was his band and he would push a rock up a hill for them. My God, was he a lunatic, screaming and yelling and jumping up and down. We ended up with such respect for each other: I am the godfather to Tony's daughter Rachel. To this day, the strangest negotiation I have ever had took place when Tony came in to discuss the record deal. We drew a pie and said, 'What part do you want, and what part do you want us to have?' It was extraordinarily fair. No one said anything and we shook hands. Then we had to figure out what those lines meant. I have never been in a negotiation like that before or since: I wish I'd kept that piece of paper.'

MIKE: Looking back it was a shame we didn't get to appear at Live Aid. I was in Air Studios in London recording the first Mike + the Mechanics album, so it was quite a key time for me. And when you are in solo mode your focus is entirely on that. We simply never got around to talking about it.

PHIL: I was in a Phil Collins phase, on tour with *No Jacket Required*. During the course of the tour I started reading articles about what Bob Geldof was planning for Live Aid. I had already been involved as the drummer on the Band Aid single: in fact, I was one of the first four people Bob asked. He called me in the studio when I was recording *No Jacket* and said, 'Did you see the television? What are you doing next Sunday?' I told him, 'I'm not doing anything', so he said, 'Well Midge, me, Sting and George Michael are getting together, and we need a drummer.' There was nobody else involved at that point, that was all he had. I figured that as I had been part of the Band Aid band, it would be logical for me to be involved in Live Aid somehow, but as I read more about it, I found myself thinking, 'This ain't gonna happen, this global jukebox can't possibly happen', especially given the technology at the time, 'it will be a disaster'.

Then I got a call from Tony Smith, I think, asking me if I was going to take part, and I told him I'd play drums if somebody wanted me to play with them. A little later I was in Dallas, and went over to see Robert Plant, who was rehearsing there. He said, 'Any chance of getting me on the Live Aid show?', because Bill Graham and Led Zeppelin had had a big bust-up. 'Maybe you, me and Jimmy could do something?' I said, 'Sure, I'll play drums. It sounds like a great idea'. Then in another hotel room Sting called me up. 'Are you going to do this Live Aid thing?' I said I thought I would. He said, 'Do you want to do it together?' And I was happy to, because Sting had sung on *No Jacket Required* and we'd become friendly.

Somewhere in amongst all that, Tony Smith said all the people you want to play drums with, including Eric Clapton, are now playing in America, but it is possible that you could get on Concorde and perform at both shows. I asked him if anybody else was doing it, because I didn't want to look like I was showing off, and he told me Duran Duran were due to be playing in London and Power Station in Philadelphia, or vice versa, so some of their members would make the journey with me. Both bands ended up in Philadelphia, so in the end there was nobody on that plane apart from me.

The event took place a week after I finished the *No Jacket Required* tour, and I wasn't in touch with Mike and Tony. I left my kids with my mother, got on the plane, went and came back, which

Previous pages: Phil enjoying the rain in Japan.
Above: Phil performs 'Mama', Philadelphia, November 1983.

became the link, and for some reason I never considered whether Genesis could have played. It would have been perfectly logical for me to have played drums in my own band and I'm sure that had it been a moment of activity for Genesis we would have been asked. But the question never came up.

TONY: I had been working on some more film music, for a low-budget science fiction film called *2084*, followed by a Kevin Bacon movie, *Quicksilver*, which was probably his least successful film ever. Unfortunately it happened to be the one I wrote the music for. I thought I'd put the music for the two films together on an album called *Soundtracks*. I included one song with Toyah Willcox, called 'Lion of Symmetry'. I thought Toyah had a great voice, but only ever sang these simple things, so I set her a challenge and she really rose to it. She wrote one set of lyrics, and I said, 'That's good, let's do it, and the next day she came round my house and said, 'No, it's a crap lyric – I've written a completely new one.' I find that a very stirring song. I also worked with Jim Diamond – I couldn't believe how high he could sing – and Fish: everyone had said Marillion were reminiscent of early Genesis, why not do something with Fish?' When we were writing the song, 'Shortcut To Somewhere' he got through one whole case of John Smiths. Great fun, nice chap. Mike meanwhile had started having success with Mike + The Mechanics, and his idea of trying to give the impression that a solo album was a group, even if technically it wasn't – although the Mechanics did end up becoming a kind of group for live performances. It was something I vaguely tried to do much later on with my *Bankstatement* project.

MIKE: I had sung on my second solo album, *Acting Very Strange*, and it was horrible. I didn't like it, I can't sing, and I thought, 'I ain't going to do that again'. I went to our publisher and told him I wanted to find some co-writers. He recommended BA Robertson and the producer Chris Neil. Chris rang me one day, and he must have been looking out the window on a cold, wet November day, and said 'Let's do it in Montserrat'. So off we went, myself and Chris and the drummer Peter Van Hooke and Adrian Lee on keyboard. Looking back, it was quite brave. We had no singers in mind. I played them my demos, which sounded so crap, you know, me singing horribly, and I could see these guys thinking, 'What the fuck is this going to be like', but it worked. They were great, great sessions, we recorded the tracks and then came back to find some vocalists. Paul Carrack came down and sang 'Silent Running' on the first day, Paul Young sang 'All I Need Is A Miracle'. It was a kind of magic, the album happened without really trying. We put the album out and no one was very confident – certainly I never am – and there was a key moment at Atlantic in America. They were about to choose the lead single, and the obvious choice was 'Hanging By A Thread', a heavy track, but Andrea Ganis, who was involved with the singles said, 'No, let's go with 'Silent Running'. It was seven minutes long so we cut it down and without that we'd never have got off the ground. The single went to American radio and they loved it. It was number one in the rock charts for two or three months. I couldn't believe it. And the pleasure was that no one quite knew who Mike + The Mechanics were. It was a chance to be reassessed without any baggage.

PHIL: I don't feel very comfortable looking at the 'me' of that period. If I look at some of the DVDs of those tours and how we performed, I can see this danger of becoming larger than life. That is the stadium effect, where you become a parody of yourself. You are very aware of how big your gestures are. I went to see the Stones at Earls Court in 1978 and watching Jagger, who was by that point obviously a little bit of a caricature. He was playing to everybody in the venue but close up, it was like, 'Whoa, turn it down a bit, Mick'. I feel that was me in that period.

TONY: The increasing size of Genesis tours brought some additional problems. I have always hated flying, and we were often flying on a daily basis, which was tedious. There were more and more interviews and these terrible meet and greets before the show. Phil would say, 'I can't do this meet and greet, because I've got to look after my voice' so we'd troop out there and of course the only person they wanted to meet was Phil. Sometimes we'd drag Chester and Daryl along to make up the numbers, poor guys, and all we could hear was people whispering to each other, 'Where's Phil, where's Phil?' It made you feel somewhat superfluous to requirements even though you knew that you were an integral part of what this was all about.

Of course even to be in that position is fun. Sitting up on stage looking out over these monster crowds throughout that period I would be thinking how absurd it all was, quite absurd. You write a little tune and then suddenly there it is out in front of those people. There is a huge satisfaction in playing something you've written and hearing that response to it. That's the nicest part about playing live. I don't get any great thrill out of being the centre of attention. But the ability to play something to an audience and to get an immediate response from them is exciting.

The gigs were becoming almost like celebrations of our whole career, especially the *Invisible Touch* tour onwards. In my mind they do start to blend into one another. They become less distinctive because you are playing endless arenas and stadiums. The very early shows when we were playing to three people in Beaconsfield always stick more strongly.

PHIL: I often thought, 'Wouldn't it be great if we could suddenly magic it together and do half a dozen shows without the six weeks of rehearsal, the three weeks of production work and the lighting run-throughs?'

Above: Tony – at this point in the band's career he says that he, Mike and Phil were working together so well, it was 'almost like being one person'.
Opposite: During a break at Shepperton Studios.
Overleaf: Ronnie and Nancy Reagan say hi.

TONY: Creating the shape and structure of these shows was something we thought about very hard – like organizing the flow of an album. I see groups on stage who still don't seem to understand how to pace sets. OK, they might end with their big number, but they don't understand how you can play with an audience in the way that you construct the set. Genesis's music really lends itself to that because it has both length and atmosphere.

We always tried to mix things together. You knew that the first time you played a piece on stage everyone would want to hear the old songs, as they called them, which was the material from the previous album which they hadn't wanted to hear at all on that album's tour. But you could introduce the new songs in a way that made them very palatable; you didn't necessarily have to play a whole string of them one after the other. On the first tour we did after *Trick Of The Tail* we even used 'Los Endos' as the end song on that tour, even though it was a new song, and it worked really well.

We also tended to avoid including the slightly more subtle and softer songs, or at least we had to be more careful about using them. We never played, which I regret, songs like 'Blood On The Rooftops', 'Many Too Many', 'Mad Man Moon' or 'Undertow'. That was cowardice on our part, because we could have slipped the odd one in occasionally. And as time went on there was less room in any case. The main problem, when there is as much material as we have, is what we aren't going to play.

TONY: Family has always been an important part of our attitude to the group. We made a decision right from the very early days that people would be able to bring their wives and girlfriends on tour and that it would be a group expense – and at the time the money was quite a factor, but we just absorbed it.

I got married in 1972 during the making of *Foxtrot*, and so we took one day off for a honeymoon down in Dartmoor and drove back the next day so we could carry on recording the album. In lieu of the proper honeymoon the others said Margaret could come out on a tour in Italy a few weeks later and that became the way.

Margaret and I didn't have children until 1978 so up until then she used to come on the road with me most of the time, as did Angie, Mike's girlfriend and later wife, and Phil with Andy in the early days. They could come when they wanted to. They had to make the decision whether they wanted to come. And of course, there were compensations. You get to see the world.

On one of our early American tours we had five or six days off between Vancouver and Fort Wayne so Margaret and I decided to drive between them with Regis Boff, who was the tour manager. It was fantastic to be able to drive through Yellowstone Park and make the journey interesting from a tourist point of view. I was never into what you might call the party life so we concentrated on being explorers wherever we went. On another tour we drove to the Grand Canyon, went down the Canyon on mules, came back up and then drove that evening to Las Vegas. We used to pack it in.

MIKE: When I talk to women friends married to other musicians, they often say, 'Isn't touring so boring, don't you hate all the travelling?' Angie always took the view that it was fun, she preferred to see the glass as half full, not half empty. And it was exciting to go round the world, even though it could be tiring. I remember on some of the early tours when our daughter Kate was a baby not sleeping for days because we couldn't afford a nanny though. But we always tried to have the approach that it was great to do, not a drag, that we were travelling with a bunch of friends. In those days Angie was modelling she wasn't so free to come on every trip, but because she used to model she had a similar lifestyle – a bit hectic, a bit crazy. A lot of friends had wives who wouldn't come on tour and when they did it was all a bit uptight. I always enjoyed touring when Angie was there.

TONY: Even when the children came along, when they were very young you could still bring them on tour. I am always reminding my son that he went to Japan when he was ten months old: they loved this blue-eyed boy who was virtually bald, he was constantly being handed round in the restaurants.

I don't know whether other bands have the same attitude. I get the impression they don't, and that bands have problems with wives getting on. We've been very lucky, we get on with each other and all the wives. And I think it has helped to keep us all sane.

MIKE: Our kids grew up knowing that this is what dad did for a living. It was a great education for them, they were very comfortable with new situations and new people, not like kids who go into a strange house, and feel nervous and apprehensive. My eldest two, Tom and Kate, came along an awful lot, Harry missed out because he was a little younger, but then later, on the *Turn It On Again* tour, he came on the road in Europe to help record the show, which he loved because he wants to go into audio recording and producing. Tom decided to become a music manager, even though I tried to warn him off.

Opposite: Mike's wife Angie takes Tom and Kate on tour. This page, clockwise from top left: Tony and Margaret with their daughter Emily at Phil and Jill's wedding; Tony's son Ben plays with Phil's children Joely and Simon backstage in San Francisco; Simon and Joely Collins again, this time with Tony Smith's son, Chris (centre); Kate Rutherford poses with Joely Collins and Ben Banks in the band room; Harry and Tom Rutherford on the 1992 tour – Mike explains: 'There was only one sandwich!'; Nicholas and Mathew follow in dad Phil's footsteps; Phil with Orianne and Nicholas; Lily Collins and Harry Rutherford 'get married' in Portugal.

Above: Phil with Pete Townshend backstage in New York. Phil says, 'We've always been big fans of the Who.'
Right and overleaf: At Twickenham Film Studios for the 'Illegal Alien' video shoot, including 'things to do with courgettes', as Phil puts it, and Tony in the car.
Overleaf, inset: Mike and Phil get a makeover for the 'Jesus He Knows Me' shoot.

PHIL: I left Genesis quite a few times in my head to play with other bands. I got this phone call from Pete Townshend, who I'd met a few times: would I come down to his place in Twickenham to work with a harpist and piano player called Raphael Rudd? By coincidence his Oceanic recording studio is built on the site of my mum and dad's boat club in Twickenham that was called Dick Waite's boatyard. I've got photographs of me as a baby in my mother's arms on that site. I sent one to Pete, a fantastic picture of all the people in the club, with all the buildings where the skiffs and punts used to be stored. And Pete wrote me back a letter on which the ink had run where he'd been crying as he was writing; he had the picture hanging in his studio.

I went there to play with him and he was, unbeknownst to me, hanging out with Steve Strange all night, but we did four or five tracks together. This was a few years after Keith Moon had died, and I said to Pete, 'If ever you need a drummer', if ever you need one, please, I know I could do this'. He said, 'Shit, I've just asked Kenney Jones and we're going out on the road with him because he used to stand in for Moon when Keith was a bit out of it'. Later the Who asked me to rehearse for a week for an Albert Hall show with them and I said no, because I didn't want to be away from home for a week. Now I think, 'If only I'd done it'. Playing with the Who would be a dream come true for me.

TONY: By the time of *Invisible Touch*, we went in with such confidence: everything was flowing out of us. We were writing songs left, right and centre. The improvisation was producing results. I think we were working really well together: we knew our strengths and our weaknesses, but we were still challenging each other. We weren't complacent. We suddenly got really good at writing these shorter songs. There's virtually no song on that album you could say was by one person rather than another. It was very much writing as a totality, three people writing almost as one. If you listen to a song like 'Land Of Confusion' you might think, 'How could three people write a song like that?' And I can't really answer that question, but that's how it was.

PHIL: From 'Mama' onward, whoever had the most energy for the song would write the lyrics, even though the song itself was group-written. I wrote the lyrics for 'Invisible Touch', sitting there with the drum machine and singing along to the music. Out of nowhere a phrase like 'She seems to have an invisible touch' will pop up.

INVISIBLE TOUCH WAS AN EASY WRITE. IT'S ALWAYS A GOOD SIGN WHEN IDEAS FLOW OUT SO QUICKLY. Mike Rutherford

TONY: Because *Invisible Touch* produced so many hit singles it's slightly strange for me: my favourite track on the album, for example, is probably 'Domino', which was not a single. I thought the album showed a real confidence, and as a writer I'm very pleased with that: lots of good songs, well done. It is a simpler album, which is maybe why I particularly like 'Domino' – which is more complicated, and less well-known. If 'Land Of Confusion' was Mike's anti-war moment then 'Domino' was mine – and I always take a lot longer to say things.

It was the idea that politicians take these sweeping decisions – and they're never easy decisions to make – but they never think of the individual and how his life or her life is completely turned upside down by the repercussions, and will never be the same from that moment on. The idea I had in mind was not the communist Domino Effect, but those huge Japanese domino patterns: one falls over, and there's nothing you can do to stop it. Sometimes with these politicians I don't think they really know what it is they have set in motion, and that's what worries me. The second half of the song took a much more detached viewpoint about our attitude to seeing war or bloodshed on television, the awful fascination.

PENSIÓN

Below: Contemplating success. Mike says, 'The success we were enjoying didn't make that much difference. You'd still go in the studio, play a couple of chords, set up a drum machine beat and a song would take place. You're not really in control of it: you can't try and chase it, you should never do that. And for a while you get good at it.'
Opposite page, above: Phil and producer Hugh Padgham in 1994: as well as his production on the Genesis albums, Hugh worked with Phil on his solo material.
Opposite page, below: Mike and Phil crank it up.
Overleaf and following pages: Backstage at Wembley, July 1987, and on stage in Toulouse, France, also on the 1987 tour.

The really poignant part of the song for me are the lines 'In silence and darkness we held each other near that night, we prayed it would last forever', the idea that some little thing could happen and it would all be over.

Invisible Touch was the first album where we suddenly felt that we were going to have a hit whatever we did. Now that may be a bad thing to think, but that's what we thought. In a way the album couldn't fail. If it had failed I think Genesis would have died there and then. Phil had an alternative career he could have gone to at any point.

PHIL: I had been responsible in some respects for bringing in new blood and Hugh Padgham in particular. There came a point, though, which was might happened in any case as a natural parting of the ways, but I remember this quote coming up when we were recording *Invisible Touch*. I try very hard not to rest on any laurels, I'm never looking back and saying, 'That one worked so this will work'. I'm as good as the next thing I do rather than the last thing I did. During the recording sessions there was a question over some aspect of the work, and Hugh said, 'Well, we won some Grammies, it can't be wrong' or words to that effect. It was probably a throwaway line and he's doubtless forgotten he ever said it, but it certainly rang a bell with me

and I felt that we were due for a bit of a change. Because doubt is a good thing, it makes you try harder, while complacency is the worst thing you want.

TONY: 'Follow You, Follow Me', which pre-dated Phil's solo success, had opened a door which had been closed to us up to that point: radio. From then on we became a radio band and even quite difficult songs like 'Turn It On Again' or 'Mama' and would get radio play. By the time of *Invisible Touch*, we were putting out songs like 'Invisible Touch', 'Land Of Confusion', 'Throwing It All Away', 'In Too Deep', and they were all hit songs. In America they were all big hits, top ten, top five even. It was a great period and audiences were massive. It was a strange thing, a bit of a dream, really. In 1987 on the *Invisible Touch* tour we played Wembley Stadium, four nights in a row; that's nearly 300,000 people.

MIKE: With the four nights at Wembley, when you're doing it you're in such a world of thinking about 'the next show after this'. There's so much going on all round that you can't really savour it.

NEARLY 300,000 PEOPLE AT WEMBLEY.
OK, THERE MIGHT HAVE BEEN A FEW REPEATS IN THERE,
BUT I THOUGHT AT THE TIME, AND I STILL THINK NOW,
THAT MOMENT WAS THE PEAK OF OUR CAREER. TONY BANKS

THE EXEC'S TALE: AHMET ERTEGUN

Tony Stratton Smith was a very good friend of mine and also of my brother Nesuhi. Nesuhi was a soccer buff – Brian Glanville once told me that when it came to obscure teams my brother was the only other person who knew what was going on – and Tony Stratton Smith was not only a music person, but also a former sports journalist who was into horses and horse racing. We enjoyed each other's company. Tony was a grandiose person and a heavy drinker, and I was a heavy drinker too. I just liked to be with him. Atlantic took over not only Genesis but a few of Tony's other groups on Charisma, although Genesis was the main thing.

The first two albums we had put out, Selling England By The Pound and The Lamb Lies Down On Broadway, were at least critically very well acclaimed and developed immediately a small but ardent group of supporters. I had had experience before with groups who didn't break big right away but who obviously possessed great talent – like Yes, where the first couple of albums didn't sell the numbers we expected but we knew the talent was there.

This particular group Genesis, to me, was one of the best groups of all time and Peter Gabriel was the genius at the heart of it. But everybody in that group was intelligent. A lot of rock'n'roll groups had talented and charismatic guys, good-looking lead singers or a flashy guitarist, whatever. But here was a group with intelligence and great musical ability, and they were venturesome and more interested in going beyond the edge than they were interested in sounding like a band that was selling a lot of records. They would have never, ever have dreamt of copying anybody else. They were anti-commercial.

I admire that because I admire people who have passion for music. So many have great passion for fame. This group had passion for music. Before we started working with them, various people, especially friends of mine, had been telling me, 'Oh my God, Genesis are playing in LA, Ahmet, I wish you were here.' It was such an experience for these people to hear the group play: Peter Gabriel is not an everyday occurrence. He is a very, very special artist and when he decided to leave the group it was a big blow. I just didn't know what would happen.

I knew that the group was not going to stop because Peter Gabriel was not 100 per cent of the group. Tony Banks and Mike Rutherford again are not your run-of-the-mill musicians: they are very special people and very special musicians. And then we had a search for another singer. When they said that they really couldn't find a singer and that Phil Collins, who was the drummer, who was a great drummer, was going to be the singer, I went out to Minneapolis or Milwaukee, some midwestern town, to hear the group without Peter Gabriel.

And I tell you I have never been so bowled over as I was by the performance that Phil gave. He took over that stage as though he had been a singer, a performer, a star, all his life. He owned the stage. He was twice as cocky and sure of himself as Bobby Darin was when he first started out. Of course Phil was also a terrific songwriter, although we didn't know that then, and he possessed a certain magic that none of the others in the group – including Peter Gabriel – had had up to that point, the magic of connecting with an audience.

Peter Gabriel's sounds and lyrics had had a totally different feel. They had been more reflective and more personal, more abstract and not as universal. With Phil upfront, what had been a very abstract rock'n'roll show became a great evening's entertainment with terrific music and the band felt it too. They all came alive and so Genesis continued to be the great band that it did.

At one point after Tony Smith had taken over the management of the band, I guess he was a little frustrated at the lack of sales, and what he thought was a lack of promotional support. Everybody always thinks that there's a lack of promotion, a lack of this and that. Tony came in to see me and said to me, 'You know, there are very few people that I haven't liked in the music business since I've been in it, and I get along with everybody, but I must tell you that I hate you! You are one of the worst, because you stay here in New York and talk about how you love this band and you don't do shit, you don't do anything.' I mean he tore into me. I said, 'Look, Tony, all I can do is promise you that we're going to try even harder but I guarantee you I can't make people like something more than they do, and I don't think that you have the kind of band who I can tell to play differently. I wouldn't do that, anyway, and if I don't like the way they're playing I won't stay with it. I happen to love Genesis and I'm sorry they don't sell as much as Foreigner, or whatever the hot-selling band that week was.

He was not at all happy and still very angry, but within a year after that, he called me up and invited me to his wedding, to which I went very happily, and we became very close friends. Not because I had done anything special, but I think he saw that there was a sincere attempt by Atlantic to work with him. If we signed a band or a singer and we kept them, not trying to sell their records would be self-destructive, foolhardy.

There are occasions where somebody is signed to the label and then the record comes out and the reaction of the public is so negative that it becomes very discouraging, because it seems impossible. But with Genesis we've had nothing but delight. Right from the time that Peter Gabriel left, the band made some incredible records and albums which were also great hits, but still retained some of the elements that *prevented the music from being 100 per cent commercial, because the Genesis sound, which they never lost, was always a different sound than a pop sound.*

They also, which was unusual for a group this big, had hits as solo artists. Phil Collins we know about. Phil took them to a new commercial place but he couldn't take them all the way because to do that he had to go on his own – but he loves the Genesis sound and the music. To me that's the sign of a great musician, somebody who will go to where he wants whether it's commercial or not and who will recreate the kind of music he believes in. Mike Rutherford had great success on his own, with the Mike + The Mechanics albums. Peter Gabriel likewise with his solo albums, some of which were with Atlantic. Unfortunately Jerry Greenberg, in a moment of total aberration – I don't know what happened – gave Peter a release, which I never quite forgave Jerry for. Tony Banks, who is true to his beliefs and represents ninety per cent of the Genesis sound, never, alas, broke through.

I think it would be great one day – when they all have time – to get both Peter Gabriel and Steve Hackett back together with the rest of the group and to have a reunion of that version of the band – the trio reunion is hot, but the five of them together, that would be met by tremendous relish on the part of all of us who love their passion.

And it would be something special for a generation who never saw that particular line-up play live, just as when I was a young kid, getting into the first great pop music I heard, which was the Duke Ellington band and Cab Calloway orchestra at the London Palladium in the early 1930s, and realising that by the time I came to America in 1935 I had missed out on the great New Orleans music. I kept wishing that I could have been in Chicago when the King Oliver band came up with the young Louis Armstrong on trumpet.

As co-founder of Atlantic Records, Ahmet Ertegun, born in Istanbul and educated in America, discovered and nurtured the careers of a roster of extraordinary talent. Atlantic's acts included Ray Charles, Bobby Darin, Aretha Franklin, Wilson Pickett, Cream, Led Zeppelin, the Allman Brothers and CSN&Y as well as the Rolling Stones and Genesis: Ahmet Ertegun had, in the industry lingo, 'great ears'. When his older brother Nesuhi joined the label he added jazz to the mix (also one of Ahmet's first loves) with John Coltrane, Ornette Coleman and the MJQ. Shortly after giving the interview for this book, Ahmet Ertegun suffered a bad fall backstage at a Stones concert, and died from complications on 14th December 2006. In an obituary in the *Guardian*, Adam Sweeting wrote that 'he wasn't merely a record mogul or talentspotter. Ertegun brought an air of refinement and sophistication to a notoriously unscrupulous business'.

CHAPTER TWELVE

THE TRAVELLERS REST

PHIL: If you go right back to *Face Value*, I never sat down and wrote anything down for that record. 'In The Air Tonight' was totally improvised. I sang what came out of my head and wrote it down afterwards. And because it worked for that first record, that's what I've always done. When I'm singing along the phrases come out. You can hit higher notes singing some words or if your throat's in a particular position. You're improvising with your voice in the same way you would improvise on a sax.

On the *We Can't Dance* album that's how I came up with the chorus of 'Jesus he knows me and he knows I'm right', 'You're no son, you're no son of mine', all that stuff. But to write 'Driving The Last Spike', I ended up getting hold of a book about the navvies. I don't know why but I just thought there was a story there to be told. And that was one of only a few story lyrics I ever wrote.

TONY: *We Can't Dance* is very much a successor to *Invisible Touch*. I see the two albums as related. In my mind, they do slightly blur together, even though they were separated by six years. Overall I feel *Invisible Touch* is the better album of the two, although I like one or two of the tracks on *We Can't Dance*. 'No Son Of Mine' is certainly one of the best songs we've ever done. By this time Phil had really developed into a very good lyric writer and that is a wonderful lyric, which communicates its ideas very, very well.

'I Can't Dance' itself was a prime example of the way we were working together at that point. Mike had been playing a riff but we had never quite found the way to build on it. It was nearly right but it wasn't very exciting. I had a new keyboard which had a drum setting on it and I started playing the drums on it. The song took on a character which became more humorous, so Phil wrote a funny lyric to reflect that.

PHIL: It was the most involved I'd ever been in any Genesis album and ironically the last I was involved with. And the tour was very relaxed – jeans, T-shirt, nothing appeared false. We still saw ourselves as a group of songwriters who were just as happy playing 'I Can't Dance' as we were with a twelve-minute song like 'Driving The Last Spike'. People all had their own agendas by that point about what they thought we should be doing. I remember Roger Waters saying that you'd never get Bob Dylan or John Lennon writing a song like 'I Can't Dance'. He failed to see the humour in it. I think Roger sometimes fails to see the humour in a lot of things.

TONY: *We Can't Dance* was very, very smooth. Our self-confidence was at a level where we played the record company just one track, 'No Son of Mine', and said 'this is the single'. We had a different producer for that album. Nick Davis was someone both Mike and I had worked with on our solo projects. Once again we couldn't change ourselves so we thought we'd change the producer because it might make us sound a little different.

On the tour Tony Smith was always going round looking a little nervous. After about three months he turned up, smiling and beaming, to tell us, 'Today is breakeven day'; we had finally paid off the expense of this tour. We put millions and millions of pounds into this bloody thing, we had trucks of stuff going round the world and people coming out of our ears. It was a very, very expensive tour to put on, but obviously once you broke even then you were making lots of money – that was the risk.

MIKE: After *We Can't Dance*, our plans were no more fixed or unfixed than before. 'Let's See' has always been our motto, 'let's see how we feel'. At the time we finished each of those last three albums, I'd think, 'God, I'm surprised and very pleased that Phil still wants to do this'. I always thought it was a testament to what Genesis stood for – and that it was good and fun to be part of – that he stayed. He had a very heavy workload, with his solo and his Genesis commitments, especially the promotional side which is so huge. Each time you were thinking, 'Maybe that's our lot'.

Opposite: Back to work, a portrait by David Scheinmann (shot at Chiddingfold Working Men's Club).

These pages and overleaf: Stage shots from the 1992 tour, including the iconic 'The way we walk' image in a few of its many manifestations.

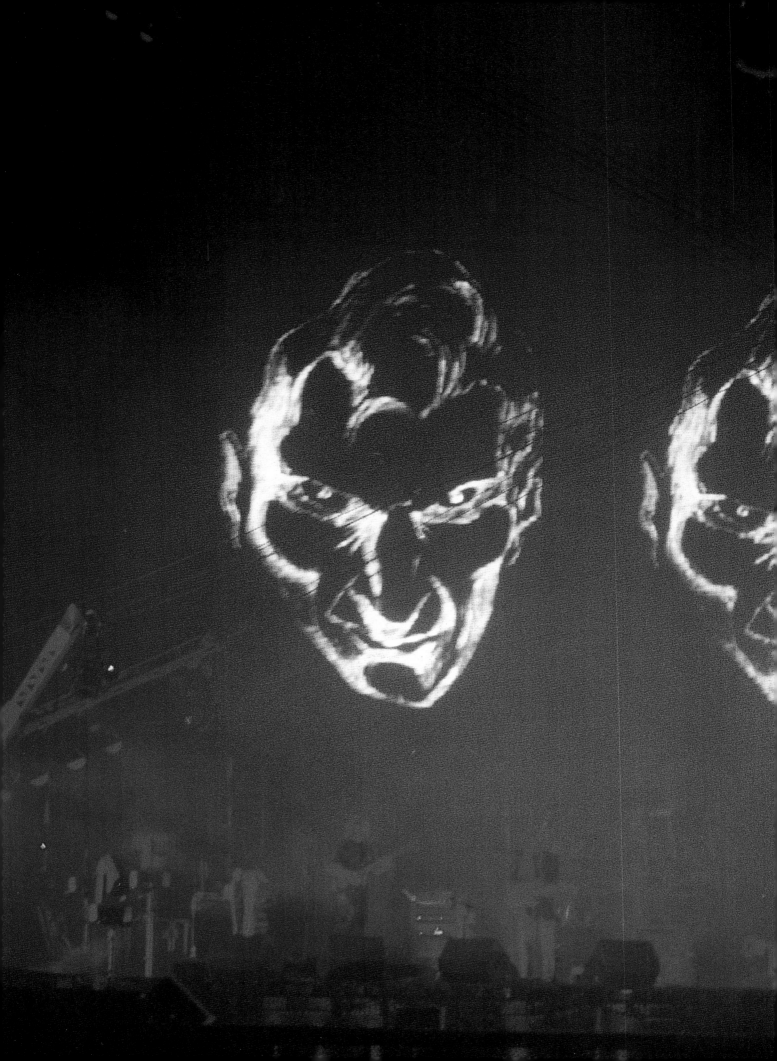

In the early days you did a solo record, put it out, and within three or four months, it had run its course and had disappeared. Nowadays the whole format has changed: there are three or four singles, videos. The process lasts a year, maybe even a year and a half if the album does well. That changed the whole timescale.

We would have these big long gaps between projects, and didn't necessarily talk that much in between. and I think it was Tony Smith who told me that Phil maybe wanted to wrap it up.

TONY: We started to get rumours back about Phil. I'd hear things from Daryl, who was playing guitar in Phil's band. It was looking unlikely that Phil would want to come back again. With the films and his other activities there was too much going on for him to fit it all in.

Above: Back at the Farm for *We Can't Dance*.

PHIL: I'll tell you what happened. We had played on tour in Vancouver and my first wife, who I had invited with the kids to the show, asked me whether I had visited this particular old schoolfriend of mine, who'd actually been the love of my life when I was at school, and who now lived in LA. I said, 'No, it's funny. I've been to LA I don't know how many hundreds of times and she's never come to the show to say hello. I know she's married, got kids and stuff.' Anyway Andy gave me her number and I took the bait and called her. It was a pivotal decision, because this woman and I had some unfinished business and we started an affair which caused the end of my marriage to Jill. Then the affair itself ended, we had closure on it, and went our separate ways.

This was the period when I started writing *Both Sides*. I was living in West Sussex, working on a 12-track Akai, doing everything, guitar samples, bass samples. I went to see Harry Connick Jr one night at the Albert Hall and he played Hoagy Carmichael's 'I Get Along Without You Very Well'. The whole premise of that song is that I get along without you right until the moment someone says something that reminds me of you and then of course I go to pieces. I went home and wrote 'I've Forgotten Everything', one of my favourite songs on that record, which was my version of the Hoagy Carmichael song. I wrote it in an hour, improvised the words. It was like *Face Value* to the power of a hundred.

And for me there was no going back. I thought, 'This is what I want to do. I don't want to go back to a band environment. How can I possibly go back to singing about double-glazing when I've done this?' I felt I didn't want to compromise any more. I was in my early forties, and wondering whether maybe this was meant to be. You outgrow things; you can't expect Monty Python to stay together forever. You naturally mature and have to leave the mother ship.

During the promotion for *Both Sides* I was flying somewhere with Tony Smith, and I told him the way I was feeling. 'I think I'm leaving it now. I don't think I want to go to that group situation where I have to sing lyrics that I didn't write when this is my life you see on this record.' We both agreed to see how we felt in a year's time when it came to the next Genesis record and I never changed my mind, but I didn't go on about it.

I knew that I'd left, and when we had a meeting at Tony Smith's house I actually announced it officially. And the others took it great. I was relieved that they were going to carry on. My biggest fear had been that suddenly there would be all these people out of work. Because hey, I'm a rich guy, and Tony and Mike are rich guys, but it's the guys who work for you who are suddenly out of a job and have got families to support and they have spent their working life supporting you.

WHEN THEY SAID THEY WERE GOING TO CARRY ON, THAT WAS THE BEST NEWS I COULD HAVE HAD. BECAUSE I DIDN'T WANT TO BREAK GENESIS UP, I JUST DIDN'T WANT TO BE PART OF IT ANY MORE. I LEFT THE OFFICE AND THE OFFICE CARRIED ON. PHIL COLLINS

TONY: We met at the house for a last supper to talk about it and Phil said he'd definitely decided not to do it again. At that point, my own inclination was to call it a day. Of course part of me felt like proving we could do it without Phil. But I didn't know whether I wanted to go through it all again. We'd had a fantastic time and now we were losing one of the major stars in the music business. It was going to be bloody difficult. But Mike was keen.

MIKE: When Phil decided to leave the critical question was whether we would carry on. From my point of view, I thought that I liked working with Tony, and that if I didn't carry on with Genesis it would mean us not working together again. Tony always says that I was the keenest at this point, but I'm not sure I remember it that way. I certainly felt it was worth a try.

I had just finished the Mechanics album, *Beggar On A Beach of Gold*, which the 'Over My Shoulder' single came off, and as alternating between the Mechanics and Genesis had always been great, I was up for a bit of that music. I'm sure somewhere in my psyche there was a little voice saying we'd survived losing one singer and we could do it again.

TONY: I had thought that *We Can't Dance* might well be the last album we did with Phil, so when I wrote the lyric to 'Fading Lights', another of my terminal songs, I had the idea of ending the song with the word 'remember'. And it is very poignant in that context, because it marked the end of a large part of our career.

PHIL: After making the decision to leave, of course I sometimes missed the environment of being in the band that wrote 'No Son Of Mine', because it is very, very special to come up with a song like that out of thin air, sitting in a room with nothing written and Tony playing something, me singing something that goes with that, and Mike reacting to what I'm singing. Something fantastic emerges from the fog for a minute, and that minute becomes the nucleus. It's very difficult to achieve that kind of chemistry.

TONY: Once Mike and I had made the decision to carry on, Mike suggested we go down to the Farm to try some writing and 'see if anything happens'.

Below: Phil miming on guitar for the 'I Can't Dance' video shoot. Overleaf and following pages: Tour shots by Armando Gallo.

MIKE: Writing with Tony had been a big part of my life but I hadn't realized how far apart we are musically. It had always seemed to me that it was 'Mike and Tony's music', with Phil somehow alongside us. What I discovered going in to write without Phil, was that Phil had actually been the guy in the middle, and that he had made Tony and me work well together by pulling on a bit there from Tony and a bit here from me, bringing in his great melodies and lines, helping complement what we did with him and what we did with each other. There had been something about the chemistry of the three of us that made me and Tony work well together. Now that Phil wasn't there, we had to find our own way to come together.

TONY: As always happens when Mike and I get together, we produced some things we were excited by. So we prepared ourselves to go through the traumatic business of trying to find a new singer. We knew neither of us could handle the singing.

RAY WILSON: I was in the kitchen in my flat in Edinburgh. I had a small studio downstairs, there were guys hanging around and making a mess, and I was having breakfast or making tea. The phone rang and it was Tony Smith, saying, 'I am Tony Smith, manager of Genesis. Phil Collins has left, we're thinking of getting a new singer, and the guys have heard your voice on the Stiltskin record'. When you get a call like that you get a rush, you know.

These pages: More tour shots. Overleaf: Phil performing 'Jesus He Knows Me': 'Give me 18 million dollars by the weekend.'

You want say 'Wow'; you feel good about yourself. You want a beer and a cigarette even if you don't drink or smoke. But two years prior to this I'd also had a phone call telling me, 'You're number one in the charts', so I had lived that high before and here it was again in a different guise.

I was torn, because there was definitely a part of me that was not sure it would be the right thing to do, because my heart was in the music and the songs I had been writing, but of course another part of me was shouting, 'You can't not do it, it's too good not to do.'

TONY: The question we couldn't ask Ray at the time was 'Why the hell do you want to do this?' I was always amazed that anybody would want to take the job on, and surprised by how many people did want to do it. Ray was always going to suffer comparisons with Phil, and there was a high chance of failure. I don't know what we did for Ray's career, but it was an experience if nothing else.

RAY: I travelled down to the Farm to audition, quite full of myself. 'Arrogant' would be a true description. I've always had that kind of self-belief and I went down there having written this album I was really proud of and thinking, 'Maybe I can use some of these songs within this new Genesis album'. Of course that wasn't going to happen, but...

I remember standing in front of Mike and Tony and Tony Smith saying, 'Look, the bottom line is I've done my own album, I've got a deal organized for it, so it's not really that important to me whether I sing with you guys or not. What's important is that it's right.' I was very confident about it, deep down probably not feeling that way, but certainly coming across like that.

TONY: I thought Ray had a lot of talent. We could have used his talent better, because he showed so many moments of what he could do with us.

RAY: It would scare the shit out of anybody really, standing there singing in front of these guys watching you from the control room. Right, here goes, sing. Headphones on, everything in the wrong key. One thing I had found out very quickly when they'd sent me the songs to learn was that the key Phil sings in is not the key I sing in and that his voice is higher and lighter than mine. I've got quite a big, round, fat voice so for me to hit a note that he hits takes an awful lot more energy for me than it does for him. I have a lot more in the lower register of my voice.

I'd assumed before the audition that they would transpose the songs for me at the audition, but the original backing tapes were loaded up on the multi-track so I was listening to Phil's and Peter's backing vocals in my ears in all the original keys. But I had a lot of adrenalin, I'd been doing a lot of singing so my voice was pretty strong, and I thought, 'Fuck it, I'll just go for it.'

I started off with 'No Son Of Mine', which is slightly easier to sing because it doesn't really get too high for a spell; you can get right into the song before you hit the really hard stuff. I had sung about three songs before I said, 'Look guys, I can't do this, I cannot hit the notes.' 'It's okay,' they said. 'Don't worry about it, we've heard enough.'

MIKE: Ray did a good job. He had a lower voice, a bit more like Peter's voice, I suppose, with a powerful sound, which with the right words was quite dark. The age difference between Ray and us didn't matter at all. He looked great, and it didn't feel like a problem. The only thing Ray lacked was that both Peter and Phil could let rip towards the end of a song. In the last quarter they would improvise, screech and just go for it. Ray could never quite do that, it's not his thing. He doesn't improvise and go mad, which has always been part of what we have done with singers. Of course, we also had to find a drummer...

NIR ZIDKYAHU: After moving to America the end of 1992, I had wanted to become a member of a working band, after the time I had spent as a session drummer in Israel. I joined a New York band called the Hidden Persuaders, who played alternative melodic rock, and spent four years with them trying, but not ever quite managing, to get a record deal.

After that I was starting to get offers to do sessions again. When the call came through, out of the blue, that Genesis wanted me to audition for them. I did not believe it – not because I doubted my talent as a drummer. I just wondered where this had come from. I went over to the Farm to audition and played for a couple of days: at the time I was a wild young guy, I have always kept that wildness as a drummer even as I have matured into a family man. I wasn't daunted by the auditions, though like any musician I knew the history and the importance of Genesis, and Phil Collins had been a huge figure and influence on me from his work with Brand X as well as Genesis.

After the album, when I was going to be on the tour, I went back to New York to prepare. I knew there was a huge interest within the drummer community, that they were all saying 'Who is this guy who got the gig?' So I isolated myself for a month to learn the material.

A couple of days into tour rehearsals, Mike asked to see me outside, and I was wondering what I had done wrong. Mike said, 'I've got to let you know, you are way ahead of us. You know the material better than we do...'

IF YOU'RE A VOCALIST IT IS VERY IMPORTANT THAT YOU'VE GOT A LOT OF SELF-CONFIDENCE. HOW THE HELL DO YOU REPLACE PHIL COLLINS IN ANYTHING IF YOU HAVEN'T GOT THE BALLS TO DO IT? Ray Wilson

NIR: Ray and I were very similar in some ways. Here we were, two young guys, one a hot-blooded Scot, the other a hot-blooded Israeli, both carrying the pressure of stepping into Phil's shoes. We were so similar, had so much the same outlook, that sometimes there were clashes, though in the end we got along great. And we were both trying to work with these two controlled Brits. It would have made a nice reality TV show...

Tony, Mike and I came from extremely different backgrounds, but the music was our bridge. Beforehand, when I had listened to the classic Genesis tracks, these masterpieces, I had imagined that every bar and every note must have been precisely arranged. I am open and emotional in my work. I'm the type of musician who likes to play what I feel without planning it out too much. But when I arrived in the studio I discovered that they had a much looser way of working than I had imagined. I found myself jamming with songs, experimenting. I could go with the flow. After the first day of working in the studio I had gone back to my room and thought, 'This is great, this is the way I like to play.' I had arrived expecting a much stiffer, squarer attitude. Instead I found I was working with two artists, two musicians, and the music was a journey, every time.

Below and overleaf: Ray Wilson joined Genesis after his time as vocalist with the band Stiltskin, the creation of Peter Lawlor, who had had a 1994 UK number one single with 'Inside', the theme from a TV ad for Levi's Jeans.

RAY: Even at my second audition we had been working on some of the material for the new album, with me singing away, making stuff up, 'bluesing away' as they call it. From that second audition a couple of songs developed, 'Not About Us' and 'There Must Be Some Other Way'.

I discovered from working with Tony and Mike that the quality of their writing is that it is never predictable; the second verse is not quite the same as the first verse. It's similar, but something subtle has changed. That for me is particularly a quality of Tony's writing.

TONY: Ray came in a bit late to contribute too much to the writing – by the time we found him, we'd written most of the pieces in musical terms – but we did definitely use a couple of his ideas. And we thought he had a fantastic voice. It was a question of what he could do with the material. We'd get him to blues along sometimes and used that as a basis particularly for 'Not About Us', and the main line in 'There Must Be Some Other Way', and he wrote the lyrics to 'Small Talk', a really good song. We should have had Ray more involved sooner so we could have got more ideas going. Previously I had been writing either specifically for Phil or for myself, and although some of the songs worked fine when they were transferred to Ray's voice, there were a couple that didn't work so well, particularly 'One Man's Fool'. The first half of the song was good, but the second half suffered. If Phil had been there I just know it would have just taken off and gone somewhere else.

I still thought the album turned out pretty well. And I thought we could do another one after that which would be better because we had learnt how Ray's voice operated and I felt he and we could work well together.

MIKE: I felt that the *Calling All Stations* album was OK, and that had we done more albums with that line-up it would have got better. However, we would have had to bring someone else in to write with us, because I think that the combination Tony, myself and Ray was not quite enough. In any case Ray arrived late in the process, but he brought some good ideas in, especially on 'Small Talk'.

RAY: All the way through working on the album I was waiting for *the* song, the 'Mama' or the 'Land Of Confusion', the song that just jumped out and said, 'I'm your hit, boys'. I never heard it and I remember thinking 'This is Genesis, it must be in there', but it never was, even though there were some great songs on the album.

MIKE: Between starting the *Calling All Stations* album and finishing it there had been a major shift in the industry. It had been coming for years: now older bands like ourselves were not getting radio play. The Mechanics had somehow managed to slip through with the 'Over My Shoulder' song, but after that, the door came down.

TONY: I wonder what Ray felt working with us two, because whether we like it or not we're still two old public school guys, for better or worse.

RAY: I'm a working-class boy and they're upper-class guys. We came from different backgrounds, different educations. But when I worked with them within music I never felt that. It felt very much like I was working with a great keyboard player and a great guitarist/bass player. I never felt that there was a divide when it came to the creative process or even when it came to performance. I felt our working relationship was good. It was painfully obvious, however, that that was where it ended. I was never invited round to the house for tea and scones. It was kept strictly business and I can understand where they were coming from. They were in their forties, I was in my twenties.

During one recording session I'd been singing 'Calling All Stations' or 'There Must Be Some Other Way', one of the songs that took a lot of energy. I came back through from the control room, my face all flushed because I'd put so much into it. And I found Tony Banks doing the Times crossword and Mike ripping some of paper into about fifty different pieces to create a little ball he could throw in the bin or tying the computer up in masking tape...

NIR: There was a lot for me to learn about working with these guys. I was in my late twenties and suffering from a classic case of insecurity, but I had to realize that the support and enthusiasm I was going to get would be given in a different way from the one I was used to. Tony came up to me during rehearsals once and said, 'I know you've come over from America, and that there when you play something good, everyone in the studio will be jumping up and down and cheering and rolling out the red carpet. With us, if we say something you've played is good, we mean it.' They played with a straight bat, literally: in all the time I was with the band I don't think I ever won against Tony at table tennis! His defence was amazing – it was like playing against a wall. However hard I attacked, the ball would always come back.

I had to come to terms and find a role in this community of the band, the crew and the support staff, many of whom had been working together for well over twenty years, and who all knew what to do without being told. And because of their accents I sometimes couldn't even undertand what they were saying, which made it even harder. In any case sometimes it was extremely difficult trying to interpret the unspoken rules. I thought it was just me but then I found out that Chester Thompson had had the same problem when he first joined the band.

TONY: We got our hands badly burned by the tour. I really felt at the time that we should just go out there, play a few theatres and test the waters. And if we had to turn people away, that would have been fine. But the feedback was that the record was going to enter the American charts at number two. We put together another massive tour. It was a mistake. The album was released and it came in at number forty-seven or something. We had to rethink very quickly, the budget growing smaller and smaller. We started downsizing the venues.

We were getting sales in places like Columbus, Ohio – where on the *We Can't Dance* tour we'd sold 80,000 seats – of twenty tickets... We had to cancel the US leg of the tour, which cost a fortune, but we decided to hold the European segment: sales of the album, particularly in Germany, had been better.

MIKE: America just disappeared, really. I think it was a difficult time for British acts in America. The acts who had done well in the past suddenly didn't mean a thing in America. It was a time of change anyway. Had it been five years earlier the result might have been different, but that's life.

TONY: The tour itself was fantastic, great fun. I particularly enjoyed doing it because with the younger guys like Nir Zidkhayu on drums and Anthony Drennan on guitar, as well as Ray, we were a new band. It was fresher. Mike and I felt like grizzled old jazz veterans hanging in there with the young guns; I liked that.

MIKE: In the studio, Nick and Nir on drums both did a good job. The odd thing was that for years Tony and I had never had to think about the drums. We would lay a track down, Phil would sing a guide vocal with the drum machine, and then put the drums down, always knowing what to do, Tony and I were not so great at those decisions, it was a new role for us. I think we suffered because of that. Anthony Drennan was also a bonus as the guitarist on the tour – and we managed pretty well considering we didn't know each other.

RAY: It had never felt like 'a band' in the studio. The only time it ever really felt that we had got to a stage where there was a band and a group of people and it was working was the day it finished. The last gig we ever did was Rock-im-Park at the Nuremburg Stadium, supported by Bob Dylan amongst others. We did that show and it felt that we had finally managed to get it together.

I have a recording on digital video tape that my brother took of the last note of the last ever gig that I did with Genesis. I am walking off the stage. I look over at Tony Smith and I ask him, 'Is that it?' and he says, 'Yes'. Now obviously he meant there was a curfew and we couldn't play any longer – but I knew deep down that that was it.

PHIL: I liked Ray. When I played Earls Court on my *Dance Into The Light* tour, he and Nir, the drummer, both came and were so nice. Ray and I e-mailed each other a couple of times. I don't know him well enough to call him a friend, but I personally felt offended by the public reaction to that line-up.

I felt sorry for them because they needed a bit of time, a bit of commitment from the audience to say, 'Hey, this could work'. My strength is immediacy in terms of my writing. You can hear one of my songs and you can kind of sing it before it's finished. Within Genesis that was tempered by Tony and Mike's longer-term skills. Sometimes I'd think I wasn't going to remember a piece of theirs and then after five or six times I would get it without any prompting. You need patience to allow the good bits to rise to the surface. But nobody had the patience with *Calling All Stations*.

Behind the trio of Mike, Tony and Ray Wilson (left) on tour, the drum seat was taken by Tel Aviv-born Nir Zidkyahu (below), who had been selected to play the majority of the drum tracks on Calling All Stations (Nick D'Virgilio of American band Spock's Beard also appeared on the album). The Corrs' guitarist Anthony Drennan was also added to the live line-up.

RAY: I was never involved in the decision not to do a second album. Tony and Mike were afraid that it might not sell at all and that that would ruin the good name Genesis had built up over thirty years, and I can understand that. But they should never have tried it in the first place if they weren't prepared to see it through. I don't think there's any doubt about that. If they didn't have the balls to do it they shouldn't have done it at all. And they didn't have the balls to do it, that's it in a nutshell.

NIR: My time with Genesis was a bitter-sweet experience, although a lot of fun, and I am proud of my performances on tracks like 'The Dividing Line'. But when it became clear after the end of the *Calling All Stations* tour that would be no follow-up album, I did feel frustration and disappointment, especially as I thought that in the final stages of the tour, the band had begun to glue together, really started sounding like a band. I was so confident at the end of the tour that there would be another album that I took quite a lot of time out back in Israel. When the news came through that the band was not going on, it took me some time to get back into the music scene in New York: the music machine moves so fast, it's difficult to climb back in when you've been away.

Previous pages: The video shoot in Malta for 'Congo': Tony and Mike with Nir Zidkyahu (far left) and Ray Wilson (second left).
This page: Time out during the 'Congo' shoot.
Opposite: Down on England's South Coast.
Overleaf: 1998 reunion of band members past and present. Standing (left to right): Tony, Peter, Ant, Jonathan Silver and Phil. Sitting: Steve and Mike.

I have to be honest, there was some anger at the time. But I came away with many positives, and I learnt a lot about myself, and with ten years' perspective I realize that what was meant to be would be. That's the way it is.

TONY: After the tour, Mike and I swapped positions. Having not wanted to do the previous album, I thought we had found something with potential; we could maybe record with the new live line-up. This time it was Mike who was worried – and maybe rightly – because he felt that a lot of people had bought *Calling All Stations* on spec, and that most of them wouldn't buy another record by the new set-up. Plus we weren't getting any radio play. We called it a day.

IT SEEMED BETTER TO MAKE A DECISION AND ARRANGE OUR OWN EUTHANASIA, RATHER THAN HANGING ON GRIMLY FOR A RATHER NASTY, LINGERING DEATH. TONY BANKS

RAY'S TALE: RAY WILSON

Many people go through the first twenty, thirty years of their life trying to figure out what they want. I found it when I was fourteen: I walked up on stage and sang. I remember singing 'Romeo And Juliet', the Dire Straits song, with my brother Steve on guitar, and seeing girls crying in the front row. I thought, "Well, that's kind of cool.'

There were lots of musicians in my family. My grandfather Fran, my mum's father, was always trying to get me to learn violin, which he played in orchestras. There's a wonderful photograph of him meeting Stéphane Grappelli at Dumfries Town Hall. I've still got a copy of that picture of my grandfather with a tear in his eye, standing next to his idol. At Christmastime our house would be full of people, and my grandfather would play a bit of violin. I don't know if he had Tony Banks's shyness or if he just couldn't be bothered but he was always quite reluctant to get his violin out. He was always reluctant to open his Christmas presents as well, because when he died we found underneath his bed a whole pile of presents he'd never opened.

On the other side of family my father's mother was a singer who performed in working and social clubs. So at least one grandparent on each side of the family was musical. And down the line I have uncles who played guitars and sang, my mother sings very well, my father too, and my brother is a musician. It runs all the way through the family. I was just the one who got lucky, or unlucky, depending on how you look at it.

At school I was in so many bands. There was a 'Bands Night' when I was fifteen or so and a school magazine called it 'The Ray Wilson Show' because I was on stage so often in different groups, including a punk group and a metal band called Electric Mistress. I was obviously already getting on people's nerves back then and making something of an impact, otherwise they wouldn't have bothered.

In one very early school band, playing with a pianist called Fred, I sang a Genesis song, 'Carpet Crawlers'. Now, I'd never heard 'Carpet Crawlers'. Even when I sang it I hadn't heard it: Fred, who wanted to play it, sang it to me. When I tell people this now, they say, 'Yeah, sure,' but it's true. The reason I sang it was not because I was a Genesis fan, it was because Fred was. I was a Bowie fan. I wasn't really interested in anything but Bowie and the rock music my brother was playing, because he was into Iron Maiden and Motörhead. I must've heard Selling England By The Pound, because the song 'The Battle Of Epping Forest' sticks in my mind: it made me think, 'What a bizarre sound.' And somewhere along the line I got a tape of Trick Of The Tail – I probably nicked it from WH Smith. I was really into that record, but not really aware that it wasn't Peter Gabriel or that it was Phil Collins; neither of these characters meant anything to me, in all honesty, back then.

My character was such that I couldn't be anything other than a front man. I was quite an aggressive teenager, and spent most of my early teenage years fighting, until when I was fifteen I fell in love for the first time with a girl who was not impressed by that. I changed the way I was because I really loved this girl and I didn't want to lose her through being perceived as being a thug, although I didn't think I was. I was fighting for recognition because I was feeling a bit lost. In the end music was where I found my place.

I was always a lead vocalist, always in control. I had this strength of character. Once I'd stopped fighting people, I channelled my energy and aggression into putting my own band together, making sure everybody turned up on time to rehearse, being a real tough person to work with, very challenging and demanding. I have only been in two bands where I wasn't in control: Stiltskin and Genesis. When I started working with Stiltskin, Peter Lawlor, who wrote the song for the big Levi's hit, owned the whole thing, and with Genesis the machine was in control, even though I had to do my job properly otherwise the machine would fall apart.

Before Stiltskin I had been doing my apprenticeship on the circuit. With three other guys from Dumfries I had a more middle of the road band called Pink Gin: we moved to Edinburgh and played the working men's clubs in Scotland and the northeast of England, places like Sunderland, when unemployment was pretty high and the mines had just closed down. It was quite sad looking at how depressed the areas had become. And we were their Saturday night. Then I started another band, Guaranteed Pure, with a singer and keyboard player called Paul. We were doing these extreme gigs, one minute some shithole in Aberdeen and the next minute a party for all these weird and wonderful people in the Palace Hotel. Each time, with each new band, I believed we would make it, even if we never did. I still believe the impossible is possible, but, hey, I'm the guy who was having his breakfast

when Genesis called up and asked me to replace me Phil Collins. Why shouldn't I believe anything's possible?

At the beginning of 1994, I bought Melody Maker magazine and a couple of other papers, and answered half a dozen ads, one of which turned out to be Stiltskin. I got a call asking if I'd come and audition, and because everything was on the line, the house was going to be repossessed, I put everything of any worth in the back of my Volkswagen van, Dick Whittington style, drove down to London, slept in the van and did this audition with Peter Lawlor. Three months later I was number one in the charts with 'Inside'. It seemed to me that all the work I'd done up to that point, travelling around playing gigs, had been in one direction and then success actually came from a completely different direction, which so often happens in life. What I'd developed was experience. My voice, a good voice like I'm lucky enough to have, had been kept strong because I'd been singing all the time.

Stiltskin was a real band, a good band. We went out on the road, sold a lot of records. And there were some good songs on the album. It had a very definite sound. Jimmy Iovine from Interscope Records in America was interested in the album, but he wanted to re-produce it and Peter Lawlor didn't want to let him. So Interscope signed Bush instead, and they went on to sell eight million albums; a dreadful waste of an opportunity.

I am often asked, 'Do you regret ever being involved with Genesis?' The answer is, 'Yes and no', because the album that I started recording just after Stiltskin folded and before Genesis called could have given me a career that was my own band. It could have done. I'll never know because Genesis came along. My character is such that as soon as something good happens I'm always thinking, 'OK, well, what bad is round the corner?' I remember hearing Sharon Osborne say that this is a Jewish trait. I'm not sure if it is or not, because I'm not Jewish, but I was always suppressing my emotions all the time, never allowing myself to enjoy anything.

I didn't find out that there wouldn't be another Genesis album for maybe eighteen months, which is a long time. I didn't need to find out. I was in contract – they were tied to me and I was tied to them. Tony Banks came up to see me in Edinburgh after Genesis finished, he is a good soul. I used the time to record a solo album, Cut, which was a continuation of the music I'd been making after Stiltskin. It had been one of my stipulations that I was able to do my own thing, and to be fair they were very pro that approach because they had all done their own solo stuff.

Cut was released in Germany, and I realize now that the timing was wrong. Its moment was when I'd come out of Stiltskin and I had a particular fan base, and a level of media interest. Five years on I'd moved away from that. I'd become a part of Genesis, and I hadn't realized just how big a deal that was. The album I'd written didn't fit the Genesis audience. It would have been better to have listened to what I had done with Genesis and written something in that vein, to use that marketplace, whereas I was using a Stiltskin marketplace which no longer existed in the same way. And the record industry had changed so much.

After my involvement with Genesis ended I was at a very low point, really down. I couldn't get my emotions together, I just felt deeply sad. Anybody's who's been through that knows how horrible it is. I had serious depression for five or six years. Every gig that was organized I wanted to cancel before I did it and then I'd do it, be really happy and want to keep going. This cycle went on and on and on and was deeply destructive to me. I came to realize the importance of music in my life because the simple truth is that if I'm not doing something like playing or recording I may as well be dead. I mean that, totally and absolutely. I don't have a purpose outside that.

When I'm on stage I talk about Genesis all the time. I like to give the audience an insight into the experience. When I do acoustic shows I play a few Genesis songs because it fits what I'm doing, 'Follow You Follow Me', 'Entangled', old songs that people love to hear. I normally do a little set in the middle of my show and tell a few stories about Genesis and my life with them.

One of the stories is from the time I was recording with Genesis down at the Farm. I used to fly from Edinburgh to Heathrow and back. One time I arrive at Edinburgh airport. It's pissing down with rain and my mobile goes. It's my mother on the phone. She says, 'Is that you, Raymie darling?' I'm getting soaked standing there in the car park but I say, 'It is, mum. What is it?' She says, 'Phil Collins wants his job back.' Those were her exact words. 'What do you mean he wants his job back?' She says, 'I just saw him on VH1 and it looks to me like he's after his old job back.' This is at the end of my first week in the studio recording Calling All Stations. What had actually happened was that Phil had said on VH1 that he would entertain the idea of doing a farewell tour at some stage – this was in 1996, ten years before they decided to get back together again. But my mother, in her wee mind, had turned this throwaway remark into a monster, thinking 'My son's going to lose his job because Phil Collins is going to come back.' And the best part about it is that after a pause she said, in a kind of quiet voice, 'It sounds to me like he's running a bit short of cash and he's wanting back in there again...'

Ray Wilson's breakthrough came when he became vocalist for Stiltskin. The band had a UK number one single in 1994 with 'Inside', the theme for the Levi's 'Creek' ad, in which two Amish girls catch a peek of a near-naked man emerging from the river. Stiltskin toured and released one album, The Mind's Eye, before breaking up. Ray joined Genesis in 1997 for the Calling All Stations album and tour. He has since released his solo projects Cut, Change and The Next Best Thing, and created a second version of Stiltskin – their album She appeared in 2006.

THE PRODUCERS' TALE, PART II: NICK DAVIS

I found my way into the Genesis camp because Mike Rutherford heard a song I had worked on, and liked the sound of it: the perfect entrée for any engineer or producer. This was in 1988 – I'd been working with Gong's Steve Hillage producing Once Around The World In 80 Days *by It Bites. There was a great song on the album called 'Kiss Like Judas', which was the track Mike heard, and that led directly to me being offered the job of engineering* The Living Years *for him.*

I was really excited to get this Mike + The Mechanics gig: I had loved 'Silent Running', which sounded glorious on the radio. On the other hand my experiences with Genesis albums had been mixed. A friend at school had lent me The Lamb Lies Down On Broadway. *I listened to the album and liked some of the music, but I thought it sounded horrible, especially the drums, so I wasn't sure whether I liked the band or not. But later I bought a copy of* Selling England By The Pound, *which I thought was fantastic*

When we recorded the schoolchildren for 'The Living Years' I was able to draw on the experience I'd gained in my early days as an inhouse demo engineer at Polygram. There was quite a lot of noise on the children's track but I was able to bring in a clever little trick that cancelled the phase on it so that the track sounded really quiet; I remember everybody was quite stunned that I could do this. It was a good brownie point.

Some time later Tony Banks asked me to produce his solo album Still. *Working with Tony was very different. When I first met him, he was incredibly shy. I am also quite shy and I definitely was even more so then, but musically I found that I could relate to him: I was a keyboard player and a flautist, and I'd also been a, not very good, drummer in my time.* Still *was not a commercial success, but the album contained some very strong material. When we finished recording Tony said, 'Oh, the band have asked me if you'd be interested in producing the next Genesis album.' I said, 'Bloody hell. Give*

me ten seconds to think about it... Yeah!' At the time Phil was absolutely colossal, he was everywhere, and the band were also huge: the previous Genesis album had been Invisible Touch.

They had frequently had a change of producer after a few albums. I am not sure why they chose me particularly to work with them on We Can't Dance. *I suspect that Tony doesn't find it easy to work with that many people and the fact we were getting on very well in the studio might have given him the confidence to recommend me.*

Of course the decision transformed my life. I have worked for Genesis ever since, pretty well every single year, in some capacity. But it was also something of a double-edged sword. In the 1990s, once people knew that you had been involved with Genesis, the music industry tended to abandon you. I can honestly say that no one has ever approached me for a job saying, 'I want that guy who worked with Genesis'. In fact, I have had instances of positive discrimination, where I haven't got a job precisely because I worked with Genesis. Many people in the music industry had an attitude that the fact the band sold such a lot of records was a bad thing, which of course is not at all fair because they are great musicians and their fanbase has stayed really loyal.

When it came to the recording sessions for We Can't Dance, *I was quite nervous about the prospect of producing Phil Collins. Early on we were working on 'Jesus He Knows Me'. We had done a take during the day and after everyone had gone home, I stayed at the studio with the assistant, listening back to the track. I heard one drum fill that either wasn't that good or was dreadfully out of time, and thought, 'Oh God, I'm going to have to tell Phil Collins that I'd like him to do that again'. I had only been working with them for two or three days. The next morning he came in and I said, 'Phil, by the way, I think there's a bit of a dodgy drum fill in the take we did yesterday.' He went, 'Oh, it's going to be like that, is it?'. He said it tongue in cheek, but my immediate reaction was 'What have I done?' But then I decided, 'Hell, they've employed me to make a record, and I've got to make it as good as I think it ought to be', so I told him, 'You listen to it and see what you think'. He listened back to it and said, 'Yeah, that's terrible. Good. Well spotted,' and from that moment on we were fine.*

A typical recording day would start each morning with a good old Farm full English breakfast – sausages, beans, eggs and mushrooms, toast – before going into the studio around half ten and working solidly, maybe with a sandwich for lunch, through to about seven o'clock, with a break for dinner, and then going in again to work through until ten. It was pretty full on.

The songs had mainly been written by the time I was involved. But 'Jesus He Knows Me' didn't have a middle section at the time and I remember suggesting to Phil, 'Why don't we try a downbeat, reggae feel,' which he tried out and which stuck.

'I Can't Dance' was written very quickly. I remember Phil scribbling the words out for it. Mike had a stomach bug that day, but he came in and played the guitar even though he wasn't feeling very well; his part took about half an hour. Tony's keyboard part took another half an hour. We had been talking about this song, using the temporary title 'Blue Jeans', for a long time, but in the end it was boshed it out in one day, including writing the lyrics, mixing, everything.

I really like the sound of 'I Can't Dance'. Phil used to use a Beyer M88 dynamic mike, which is a great microphone, but for a couple of tracks, this one and 'Hold On My Heart', I hired in a big old valve mike and persuaded him to sing into it. 'Hold On My Heart' is a lovely-sounding track, one of those tracks that has really interesting chords, but which sounds incredibly simple. For me, music should sound effortless, but I like it when there is also a bit of something clever going on inside it.

'Elephantus' was the working title for 'No Son Of Mine', because of the elephant sound that comes in at the beginning, and we had another song we called 'BB Hit' which stood for 'Big, Big Hit' – because that's what we thought it would be. It eventually became 'Never A Time', but it never did become a big, big, hit. We were being filmed by a TV crew who used to come in one day a week – they call them 'fly on the wall' documentaries, but I've never seen a fly as big as a camera. Phil is probably used to performing in front of the camera but I know Tony hates it. We did the vocal for 'Never A Time' one day while they were filming and I think the song never recovered from that.

We had different ways of discussing what we wanted to do. Mike draws everything. He visualizes things in a completely bizarre way: he'll draw you a hairy testicle in a box and say, 'Look, that's how I want the track to sound'. I'll look at it and go, 'What the hell are you talking about, Mike?' Phil would probably talk in terms rhythm and bars, and Tony about the chords, keys or melody. I seemed to be able to relate to all of them, thankfully.

Producing is like plate spinning. When you're working on an album you get all your plates, the tracks, spinning and then suddenly one track will go a bit wobbly because you haven't got the right keyboard part or the vocal is rubbish, so you give that one a quick spin by making some repairs. And then another track will start going wobbly. The songs you think are really powerful at the beginning of the process are not always the ones which are strong by the end, like 'BB Hit', which we all thought was going to be a huge hit. That was a plate that definitely had a bit of a wobble. On the other hand, 'I Can't Dance' started out as nothing more than a weird guitar riff, but at the end that song was spinning really strongly.

My theory about Genesis is that Tony triggering against Phil was what made things happen. Tony, if he's left to his own devices, will always put in an extra chord change. Phil is completely the opposite. So there is a spark between the two of them in the studio. It's not an argumentative relationship, but they will contradict each other. Mike, with his interesting guitar parts, is the glue that makes those two stick together.

By the next album, things had changed, of course. Phil had left. Mike and Tony were reasonably positive, however. The weakness of Calling All Stations is not the songwriting, but not knowing who was going to sing the songs or play the drums. It was a weird situation, because the album was virtually written, but there we were auditioning musicians to play on it. With the drums, for example, although I think the drums sound pretty good, we had used a drum box throughout the writing, which means they had never written an ending for any of the songs, so unusually every track on that album fades out.

A second album with that line-up would have definitely been an improvement, because the Calling All Stations album was done with so many limitations. Ray was great, a good character, and fun to work with. He was very concerned that it wasn't quite good enough at times, but he worked really hard. I think he must have taken quite a battering, and he had a tough gig to fill. The expectation was so huge and the reality was not so huge. But the atmosphere in the studio while we were making it was actually very positive, a very good vibe.

I recently spent a lot of time remixing all the Genesis albums into the 5.1 format for re-release. I discovered so many things on those old tapes that were really inventive, probably far more imaginative than the more modern albums, little musical parts that embroider the whole. And I could observe the relationship between Tony and Peter during the process, rather like the one that exists between Tony and Phil, but probably a bit more antagonistic. Although they are great friends they both want to control the band. The albums do definitely fall into eras. The Peter Gabriel era is musically very strong. Lyrically it has moments of brilliance and moments of utter nonsense, where I find myself sitting there thinking, 'What are they on?'

Back when I first heard The Lamb I was so disappointed in its sound quality, and that was before I became a studio engineer. When I was working on the remixes I aimed to make all of the albums reward the listener sonically. The perfect response is for people to come away saying, 'Yeah, Genesis sounded great'.

Nick Davis started out as an assistant at Polygram demo studios in the early 1980s. He has since gone on to produce and engineer both Grammy and Mercury Music Prize nominated albums. As well as his production work on the Genesis albums *We Can't Dance* and *Calling All Stations*, Nick has worked on solo projects with Phil Collins, Mike Rutherford and Tony Banks, as well as releases by Deep Purple, Marillion, XTC, Aha, and It Bites, whose single 'Kiss Like Judas' first caught the ear of Mike Rutherford. Nick has spent three years mixing Genesis's back catalogue in the surround sound 5.1 format, and was audio consultant for the 2007 *Turn It On Again* tour.

THE MANAGER'S TALE, PART II: TONY SMITH

You never plan for failure. As a manager you have to be positive, you've got to lead from the front, for my style of management anyway, and I have to be a fan. I've got to love the guys and the music, otherwise I don't think I could do my job. Because it's you and the band against the rest of the world. Certainly in the early days it felt like that.

When Pete left the band, I don't think he felt for one moment that the band wouldn't be able to do a record because he'd left. He thought they would carry on fine. They just needed to find another singer. The big issue was whether the band would be able to perform live and that was another little hill to climb. The decision to use Phil was certainly the best result, although it hadn't been thought through or planned out. It happened by accident, as is true of much of this band's career.

Then Steve left. I remember Peter saying to me quite early on, in terms of how Genesis worked as a band, that Phil was very much a member of the band, one for all and all for one, but that he felt Steve was less committed, always a little bit outside the rest. I'd have to agree with him. I think Steve was highly underrated from a musical point of view but he wasn't really a team player. And in the end it was the same old story, a question of writing. Steve felt that he wasn't getting his fair share of the writing and that he'd got more to offer than was appearing on the records. I suspect, though I may be wrong, that he was being told from other sources that he had more going for him as a solo artist, and that he could do better elsewhere.

His decision to go freed up the band, especially once Mike had decided to handle the guitars, because a three-man unit is a much easier relationship to make work. It opened the door to a new way of writing in which Phil could participate more. 'Turn It On Again' was one of the many things to emerge from jam sessions, complete improvisation – and on subsequent records that was a major part of how they wrote. The music took on a different feel. And that might not have happened if Steve had still been there.

We had our first real hit with 'Follow You Follow Me'. Ahmet Ertegun played a small but significant part in that. When he first heard the record, he called up and he said, 'There's a bit more you can do with this track' and he was absolutely right. He made a subtle difference to it, made it more radio friendly. Ahmet had good ears; he was a music fan first and foremost.

Up until then eighty per cent of our audience had consisted of earnest spotty young men. Suddenly we had this hit single and girls started turning up. It created a new constituency out there for the band. The single had been a bit of a throwaway on the album – in fact it almost didn't make it on because we felt it was a bit light – but by its very nature it lightened the whole thing up a bit, because otherwise there was a danger of disappearing down the navel-gazing Yes route. We had always been very

serious about what we did, but we also didn't take ourselves too seriously. And in fact there wasn't much navel-gazing going on. It was more an impression the band's music gave out.

I have a phrase about producing a 'single with credibility' – which 'Follow Me Follow You' was not. But with 'Turn It On Again' on Duke, we had found one: it's in a really odd time signature that you can't actually dance to. I think that was when things really came together. Certainly a lot of the critics say, 'The band didn't really progress from there on', but I disagree with them. I think if you listen to every album, each one has moved on musically from the previous album, and the interesting thing from a manager's point of view is that during this period each album outsold the previous album. We never had that big Dark Side Of The Moon record. Each album was progressively more popular than the one before.

As the band's sales grew and Phil's solo career escalated, I was able to view them as two very different things. I've always said that Genesis really is unique, it's the particular combination of Tony, Mike and Phil, what comes out of the three of them; anything else is separate and doesn't really affect it. Phil's solo success didn't really alter the dynamic of the three of them, but it did affect the media perception of Genesis. Because Phil had a lot of hit singles, people started to think that maybe Genesis were less of a rock band and more of a singles band, which wasn't helped by the fact that the band had a very successful period of singles. For a long time one success fed off the other. Phil benefited from Genesis because he still had his rock credibility and his rock roots. The band benefited from the fact that Phil was so popular. It was a mad period, jumping from a solo record to a Genesis record and a Genesis tour. We didn't stop for ten years. I often think, 'How the hell did we do it all?' because it was really non-stop.

When Band Aid and Live Aid came up, and Phil was shuttling across the Atlantic on Concorde, it never occurred to

me that Genesis could perform there too. At that point we were doing spectacular stage shows, and for us to have played at Live Aid, we would have needed the whole production to do it properly. Phil as a solo artist could go on and do a couple of songs, not a problem, but Genesis, forget it, it wouldn't have worked, we'd have needed an hour and total darkness. The question never come up and I'm sure that from Tony and Mike's point of view it wasn't even an issue. In any case the following year we played Knebworth, twice. And by 1988 we played four sell-out shows at Wembley Stadium, which is still the record at the old stadium. 288,000 tickets at Wembley, amazing.

Tony was frustrated that he couldn't have solo success, but I would say of Tony – and this doesn't really help him – that really his solo albums were the Genesis albums. Ultimately the Genesis records are Tony's legacy; that's my opinion. Mike and Phil are clearly super-talented and have shown that in their own solo careers and ultimately it's the combination of three of them that makes the magic. Each of them would be sorely missed, but Tony's part in that is pivotal. Because I think Tony is the one element of Genesis which is irreplaceable. I think of him as the conscience of Genesis, the one who will say, 'No, we shouldn't do that because it's not right for what we are'. And if he felt strongly about anything, then that's the way the decision would go. Whereas if there was a tough decision to be made and Tony didn't have a strong view on it, it could go either way.

When Phil said he wanted to leave, we'd been on hold with Genesis for quite a while. Tony and Mike were amazed that Phil was still doing Genesis records, when he had this fantastic solo career; why would he bother?

If you listen to Calling All Stations from a compositional point of view there's some bloody good stuff on there. As good as anything on any of the other records. Unfortunately we just couldn't find the right front man, the right singer to deliver it in quite the same way as Phil. I don't think that person didn't exist. We just didn't find him. Ray Wilson did a pretty good job but they were enormous boots to fill and I admire Ray for having the guts to try, but there's no getting round the fact that it just wasn't as strong live. And the record came out at a time when the band had become deeply unfashionable in any case. Even if we'd brought out a Genesis record with Phil singing, I'm not sure how it would have been received. There had been a real sea change in taste and in public perception. That said, everyone perceives Calling All Stations as a failed record, but we sold over a million copies. Afterwards Tony, Mike and I sat down and decided there was not much point in continuing. I think Tony would have been willing to do another record, but Mike wasn't enthusiastic; it was going to be a real uphill battle.

It was very depressing. I was also going through a divorce at the same time, so it was an extremely difficult phase, not one of the great periods of my life. It was very sad after all those years to see Genesis sputtering and petering out. It was not the way to finish. And personally it was hard, because you do your best, you make the decisions and when things don't work as well as they should, you feel you've failed the band. I'd spent the best part of thirty-five years with Genesis, and that's a huge part of your identity. It's not like having a job where you can knock off at 5.30 and put your work to one side. It was a tough, tough thing for everyone to go through, and much tougher for the guys than me: I still had Phil and Mike's solo careers to manage and a whole Genesis industry with the back catalogue going on.

We decided to remix all the records into 5.1 SACD to renew the catalogue. Some of the earlier records had not been particularly well recorded or engineered and technology had moved on. We felt there was a better version of those records in there. The first album Tony, Mike and Nick Davis remixed was The Lamb. It sounded fantastic, but I was trying to get my head round the fact that I didn't want to release all this material into a vacuum. There was no activity going on at all. We started various conversations about promotional activity to support the launch. I was talking to Phil all the time, and although there was clearly no space in his life for anything else, I kept on keeping on. 'It's a shame, we should be doing something.'

And then I had lunch with Peter Gabriel and Mike Large, his associate at Real World Records, specifically to talk about The Lamb, to find out Peter's time frame, and whether there might be a period in the next couple of years when he'd be free to do a bit of promotion. Peter disappeared off to the loos and Mike and I were chatting about this. I said, 'Of course the best thing would be a live show'. Mike replied, 'Why don't we ask him?' When Peter came back, I said, 'We've just been talking and the most effective promotion would be to put on a live show. And then being a little bit Machiavellian and a little bit mischievous, I added, 'But you probably couldn't sing it now, could you?' To which Peter rose, like a fish to bait. 'Of course I could, if Tony changed some of the keys, I'd be fine'. Now that idea didn't go anywhere in the end, although we did have a meeting in a hotel room on Phil's solo tour in 2004, with Peter and Steve Hackett to discuss it, but what it did trigger was the realization of how well they got on. After Peter and Steve had left that particular meeting, Tony, Mike and Phil continued talking: 'We might be waiting for five years for Peter, you know what he's like. Why don't we do something in the meantime?'

Since taking over the management of Genesis in 1973, Tony Smith has continued to run their affairs as well as overseeing the solo careers of Phil Collins, Mike Rutherford and Tony Banks. In 1977 he set up Hit & Run Music Publishing with Jon Crawley; the company's client list, in addition to the Genesis musicians, has included Kula Shaker. In September 2000 Tony received the prestigious Peter Grant Award for Outstanding Achievement at that year's British Music Industry Roll of Honour event.

CHAPTER THIRTEEN

BEYOND THE POINT OF NO RETURN

MIKE: After the end of *Calling All Stations*, I felt there were two options. One was to try and become a different Genesis by doing album, tour, album, tour for about three years. I thought that would be the only way to establish ourselves. If we were going to move on we would have to create a new identity very quickly. But I was still keen on Mike + the Mechanics, and concentrating on building up a new Genesis identity would have meant not doing the Mechanics.

In the end I felt that the road was going to prove too long. At my stage of career, having done Genesis, having got through Peter and Phil leaving, and having made the Mechanics succeed, which had been a lot of hard work, I didn't have the energy to do it again. Tony and Ray would have carried on. I felt I wasn't up to what was needed. Perhaps if we had called the band by a different name things would have been different, but that in itself would have required another kind of energy. The decision floated for a while, a few months, maybe a year, and then it was gone.

TONY: When we made the decision to call it a day, my first thought was not to rush into anything at all. I wanted to spend time at home and not feel the pressure to get into any particular project. I had still been trying to find work in films and TV, but nothing seemed to be happening, partly because I'm not a pushy person. I even got an agent, but that didn't seem to work either. So I asked myself, 'What would I really like to do if I was never going to do any more music again?', and my feeling was I would like to work with an orchestra, something I had done briefly with the *Wicked Lady* soundtrack back in the early 1980s: I'd written a fairly reasonable theme but once we'd orchestrated it the piece had sounded beautiful.

I was happy for two or three years to go by while I played some more golf, did some gardening – the things I love doing apart from being a musician – but I would still play every day. I continued with the idea of an orchestral piece and how I could do it; I wrote one slow piece specifically for the project using a string synthesizer and loved the way the piece moved. I improvised for hours and then joined the pieces together, left bits out, added other sections. That was the piece that became 'Black Down', the heart of my *Seven* record, and the key reason for doing the album.

I had a contact within the London Philharmonic Orchestra. I hired them to play on the album, found myself an arranger and booked some time at the Abbey Road studios. The recording was quite traumatic – we initially put down four pieces and I really wasn't happy with them, even though the musicians were great. The difficulty with an orchestra is that you go into the studio and what you capture there is the mix you're stuck with; there's no overdubbing. I found it quite depressing because I knew it wasn't right. So I decided to try and take more people from my side into the studio and asked Nick Davis, who is a good friend and likes the music I write, to help. With his input I think I was able to get my end slightly stronger. That whole process took me a period of four or five years, because I wasn't working on it full time.

PHIL: While I was doing press for *Dance Into The Light* – which came out in 1996 – and for the tour that went with it, the Peter Gabriel era Genesis box set came out. I thought to myself, 'Surely someone's going to call me and say, "We've had an idea. The box set's coming out, so let's get together and do some gigs with the five of us"'. So in interviews, whenever a journalist asked if I minded talking about the Genesis box set, I'd say, 'It includes all the early stuff... and maybe we'll even do some shows.' People started writing about what I'd said and then the fan websites picked up on the fact that I had mentioned this, which I got good and bad feedback on, especially comments along the lines of 'Don't titillate us if you can't come up with the goods.'

MIKE: There was a charity show with Phil in Switzerland for his Little Dreams foundation where we discussed the idea, but we never got further than talking about it. And I'd occasionally read interviews with Phil or people would tell me that he had said it would be fun to do.

Opposite: Chester, Mike, Phil, Daryl and Tony back together for the *Turn It On Again* tour in 2007. Chester remembers that there was a reception with all the others after one of Phil's solo concerts at Wembley Arena some years before. 'That particular night I thought it felt amazing. I was really shocked at how great it felt to be there, I felt like I was with really good friends, and it caught me way off guard. I think everybody felt it because that night Phil said, "Well, we're all here, when's the tour?" I looked at Tony Smith, and he had a big grin on his face. He was beaming. And it just never went away after that. I thought that was a major turning point.'
Overleaf: The *Turn It On Again* set during rehearsals in Brussels.

TONY: I think we were always quite open to the idea of playing together again. Even in the days when Phil first left I thought there was no reason why we shouldn't do so at some point in the future, but I felt that a certain period of time had to pass after the *Calling All Stations* album. It became more and more likely. Every time we met to promote the Genesis *Archive* box set, we'd talk about it. Phil always seemed the keenest of us on it in many ways. One time in Cologne we started off at the beginning of the day saying 'Let's do it', and by the end, 'Maybe not'; so we put the idea on hold. But it was something that was always going to rear its head.

PHIL: We sat round the table in a German hotel discussing the idea of doing something. Tony Banks was very reluctant at that point: he thought we should just leave it alone. And by the end of the day we had talked ourselves out of it. But I kept on being asked about the idea; every interviewer would say, 'Can we just ask about a Genesis reunion?'

MIKE: One day we did a bunch of press interviews for the *Archive* set or the *Platinum* collection in Home House in London, for about three days. It was really boring. It was either then or in Germany that we started talking about maybe doing something together, and by the end of day three, we all thought 'No'. The press interviews had reminded us of what we might be letting ourselves in for. There are days when you're a little bit tired, keeping your head up, and then you get some twerp asking dumb questions. I know that's part of the job, but the prospect was too offputting.

PHIL: I was in a car doing something in Europe. Tony Smith turned round to me and said, 'By the way Pete's been in touch. He's been reading about doing something together and I'm having a meeting with his manager.' It seemed Pete would be interested if it was the right project and they were talking about doing *The Lamb*. I thought, 'Fantastic', because *The Lamb* certainly could have been done better the first time round. Only a handful of those hundred-odd shows worked as they should have done, so the idea of doing it again made sense. Tony, Mike and Steve were up for it, and we decided to meet. The only date all five us could get together was in November 2004; the meeting was in Glasgow because I was playing there on tour.

TONY: The possibility of doing *The Lamb* came up. Initially I wasn't sure, but Peter seemed quite keen. And if he was keen, I could be too. It surprised me Peter even entertained the idea: I thought he'd put Genesis well into his past, but as you get older you do mellow a bit. *The Lamb* was a naturally theatrical piece to perform in its entirety, but it would be quite demanding to do.

PHIL: By the time we got to the date of this get-together even the fan websites knew about it; I still don't know how they found out. Pete had his manager and Tony Smith was there, and Steve, Mike, Tony and me. And it transpired that there was still a question mark over whether Peter wanted to do it, which was not quite what we had thought. I had figured this meeting was for us to talk about how we were going to do the show, and when to schedule it, not if we were even going to do it.

But Peter said he hadn't finished his album yet, and God knows how long that might take, and he was going to go on the road with the album, but he would let us know by that Christmas of 2004. As far as I know he never came back to us and said he wasn't doing it, he just never came back to say he would do it.

For the two or three hours we were together in Glasgow, everybody assumed their old positions. Pete was the way he always was: knowing exactly what he wanted to do but stumbling a little bit, and being indecisive about committing. Steve was very dark, as I remember him being. Tony was still best friends with Peter, but there was also a little bit of the old antagonism between them. You could see Pete knew what he'd have to deal with if he came back into this. Mike was somewhere in the middle, and I was the joker trying to defuse the situation as I had always spent so much of my time doing.

TONY: When we met I thought we were going to do it. It was just a question of working out timings. Pete suddenly said, 'This is a meeting to find about whether we might be doing this or not'. And I thought, 'Surely we've been through this already?' Pete and I go back for ever, we're great friends, and this was very typical of him. I wasn't surprised by it. I just thought, 'OK, here we go'.

PHIL: I think Peter always felt threatened by going back, and clearly it represented a much longer time period for him. He has built an extremely impressive solo career, which he feels would be dented if he was to go back with Genesis in any shape or form. I have always done lots of different things. For me it's a case of 'Write a musical? Sure. Get back with Genesis? Of course.' I've always lived like that. The variety is what keeps me going. So for me reuniting was a bit of fun, without wanting to trivialize it.

If you think about it, Peter used to spend most of the *Lamb* show in a leather jacket without a shirt. Pete doesn't look like that any more. None of us do. Apart which there was the issue of whether he would want to go back into what he probably remembered as being a hornet's nest of compromise. Which I don't really think it is. We've all grown up. We all know when to back off. We didn't before. We used to argue a bit, although not much in reality. It wouldn't harm Pete, it would be great fun. So it was a shame. I would have loved to have played the drums on *The Lamb* behind Pete, and I still hope that at some point it will happen.

MIKE: *The Lamb* was visually a very exciting piece but it was never done very well. It was always hard to do it with the budget we had. However Peter would have had to work out how to sing his part as a young Puerto Rican kid called Rael. Plus Peter has had thirty-odd years of being the ex-singer of Genesis. It's a tag that never really goes away, unfortunately.

PHIL: Pete left, Steve left. Tony Smith and the three of us sat around and we said, 'If the *Lamb* shows don't happen, do we want to do something with the three of us?' And Tony and Mike said 'Yes' straightaway, probably thinking 'This is going to be very easy to do considering how difficult the five-piece idea is already', and we agreed there and then that we would do it. We never thought about going out as a four-piece. It's either been the three-piece or the five-piece. I feel a bit sorry for Steve because there's never been any suggestion of compromising between the two options.

AFTER TWO HOURS WITH PETER AND STEVE DISCUSSING THE IDEA OF THE LAMB, TONY, PHIL AND I – AS WE ALWAYS DO – DECIDED IN ABOUT FOUR MINUTES TO PLAY AGAIN. IT REMINDED ME HOW WELL THE THREE OF US WORK TOGETHER. Mike Rutherford

TONY: The person I felt sorriest for was Steve, but there was no option. I am a great fan of Steve's, but the four-piece line-up only represents a very small period in the band's career. Daryl joined us in 1978, so for fourteen years he was the guitarist of the band live, and it would be a strange thing to use Steve on our later material: I don't think he would be too keen to sit down and play 'I Can't Dance'.

PHIL: I was a little reluctant at first because my marriage was falling apart and I didn't want to commit to something I would live to regret. In principle I was happy to do the tour, but I needed some time. This conversation took place in November 2004 and I knew I had to finish the *Tarzan* musical and spend at least a year in New York. It was, yes, it's going to happen, but when? It was very much in the distance. In any case, it was better to do the three-piece first. If we had gone out and performed *The Lamb* the critics would have loved it: everybody thinks of it as a great album now, although they didn't when it first came out. And Peter is critically very well respected. For us to go back and do a crowd-pleasing show after that would not be the right thing.

TONY: When the *Lamb* project was obviously not going to work in the near future, we talked about the three-piece period, which is an easier thing to do and closer to my heart: my favourite era is from *Foxtrot* to *Duke*, and my favourite albums are *Wind And Wuthering* and *Duke*. It also meant we could play more ambitious songs like 'Domino' and 'Home By The Sea'.

PHIL: Tony, Mike and I had booked some time on spec in the SIR rehearsal studios in New York during October 2006. This was in case we did decide to go ahead and perform *The Lamb*, because if we did we needed some rehearsal time to know if we could still play the material, let alone whether Peter could sing it. We needed to make sure we weren't shooting our mouths off without being able to follow it up. I had also sat in with The Musical Box, the Canadian Genesis tribute band, after watching them perform *The Lamb* and wondering if I could actually play it. But by the time we got to that October the idea of putting on *The Lamb* had fizzled out, so we used the time to rehearse the three-piece version along with Daryl and Chester.

TONY: Mike and I were sure we wanted to play together again. Phil was still caught up in *Tarzan* and his personal life was quite difficult, so at times he appeared a little distracted, but he certainly seemed to be into it. We knew we had to get our playing chops together again, especially the drummers, because Phil hadn't played our kind of songs for years. But I knew he'd get it. And once we knew we were going to do it, we could do our homework.

Below: At rehearsals for the
Turn It On Again tour.

PHIL: In the New York rehearsals we were there to break the back of the music. We worked out a lot of stuff we would have had to resolve eventually. What became apparent to me was that both Tony and Mike had become a lot looser than when I had last played with them in 1992-93. Tony, not being a natural performer, would occasionally drift in time, which is a drummer's nightmare. Before, I had never been able to acknowledge it, whereas in New York I could mention it and Tony would say, 'I know, I know, I know!' That was a great barrier gone. We had actually arrived at the point where were comfortable saying to each other that something wasn't quite as good as it should have been. We could have those conversations and laugh at each other, which was very refreshing, and something Pete would probably not be aware of.

TONY: We played everything we knew and thought about a couple of other songs we might do. Afterwards we had a series of e-mail conversations. I was always keen to include 'Behind The Lines', because I thought the intro was so arresting. The others didn't want to do the whole song, but felt that the first part was appealing, which I thought was fine. And because *Duke* was one of my favourite albums, we took a short section of 'Duke's Travels' as part of a solo combination. I was also keen to do an older song, ideally one we had never done before. I suggested 'Blood On the Rooftops', a song I've always loved, and 'Many Too Many', but I also said, because I knew 'Blood On the Rooftops' doesn't go down well with everybody, let's do 'Ripples', which we hadn't played for a long time. For me it really evokes that first period when Phil took over the vocals, and would give a very distinctive flavour to the set.

PHIL: In April 2007 we organized music rehearsals in Switzerland and for the end of May the full production rehearsals in Brussels. The guys had said they would come and rehearse wherever I wanted because their kids were grown up, and I needed them to come to Switzerland because I had to be there for my children. They were absolutely wonderful about it, I have to say. They went the extra yards to help make the reunion happen, taking in all my problems.

We used to allow weeks and weeks for rehearsals and production rehearsals but for the *Turn It On Again* tour we kept it much more streamlined. I also reverted to more of the original way the songs were sung. When I was listening back to live versions from the past I found I was inventing and adding little extras, so I went back and tried to simplify the vocal performances to the way they were when they were written, and from a drumming point of view I tried to bring the playing into this century.

THERE WAS NO ALBUM TO PROMOTE. WE WERE ONLY PLAYING BECAUSE IT WAS FUN. WE WEREN'T TRYING TO PROVE ANYTHING.
TONY BANKS

TONY: Because I had been doing so much work on the 5.1 versions of our back catalogue I knew all the material backwards, so there were no particular surprises for me in that sense. What was weird was that I found it difficult to believe it was fifteen years since the three of us and Daryl and Chester had all played together.

PHIL: A Chicago band called Disturbed had done a cover version of 'Land Of Confusion', and taken it into a heavy metal-grunge area. We thought we would bring a little bit of that into the song as well, to acknowledge the fact that it could sound a little bit different, more modern.

MIKE: The combination of these five guys playing on stage had worked for so long, there was no particular reason why that chemistry wouldn't work again. It just took a little longer than normal. For some of the early songs you had to get back into the mindset we had fifteen years ago. But not having a new album to promote meant we could draw together a different kind of set, more instrumental: Phil would be playing drums for about forty minutes, where it used to be about fifteen. It was a slightly heavier set, which I enjoyed.

Opposite: Tony on the reunion – 'We had talked about doing this many times. The rehearsing was great fun because you're back with friends again, and the music was sounding good. It's like being part of an orchestra; you do your little bit and the whole effect works and everything. The ticket sales for the tour amazed me. In England we get such bad press. We are never in anybody's 'best' of anything, so I really thought that in the UK it had died for us. And then we put the tickets on sale and Twickenham sold out in a couple of hours. It was very bizarre.' Overleaf: Genesis live in Hamburg on the *Turn It On Again* tour.

PHIL: Most of the time we realized that to go in and change things for the hell of it just frustrates fans. I once went to see Prince in concert. I was waiting for him to sing 'Little Red Corvette' and he just played a verse and a half of it on the piano. I remember thinking, 'I don't want to hear that, I want to hear 'Little Red Corvette''. You have to keep the fans in mind; you can't mess with the material too much.

'Home By The Sea' and 'Domino' are mainly Tony-biased songs which I found I enjoyed much more fifteen years on. There was a moment with 'Domino' during the New York rehearsals when we started the song and I didn't know what to sing. I couldn't remember anything. We put the CD on, I listened to it and I thought, 'I'll never be able to remember this'; but suddenly it came back, and this time it was much more fluent. I was even fine with the famous 'double glazing' and 'nylon sheets and blankets' lyrics I'd had problems with before. They're not the kind of lyrics that I would write, but I realized, 'I can find it, I can see it now, I can do it.' And that was a pleasant surprise.

TONY: In the new staging, we had a massive video screen. It was quite a challenge to work out how to use the screen and what imagery to put on it. We went through various possible ideas with the video guys over a period of time trying to create a look for each song. One of the most effective, I thought, was on 'Tonight, Tonight, Tonight', when all we had was what looked like a theatre backdrop. I thought that was fantastic. I had always dreamed of being able to change the environment we were in. And the videos for 'Domino' and 'Home By The Sea' were even more spectacular because of the sheer scale of the screens.

In terms of the sound we were trying to address some of the problems we had had with sound mixers in the past, particularly when the keyboards would be dropped way back, which could be very frustrating for me. I had heard live tapes and often thought, 'Why was I there?' It was as bad as that: on three or four songs I would be inaudible. So for the *Turn It On Again* tour, as well as using as a very good sound guy, Nick Davis came to the rehearsals as well, and sat in for the first few shows, because he could listen to the sound from the group's point of view.

MIKE: One thing I said quite early on was that we should include more double drumming, because outside Genesis I have never experienced that; not many bands do it. It adds a really powerful sound, a strong moment, into our show. And it shows Phil as a drummer. People tend to forget he is a fantastic drummer, because he's been singing so much, and the new set showed his talents off much more.

PHIL: The singing was easier but the drumming was terribly difficult for me in the New York rehearsals. It used to be the other way round; the drumming was easy and the singing was difficult. I got very down about the drumming and wondered what the matter was, but of course I hadn't played at all for the year I was in New York writing the *Tarzan* musical. And when I was out on my own tour I did a duet with Chester at the beginning of the show, and then played on 'In The Air Tonight' and that was it. I had to get myself back into shape.

Then there was the tambourine dance in 'I Know What I Like'. We had some footage of me on the screen doing the dance in 1976. I looked at it and thought 'I'll never get my legs up there'. But I spent fifteen minutes on my own in a corner of the rehearsal hall hitting my head, banging the tambourine, and went back on stage and did it. And everyone was very surprised. It was one little step at a time.

I WROTE A SHORT PIECE FOR THE TOUR PROGRAMME, SAYING THAT SINCE 1970 GENESIS HAS BEEN A BIG PART OF MY LIFE, AND THAT ALTHOUGH I THINK OF MIKE AND TONY AS THE GUYS IN THE BAND, THEY'RE FIRST AND FOREMOST MY FRIENDS.

PHIL COLLINS

1950

12 February	Steve Hackett is born in Pimlico, South London.
13 February	Peter Gabriel is born in Chobham, Surrey.
27 March	Tony Banks is born in East Hoathly, Sussex.
2 October	Mike Rutherford is born in Guildford, Surrey.

1951

| 30 January | Phil Collins is born in Chiswick, London. |
| 23 December | Anthony Phillips is born in South London. |

1952

| 27 November | Daryl Stuermer is born in Milwaukee. |

1963

| September | Tony Banks, Peter Gabriel and Mike Rutherford enrol at Charterhouse School. |
| | Anthony Phillips forms his first band, the Spiders, with Rivers Job at St Edmund's School, Hindhead. |

1964

| | Phil Collins appears an an extra in the Promo for the Beatles' 'Hard Day's Night'. |

1965

| April | Ant Phillips moves to Charterhouse. It is around this time that three bands are formed at the school: the Garden Wall (Peter Gabriel, Tony Banks, Johnny Trapman, Chris Stewart and Rivers Job), Anon (Ant Phillips, Rob Tyrell, Rivers Job, Mick Colman and Richard Macphail) and the Climax (including Mike Rutherford and Chris Stewart). |
| | 1965 is also the year that Phil Collins appears as the Artful Dodger in the West End production of *Oliver!* for nine months – until his voice breaks. |

1966

| | The end of Anon as a three-piece after they perform (alongside the Garden Wall and the Climax) at the Charterhouse Charity Beat Concert. |

1967

| | Banks, Gabriel, Phillips and Rutherford record a demo together after the other Charterhouse bands are disrupted as members leave school. The demo is passed to Jonathan King, an Old Carthusian. Chris Stewart comes on board as the percussionist. Later in the year, Chris Stewart leaves the group to continue with his studies. |

1968

February	Genesis release their first single, 'The Silent Sun'/'That's Me' on Decca. The group's name does not appear on the sleeve. It is also at this time that their first publicity picture is issued by Decca.
May	'A Winter's Tale'/'One-Eyed Hound' (Decca) is released. Over the summer, John Silver is drafted in as a replacement for Chris Stewart and *From Genesis to Revelation* is recorded at Regent B studios, London.
8 September	Ray Wilson is born in Dumfries, Scotland.
11 December	Chester Thompson is born in Baltimore.

1969

March	*From Genesis to Revelation* released. Again, the group's name does not appear on the sleeve other than in the title. It is not until 1974, when Genesis begin to achieve success with subsequent albums, that this first attempt charts at US #170.
June	'Where The Sour Turns To Sweet'/'In Hiding' is released on Decca.
August	John Silver leaves Genesis and is replaced by John Mayhew.

Autumn	The band leaves Decca and is signed by Charisma. Peter Gabriel has said, 'The contrast between Decca and Charisma is amazing: Charisma is like a family.' Atlantic records are responsible for the band's US releases.
November	The band moves into Christmas Cottage, where they will stay until April 1970.
	Also this year, Phil Collins becomes the drummer for Flaming Youth. They will go on to release one album, *Ark 2*.

1970

April	Genesis play their first gig at the Friars, Aylesbury.
July	*Trespass* is recorded at Trident Studios, London. Over the summer, Anthony Phillips and John Mayhew both leave the group. Ads are placed and auditions held to find replacements.
August	Phil Collins is recruited as the new drummer after responding to an ad in the *Melody Maker*.
October	*Trespass* is released. It will go on to peak at UK #98.
December	Genesis play a free Christmas gig at the Lyceum, London.
	Also this year, Steve Hackett joins the band Quiet World.

1971

January	After auditions in December, Steve Hackett joins as the new guitarist. Peter Gabriel had contacted him after seeing his ad in the *Melody Maker*, in which Hackett sought a band 'determined to strive beyond existing stagnant music forms'. Almost immediately after Steve joins, The Six Bob Tour starts at the Lyceum, London, featuring Genesis, Lindisfarne and Van der Graaf Generator.
May	'The Knife (Part 1)'/'The Knife (Part 2)' is released on Charisma.
June	Peter breaks his ankle leaping from the stage at the Friars, Aylesbury.
August	*Nursery Cryme* is recorded at Trident Studios, London. It is released in November and goes on to achieve moderate success, peaking at UK #39.

1972

January	Genesis play their first overseas gig, in Brussels.
April	The band embark on their first seven-date Italian tour.
May	'Watcher of the Skies' is premiered at the Great Western Express Festival in Lincoln.
29 July	Tony marries Margaret in Farnham, Surrey.
August–September	*Foxtrot* is recorded at Island Studios, London.
October	Both the single 'Happy The Man'/'Seven Stones' and the album *Foxtrot* are released. *Foxtrot* will go to UK #12.
November	Live premiere of 'Supper's Ready' at Brunel University.
December	Genesis play their first gigs in the US.

1973

February	Genesis headline at the Rainbow Theatre. They then embark on a series of gigs at the De Montfort Hall, Leicester and the Free Trade Hall, Manchester, which are recorded for *The King Biscuit Hour Show*. These recordings are released later in the year as *Genesis Live*, which goes on to achieve success at UK #9; US #105.
March	The band begin their first American tour.
August	*Selling England by the Pound* is recorded at Island Studios, London. It is released in October and goes on to achieve UK #3; US #70.
December	Three nights at the Roxy, LA.

1974

January	Five sell-out nights at the Theatre Royal, Drury Lane, London, where Peter 'flies' during 'Supper's Ready'.
February	'I Know What I Like (In Your Wardrobe)'/'Twilight Alehouse' is released and charts at UK #17.
August–October	*The Lamb Lies Down on Broadway* is recorded at Glaspant, Wales on the Island Mobile studio.
November	'Counting Out Time'/'Riding The Scree' and *The Lamb Lies Down on Broadway* are released. The album goes to UK #10; US #41.
December	*The Lamb Lies Down on Broadway* album tour begins. It is during this six-month, 102-show tour that Peter decides to leave the band – but he agrees to honour all gigs booked.
	It is also this year that an *NME* Readers' Poll votes Genesis 'Top Stage Band'.

1975

April	'The Carpet Crawlers'/'Evil Jam (The Waiting Room Live)' is released.
May	Peter's last gig with Genesis in St Etienne, France. In spite of the band's efforts to keep it under wraps while they search for a new singer, the news breaks on the front cover of *Melody Maker*. Phil Collins is eventually confirmed as the new frontman – whilst remaining as the group's drummer.
September	Phil Collins marries Andrea Bertorelli.
October	Steve Hackett releases his first solo album, *Voyage Of The Acolyte*. Hackett is the first member of Genesis to embark on a solo project. Both Phil Collins and Mike Rutherford are involved in the recording of this album.
November	*A Trick Of The Tail* is recorded at Trident Studios, London.

1976

February	*A Trick of the Tail* is released and reaches UK #3; US #31.
March	'A Trick Of The Tail'/'Ripples...' is released.
Summer	The *A Trick Of The Tail* world tour begins – the first with Phil Collins as vocalist. Although Phil has continued to play on recordings, King Crimson drummer Bill Bruford is drafted in to augment him on drums during the live shows. The tour is filmed and later released as *Genesis: In Concert*.
September	*Wind And Wuthering* is recorded at Relight Studios, Hilvarenbeek, Holland.
November	Mike Rutherford marries Angie. They will go on to have three children together.
	Also during 1976, Phil Collins joins in recording sessions as percussionist for Brand X, and appears on their first album, *Unorthodox Behaviour*.

1977

January	Genesis reopen the Rainbow Theatre, London with three sell-out shows. This is also Chester Thompson's first appearance with the band. Also this month, *Wind And Wuthering* is released. It will go on to reach #7 in the UK; #26 in the US.
February	'Your Own Special Way'/'It's Yourself' is released, and goes to UK #43; US #62. It is also during this month that Peter Gabriel releases his first album.
June	The *Wind And Wuthering* tour includes three sell-out dates at Earl's Court, London and five sell out nights at Palais des Sports, Paris. The lighting rig boasts 48 jumbo jet landing lights.
July	Steve Hackett decides to leave the band. Rather than finding a replacement it is agreed that Mike Rutherford will combine the roles of bass and lead guitarist.
September	*And Then There Were Three* is recorded at Relight Studios, Hilvarenbeek, Holland.
October	Steve's departure is announced and the following week Genesis's second live album, *Seconds Out*, is released. It will go on to achieve UK #4; US #47.
November	Daryl Stuermer joins the touring band.
	This is also the year that a Melody Maker Readers' Poll votes Genesis 'Best Live Band in the World'.

1978

March	'Follow You, Follow Me'/'Ballad Of Big' is released. It will peak at UK #7; US #23.
April	*And Then There Were Three* is released. It rises to UK #3; US #14.
May	*Peter Gabriel II* and Steve Hackett's *Please Don't Touch* are released.
June	'Many Too Many'/'The Day The Lights Went Out'/'Vancouver' is released. It goes to UK #43. Also this month, Genesis play the Knebworth Festival in front of 100,000 fans.
September	Genesis play the Fete de L'Humanite, Paris, in front of 120,000.
November	The band embark on their first tour of Japan.

1979

	1979 is a quiet year for Genesis as Phil takes time out and the others concentrate on their solo projects. Tony Banks releases his album, *A Curious Feeling*, in October. Phil Collins is involved in another Brand X release, *Product*. Steve Hackett also releases a further solo album, *Spectral Mornings*, and headlines the Reading Festival.

1980

January	Mike Rutherford's solo album, *Smallcreep's Day*, is released.
March	*Duke*, a real turning point for Genesis, is released and reaches UK #1. In the US it peaks at #11. 'Turn It On Again'/'Behind The Lines Part 2' is also released this month. It achieves UK #8; US #58.
March–May	Genesis embark on a 'small venue' tour of the UK.
May	'Duchess'/'Open Door' is released. It goes to UK #46.

June	Peter Gabriel founds WOMAD and releases *Peter Gabriel III*.
June	Steve Hackett releases *Defector*.
September	'Misunderstanding'/'Evidence Of Autumn' goes to UK #42; US #14
	It is also in 1980 that Phil Collins and Andrea Bertorelli divorce.

1981

February	Phil Collins releases his first solo album, *Face Value*.
August	'Abacab'/'Another Record' goes to UK #9; US #26. The same month, Steve Hackett releases *Cured*.
September	*Abacab* hits the bigtime on both sides of the atlantic, with a UK #1; US #7. The *Abacab* tour starts in Barcelona, featuring the new phenomenon of the Vari-Lite series 100 computerized lighting system.
October	'Keep It Dark'/'Naminanu' reaches UK #33.
November	'No Reply At All' reaches US #29.

1982

March	'Man On The Corner'/'Submarine' goes to UK #41; US #40.
April	Steve Hackett releases his most successful solo album, *Highly Strung*.
May	The *3 X 3* E.P. goes to UK #10.
June	*Three Sides Live* is released and achieves UK #2; US #10.
July	'Paperlate' is released and reaches US #32.
September	*Peter Gabriel IV* emerges, released in the US as *Security*. The first WOMAD festival takes place.
October	The classic Genesis line-up re-forms for a special 'Six of the Best' gig at Milton Keynes Bowl, held to raise money for Peter Gabriel's WOMAD.
November	Phil Collins releases *Hello I Must Be Going*.
	Also in 1982, Mike Rutherford releases another solo album, *Acting Very Strange*.

1983

	A 72-date arena tour of the US takes up most of the year.
April	Tony Banks releases *The Wicked Lady* soundtrack.He follows it with *The Fugitive* in June.
August	'Mama'/'It's Gonna Get Better' is released and hits UK #4; US #73.
October	*Genesis* is released and is another hit, with UK #1; US #9. The single 'That's All'/'Taking It All Too Hard' is also released this month and goes to UK #16; US #6.
	Also this year, Steve Hackett releases *Bay of Kings*.

1984

January	'Illegal Alien'/'Turn It On Again' (Live) goes to UK #46; US #44.
February	Genesis play five nights at the NEC, Birmingham – their only UK concerts of the year.
	Also this year, Charisma Records is bought out by Virgin but continues to release under the Charisma name; Phil Collins marries Jill Tavelman; Peter Gabriel contributes the soundtrack to Alan Parker's film *Birdy;* Steve Hackett releases *Till We Have Faces*.

1985

January	Phil Collins releases *No Jacket Required*.
	Mike Rutherford forms a new group called Mike + the Mechanics, and in November they release their debut album, *Mike + the Mechanics*.

1986

March	Tony Banks releases *Soundtracks*.
May	'Invisible Touch'/'The Last Domino' is released and reaches UK #15; US #1. The same month, Peter Gabriel releases the album *So*, which includes the multi-platinum single 'Sledgehammer'.
June	*Invisible Touch* is released and hits UK #1; US #3.
August	'In Too Deep'/'Do The Neurotic' goes to UK #19; US #3.
November	'Land of Confusion'/'Feeding The Fire' reaches UK #14; US #4.
	Also this year, Steve Hackett forms the group GTR along with Steve Howe (ex-Yes), Max Bacon, Phil Spalding and Jonathan Mover. They release the album *GTR*.

1987

March	'Tonight, Tonight, Tonight'/'In The Glow Of The Night' reaches UK #18; US #3.
June	'Throwing It All Away'/'I'd Rather Be You' reaches UK #22; US #4.
July	As part of the *Invisible Touch* tour, Genesis play four nights at Wembley Stadium to nearly 300,000 seats – a record that remains unbroken.

1988

January	Phil Collins releases *12"ers*. He also appears in the film *Buster* and records the accompanying soundtrack.
October	Mike Rutherford releases *The Living Years* with Mike + the Mechanics.
	Also this year, Steve Hackett releases *Momentum*, having left GTR in 1987.

1989

August	Tony Banks releases *Bankstatement*.
November	Phil Collins releases *But Seriously*.
	Also this year, Peter Gabriel releases the soundtrack to Martin Scorcese's *Passion*, called *Passion: Music For The Last Temptation Of Christ*.

1990

| November | Phil Collins releases *Serious Hits Live* and appears in the film *Hook*. |
| | The same year, Peter Gabriel releases the compilation *Shaking the Tree*. |

1991

April	Tony Banks releases *Still* and Mike Rutherford releases *Word of Mouth* with Mike + the Mechanics.
October	'No Son of Mine'/'Living Forever' goes to UK #6; US #12.
November	*We Can't Dance* gets a UK #1; US #4.
December	'I Can't Dance'/'On The Shoreline' reaches UK #7; US #7.
	Also this year, Steve Hackett releases *Time Lapse*.

1992

April	'Hold on My Heart'/'Way Of The World' goes to UK #16; US #12.
May	Genesis embark on a 26-show US tour, to be followed by a 26-date European tour, culminating at Knebworth in August.
July	'Jesus He Knows Me'/'Hearts On Fire' goes to UK #20; US #23.
September	Peter Gabriel releases the album *Us*.
October	Genesis play another eleven-date UK tour.
November	'Invisible Touch' (Live)/'Abacab' (Live) charts at UK #7 and *Live/The Way We Walk, Volume One: The Shorts* achieves UK #3; US #35.
	Also this year, the name Charisma disappears following Virgin's merger with EMI, and Steve Hackett releases *The Unauthorized Biography*.

1993

January	*Live/The Way We Walk, Volume Two: The Longs* gets to UK #1; US #20.
February	'Tell Me Why'/ 'Dreaming While You Sleep' (Live) reaches UK #40.
November	Phil Collins releases *Both Sides*. The same month he stars in two films, *Frauds* and *Calliope*, and has a cameo in *And The Band Played On*.
	Also this year, Steve Hackett releases *Guitar Noir*; WOMAD tours across the US, and Peter Gabriel embarks on a Secret World Tour, which lasts 18 months and covers 5 continents.

1994

| | Peter Gabriel releases *Secret World Live* and the CD-ROM *Xplora*. |

1995

March	Mike Rutherford releases *Beggar On A Beach Of Gold* with Mike + the Mechanics.
September	Tony Banks releases *Strictly Inc*.
	Also this year, Steve Hackett releases *Blues With A Feeling* and *There Are Many Sides To The Night*.

1996

March	It is announced that Phil Collins has left the group. Mike Rutherford releases *Hits* with Mike + the Mechanics.
October	Phil Collins releases *Dance Into The Light*. His marriage to Jill Tavelman is dissolved.
	Also this year, Steve Hackett releases *Watcher of the Skies: Genesis Revisited*.

1997

June	Mike Rutherford and Tony Banks announce that Ray Wilson of Stiltskin will replace Phil Collins.
September	*Calling All Stations*, the first and only album with the new line-up, is released and reaches UK #2; US #54. 'Congo'/'Papa He Said'/'Banjo Man'/'Second Home By The Sea' is released and reaches UK #29.
December	'Shipwrecked'/'No Son of Mine'/'Lover's Leap'/'Turn It On Again'/'Phret'/'7/8' is released and gets to UK #54.
	Also this year, Steve Hackett releases *A Midsummer Night's Dream*. He is also involved in the release of *GTR Live*.

1998

	The new Genesis line-up goes on tour with *Calling All Stations*.
February	'Not About Us'/'Dancing With the Moonlit Knight' (Live)/'Follow You, Follow Me' (Live)/'Anything Now'/'Sign Your Life Away'/'Run Out Of Time' reaches UK #66.
May	A press conference held at Heathrow airport reunites Steve Hackett, Phil Collins, Peter Gabriel, Anthony Phillips and John Silver with the two remaining original members, Tony Banks and Mike Rutherford. The gathering precedes the June release of the first Genesis box-set.
June	The box-set *Genesis Archive 1967–75* is released and reaches UK #35.

1999

May	Mike Rutherford releases *M6* with Mike + the Mechanics. Phil Collins releases *A Hot Night in Paris* and writes the soundtrack for the animated movie *Tarzan*. He marries Orianne Cevey the same month.
October	*Turn It On Again: The Hits* reaches UK #4; US #65.
November	'The Carpet Crawlers' 1999/'Follow You, Follow Me'/'Turn It On Again' is released.

2000

August	Peter Gabriel releases *OVO*, a soundtrack for London's Millennium Dome show.
November	*Genesis Archive 2: 1976–92* is released.

2002

September	Peter Gabriel releases the album *Up*.
November	Phil Collins releases *Testify* and performs at the Queen's Golden Jubilee concert at Buckingham Palace as house drummer and bandleader.

2004

	Phil Collins releases *The Platinum Collection* and *Love Songs… A Compilation… Old and New*.
March	Tony Banks releases *Seven: A Suite for Orchestra*.
June	Mike Rutherford releases *Rewired* with Mike + the Mechanics.

2006

November	After much speculation it is announced that the three-piece Genesis of the mid-1970s – Tony Banks, Mike Rutherford and Phil Collins – is to re-form for a world tour in 2007. They will be joined by touring members Chester Thompson and Daryl Stuermer.
	The same year, 'Silent Sun 2006' is released on iTunes and Phil Collins separates from Orianne Cevey.

2007

11 June	The *Turn It On Again* tour opens in Helsinki. It will incorporate a performance on 7 July at Live Earth, a concert to heighten awareness of climate change, and culminate at the Hollywood Bowl on 13 October.

ACKNOWLEDGEMENTS

Philip Dodd would like to thank everyone who agreed to be interviewed for this book for giving up their time, energy and memories: in addition to the band, Geoff Banks, Bill Bruford, Rusty Brutsché, Geoff Callingham, Gail Colson, Nick Davis, Ahmet Ertegun, Ed Goodgold, Steve Jones, Jonathan King, Nancy Lewis, Richard Macphail, John Mayhew, Doug Morris, Dale Newman, Hugh Padgham, Anthony Phillips, Brian Roberts, John Silver, Chris Stewart, Daryl Stuermer, Chester Thompson, Ray Wilson and Nir Zidkyahu. For their help in organizing and scheduling those interviews thanks are due to Carole Broughton, Billy Budis, Frances Chantly, Jane Ellis and Annie Parsons. A big thank you as ever to Michael Dover and Debbie Woska at Weidenfeld & Nicolson; to David Costa and Nadine Levy at Wherefore Art?; to Emily Hedges and David Penrose for turning up some wonderful photos; and to Adèle Herson at Adèle's Typing Works. And finally, without the help and support of Carol Willis and Jo Greenwood at TSPM, and of Tony Smith and the band, this book would not and could not have existed.

SPECIAL THANKS...

In addition to the many friends who have contributed to and appeared in this book, Genesis would like to thank the following people:

Les Adey, John Alexander, John Anthony, Geoff Banks, Marcus Bicknell, Una Billings, Regis Boff, Mike Bowen, Tim Brockman, John Burns, Danny Busch, Geoff Callingham, Chiddingfold Working Men's Club, Michael Cohl, Cubby Colby, Michel Colin, Paul Conroy, Carol Coombes, David Costa, Mal Craggs, Justin Crew, Michael Farrell, Mark Fisher, John Flynn, Holly Fogg, Dik Fraser, John Giddings, Danny Gillen, Harvey Goldsmith, Sheryl Gordon Martinelli, Joanne Greenwood, Chris Hedge, Dave Hentschel, Dave Hill, Howard Hopkins, Dave Jacobson, Jeffrey and Theo, Steve Jones, Sue Kennedy, Mike Kidson, Ian Knight, Morris Lyda, Andy Mackrill, Danny Marcus, Brad Marsh, Mauricio, Sandro and Walter, Robin Moore, Doug Morris, Brian Murray-Smith, Dale Newman, Maurice Plaquet, ML Procise, Tex Read, Colin Richardson, Peter Rieger, Theo Roos, Dave Rule, Alain Schneebeli, Adrian Selby, Gerard Selby, Showco, Alex Sim, Wiff Smith, David Stopps, Rob Sworder, David Thomas, Wally Versen, Jon Webster, Steve Weltman, Carol Willis, Patrick Woodruffe

...and especially Tony Smith.

And also those who are no longer with us:

Perry Cooper, Tunc Erin, Ahmet Ertegun, Alan Owen, Craig Schertz, Tony Stratton Smith, Monty Wynne.

The publishers would like to thank the following sources for their kind permission to reproduce the photographs and illustrations in this book. Every effort has been made to contact the copyright holders. Should there be any errors or omissions we would be happy to correct them in future editions of this book.

2 Stephanie Pistel, 4 Genesis Archive/Henry Diltz, 6-7 Genesis Archive, 9-11 Guido Karp, 12 top left Peter Gabriel, 12 top right Mike Rutherford, 12 bottom left Anthony Philips, 12 bottom right Tony Banks, 18 Charterhouse, 20-23 Tony Banks, 25 Mike Rutherford, 26-27 Chris Hollebone, 28 Rex Features, 29 Rex Features, 30-31 Brian Roberts, 32 Genesis Archive/Decca Records, 33 Jonathan Silver, 34-35 Jonathan Silver, 36 Genesis Archive, 39 Jonathan Silver, 39 inset Genesis Archive, 40-43 Jonathan Silver, 44 Gems/Redferns, 46 David Penrose, 48 John Firth, 50-51 Anthony Phillips, 53 Genesis Archive/East Grinstead Courier, 54-61 Jonathan Sliver, 62 Genesis Archive, 65-67 Jonathan Silver, 69 Jonathan Silver, 70 Genesis Archive, 73 Tony Banks, 74 top Genesis Archive, 76-77 Barrie Wentzell, 78 Genesis Archive, 79 Tony Banks, 82-83 Barrie Wentzell, 84 Armando Gallo, 86 Milton Mclachlan of Milton's Fingers, 88 Barrie Wentzell,90 Gered Mankowitz, 92-93 top Phil Collins, 93 bottom Gered Mankowitz, 94 & 96 Richard MacPhail, 97 Mike Rutherford, 98-99 Barrie Wentzell, 100-101 Armando Gallo, 104 Mike Rutherford, 107 top Armando Gallo, 107 bottom Genesis Archive, 108-9 Armando Gallo, 111 Richard Macphail, 112 Barrie Wentzell, 114 left and left of centre Armando Gallo, 114-115 centre Genesis Archive/Neal Preston/Andy Kent, 115 right Armando Gallo, 116-117 John Lynn Kirk/Redferns, 116 top inset Rex Features, 116 above centre inset Genesis Archive, 116 centre Robert Ellis/Repfoto, 116 bottom centre inset & 116 bottom Armando Gallo, 118 Genesis Archive/Barry Plummer, 119 top Mike Rutherford, 119 bottom & 120 Richard Macphail, 121 left David Warner Ellis/Redferns, 121 right Genesis Archive, 122 top Armando Gallo, 122 bottom Robert Ellis/Repfoto, 123 Rex Features, 124 top Mike Rutherford, 124 bottom Armando Gallo, 125 left & right Ian Dickson/Redferns, 126-127 left Armando Gallo, 128-129 inset-129 Tony Banks, 130 Mike Rutherford, 131 Cliff Lipson, 132-135 Barrie Wentzell, 136 top Tony Banks, 136 bottom Jill Furmanovksy, 137 Barrie Wentzell, 138-139 Jill Furmanovksy, 140 Robert Ellis/Repfoto, 141 Jorgen Angel/Redferns, 142-143 Andre Csillag/Rex Features, 144-146 top left Robert Ellis/Repfoto, 146 top right & bottom Armando Gallo, 147 Ellen Poppingka/Redferns, 148 & 149 top Robert Ellis/Repfoto, 149 bottom Mike Rutherford, 150 top Tony Banks, 150 bottom Mike Rutherford, 151 courtesy Steve Hackett, 152-153 Armando Gallo, 154 Robert Ellis/Repfoto, 155 Armando Gallo, 156 Genesis Archive/Suzan Carson, 159 Robert Ellis/Repfoto, 160-161 Jorgen Angel/Redferns, 163 Barrie Wentzell, 164-168 top Robert Ellis/Repfoto, 168 bottom Tony Banks, 169 Melody Maker/IPC+ Syndication/Barrie Wentzell, 170 Genesis Archive/Retna Michael Putland, 171 Genesis Archive/Graham Wood, 172-173 Jill Furmanovsky, 174-175 Genesis Archive/Retna Michael Putland, 176 Genesis Archive/Waring Abbott, 177 Robert Ellis/Repfoto, 178-179 Tony Banks, 180-181 Robert Ellis/Repfoto, 182 Getty Images, 183 Robert Ellis/Repfoto, 184-187 Genesis Archive/Graham Wood, 188-189 all Robert Ellis/Repfoto except 188 top left Genesis Archive/Graham Wood, 190 top left & 190-191 centre Robert Ellis/Repfoto, 190 bottom left Jill Furmanovsky, 191 top & bottom Robert Ellis/Repfoto, 193 Genesis Archive/Graham Wood, 194-195 Jill Furmanovsky, 197 Genesis Archive/Hit + Run, 199 Genesis Archive/Waring Abbott, 200 Jill Furmanovsky, 202 & 203 top Tony Banks, 203 bottom & 204-207 Robert Ellis/Repfoto, 208 left Robert Ellis/Repfoto, 209 Lisa Tanner, 210-211 Robert Ellis/Repfoto, 212-213 Genesis Archive/Daniel Simon/Gamma, 214 top Phil Collins, 214 bottom Genesis Archive, 215 Genesis Archive/Warren Linhart, 216-217 all Robert Ellis/Repfoto except 216 right of centre & 217 left of centre Phil Kaman, 217 top right Alain Dister/Redferns, 217 bottom David Redfern/Redferns, 218 Robert Ellis/Repfoto, 220-221 Genesis Archive/Hit + Run, 223-225 Jill Furmanovsky, 226-233 Robert Ellis/Repfoto, 234 Tony Banks, 235-238 Robert Ellis/Repfoto, 239-243 Tony Banks, 244-251 Robert Ellis/Repfoto, 252 Tony Banks, 253 Gered Mankowitz, 254-255 Tony Banks, 256-257 Daryl Stuermer.com, 258 Robert Ellis/Repfoto, 260 Rusty Brutsche, CEO of Vari-Lite/photo Lewis Lee, 262-265 Robert Ellis/Repfoto, 266-267 Tony Banks, 268 Robert Ellis/Repfoto, 269-271 Robert Ellis/Repfoto, 272-275 Genesis Archive/Lewis Lee, 276 Genesis Archive/Hotshoz inc, 277 Gered Mankowitz, 278-279 Tony Banks, 280 top Mike Rutherford, 281 Private Collection, 282 Phil Collins, 283 Andre Csillag/Relay Photos, 284 inset Tony Banks, 284-285 Andre Csillag/Relay Photos, 285 inset Tony Banks, 286 Gered Mankowitz, 287 top Robert Ellis/Repfoto, 287 bottom Ilpo Musto/Redferns, 288 Genesis Archive/David Kennedy, 289 Genesis Archive/Malcolm Heywood, 289 insets Genesis Archive/Lewis Lee, 290 top Hotshoz inc, 290 bottom Genesis Archive/David Kennedy, 291 Linda Matlow/PixIntl, 292-293 Genesis Archive/Malcolm Heywood, 294-295 Robert Ellis/Repfoto, 297 Getty Images, 298 Genesis Archive/David Scheinmann, 300 All Genesis Archive/Lewis Lee except 300 bottom Genesis Archive/Henry Diltz, 301 top Genesis Archive, 301 bottom Lewis Lee, 302-303 Armando Gallo, 304 Andre Csillag/Rex Features, 305 Genesis Archive/Henry Diltz, 306-314 Armando Gallo, 316-317 Kevin Westenberg, 318-319 Genesis Archive/Peter Robathan, 320-324 Armando Gallo, 325 Kevin Westenberg, 326-7 Genesis Archive/Lauren Haynes, 328 Armando Gallo, 330 Nick Davis, 332 Tony Smith Personal Management, 334-337 Guido Karp, 338-339 Stephanie Pistel, 341 Guido Karp, 342-345 Stephanie Pistel, 346-347 Sebastian Schmidt.

First published in Great Britain in 2007
by Weidenfeld & Nicolson
10 9 8 7 6 5 4 3 2 1

A CIP catalogue record for this book is available from the British Library.

ISBN: 978 0 297 84434 1

Interviews: Philip Dodd
Design: David Costa and Nadine Levy at Wherefore Art?
with jacket and endpapers designed by Chris Peyton
Picture research: Emily Hedges and David Penrose
Managing editor: Debbie Woska
Editorial assistance: Alan Ewers, Brónagh Woods

Colour reproduction by DL Interactive UK
Printed and bound in Italy by Rotolito Lombarda

Weidenfeld & Nicolson
The Orion Publishing Group Ltd
Orion House
5 Upper St Martin's Lane
London WC2H 9EA

An Hachette Livre UK Company

The Orion Publishing Group's policy is to use papers that are natural, renewable and recyclable products
and made from wood grown in sustainable forests. The logging and manufacturing processes are expected to conform
to the environmental regulations of the country of origin.